# WASHING WINDOWS V

*honouring*
all women who have contributed to the flowering of Irish writing, reading and literacy, including:

JANE ALGER
*co-founder, Dublin UNESCO City of Literature*

CAITRÍONA BENNETT
*Argosy Books*

MARY FALLON
*Alan Hanna's Bookshop*

MARIAN KEYES
*inaugural LexIcon Librarian*

JOSEPHINE VAHEY
*Galway Libraries*

RUTH WEBSTER
*Books Upstairs*

*remembering*
EILEEN BATTERSBY
*literary critic extraordinaire*

ANNE BRENNAN
*Kenny's Bookshop, at its heart*

JULIA DORIAN (AUNT JUDY)
*Senior management, Dublin City Libraries*

CAROL FITZPATRICK (AUNTY CAROL)
*Dublin cultural expert*

MRS MAUREEN KENNY
*c/o founder, Kenny's Bookshop, literary expert/bible*

BERTHA MCCULLOUGH
*Limerick literary legend*

*Celebrating 50 years of Arlen House*

# Washing Windows V
*Women Revolutionise Irish Poetry, 1975–2025*

Alan Hayes and Nuala O'Connor
*editors*

Washing Windows IV
*Women Revolutionise Irish Poetry, 1975–2025*

is published in May 2025 by
Arlen House
42 Grange Abbey Road
Baldoyle, Dublin D13 A0F3, Ireland
arlenhouse@gmail.com
arlenhouse.ie

978–1–85132–555–9, *paperback*

Distributed internationally by
Syracuse University Press
621 Skytop Road, Suite 110
Syracuse, New York, 13244–5290
syracuseuniversitypress.syr.edu

poems © individual authors, 2025
selection/introduction © Alan Hayes, 2025
afterword © Nuala O'Connor, 2025

The moral right of the authors has been reserved

Typesetting by Arlen House

cover image: 'Dinner in the College' by Pauline Bewick
• watercolour, acrylic and silver leaf • 2003
is reproduced courtesy of the Artist's Estate

Tá Arlen House buíoch de
Chlár na Leabhar Gaeilge
agus d'Fhoras na Gaeilge

## Contents

15  *Writing Women:*
    *Power, Politics, Patronage, Privilege and Pricks*
    Alan Hayes

55  *In Her Own Image*
57  *Night Feed*
    Eavan Boland

WASHING WINDOWS V
61  Amy Abdullah Barry / *Times of War*
62  Sonia Abercrombie / *The Singer*
63  Síle Agnew / *Murty Magic*
64  Michelle Ivy Alwedo / *TK Maxx Christmas Temp*
65  Nathalie Anderson / *Magpies*
67  Nuala Archer / *Memoir*
73  t c arkle / *The Parable of the Green-Eyed Monster*
75  Bebe Ashley / *Chloe, on Chesil Beach*
76  Ivy Bannister / *Walking with the Saint*
77  Terry Barrett / *This Morning*
78  Marie Bashford-Synnott / *Garrykennedy Forest Walk ...*
79  Amanda Bell / *Light Years*
80  Trish Bennett / *On the Turn*
81  Clodagh Beresford Dunne / *Stabilisers*
82  Sara Berkeley / *Where We Are Going*
84  Clíodhna Bhreatnach / *Johnny Depp v. Amber Heard ...*
87  Claire Blennerhassett / *Reverse Progress*
89  Roslyn Blyn-LaDrew / *Seothín Seó d'Oklahoma ...*
91  Fióna Bolger / *Canal Bank Poem 2024*
92  Eva Bourke / *Starlings over Nimmo's Pier*
95  Niamh Boyce / *The Trinity*
96  Sara Boyce / *Black Sand*
98  Maureen Boyle / *Trinity, Christmas 1980*
100 Yvonne Boyle / *Swimming with my Cousin in the Lake*

101 Caroline Bracken / *Amygdala*
102 Julie Breathnach-Banwait / *comhairle*
103 Marie Breen-Smyth / *Painting my Father*
104 Clodagh Brennan Harvey / *The Call to Mass*
105 Deirdre Brennan / *Na Cailleacha Ghána*
106 Heather Brett / *Signings*
108 Lynn Caldwell / *Button Necklace*
110 Louise C Callaghan / *Winter Morning Run*
111 Mary Rose Callaghan / *The Green Tin House*
112 Rosaline Callaghan / *Granite*
113 Siobhán Campbell / *Blush*
114 Moya Cannon / *Soup*
115 Caitríona Caomhánach / *Cadhain Aonair*
116 Eibhlís Carcione / *Iníon*
118 Ruth Carr / *Here We Are*
119 Alvy Carragher / *The Neighbour's Voice at Night*
120 Deirdre Cartmill / *War Wound*
121 Anne Casey / *War Cabinet*
122 Eileen Casey / *Posting Home*
123 Pratibha Castle / *Recalling Kells*
124 Sarah Clancy / *Anois Teacht an Earraigh*
125 Jane Clarke / *Cherry Trees, Charente*
126 Marion Clarke / *Capricorn Child*
127 Catríona Clutterbuck / *The River in Fethard*
128 Louise G Cole / *Eating Yoghurt with a Fork*
129 Susan Condon / *Heated Words*
130 Áine Rose Connell / *A Double-Volted Antigen Test*
132 Monica Corish / *Love Rises Like Bread, Each Day ...*
133 Polina Cosgrave / *Fireworks 2025*
134 Enda Coyle-Greene / *Instead of the Sniper*
135 Bernie Crawford / *Looking for my Grandmother in ...*
137 Catherine Ann Cullen / *My Bones Sing*
138 Majella Cullinane / *Pinch*
139 Denise Curtin / *Margo: The Love Pattern*
140 Martina Dalton / *The Return*
141 Maureen Daly / *How We Do Things Now*
142 Ailbhe Darcy / *Fear*
144 Eilín de Paor / *Pishogue*

145  Celia de Fréine / *An Fásach : The Wasteland*
147  Helen Dempsey / *Turning*
148  Annie Deppe / *The Music of the Nails*
150  Deirdre Devally / *Dressed to Kill*
151  Zoë Devlin / *Two Hearts*
152  Déirdre D. Dodds / *Bearáilte*
153  Moyra Donaldson / *Where Was I Looking*
154  Rosemary Donnelly / *Nighttime*
155  Katie Donovan / *The Midnight Baker*
156  Mary Dorcey / *Our Heart-Stricken Earth*
158  Doreen Duffy / *I Watch You Dance*
159  Ger Duffy / *Anchorite*
160  Katherine Duffy / *Apparition*
162  Ann Marie Dunne / *Annie Morley*
164  Áine Durkin / *Forainm*
165  Micheline Egan / *She Shaped our Faith*
166  Orla Egan / *Stand Strong Together*
168  Attracta Fahy / *Inishbofin*
170  Emer Fallon / *Gardening with my Mother*
172  Helen Fallon / *Our Country*
173  Carole Farnan / *Women, Life, Freedom*
174  Tanya Farrelly / *Canvassing*
175  Orla Fay / *Mil na Fianna*
177  Pauline Fayne / *Luas Lass*
178  Felispeaks / *Green Lady*
180  Anne Fitzgerald / *Heatwave 1976*
182  Deirdre Flaherty Brady / *Circadian Rhythms*
183  Deirdre Flannery / *Son*
184  Siobhán Flynn / *How to Find the Witch*
185  Catherine Foley / *Downhill : Síos le Fána*
187  Bernadette Fox / *Habit*
188  Anne-Marie Fyfe / *Wishbone*
189  Amy Gaffney / *Holy Trinity*
190  Bernadette Gallagher / *Dancing in the Dark*
191  Peggie Gallagher / *The Gift*
192  Elaine Gaston / *On Round the Coast Road*
194  Shauna Gilligan / *Beverly Allitt's Push of Dreams*
195  Aimee Godfrey / *Devotee*

196  Trudie Gorman / *Synonyms for Loss*
197  Anita Gracey / *The Lonely Passion*
198  Angela Graham / *It Broke my Mother's Heart*
200  Mim Greene / *Beloved*
201  Anita Greg / *Sweeter than Ashes*
202  Nicki Griffin / *Another Life*
203  Sinéad Griffin / *The Score*
204  Sharon Guard / *For Fear*
205  Christine Hammond / *Perpetual Motion*
206  Eithne Hand / *That Datsun was our First Bedroom*
207  Rachel Handley / *A Soft Reckoning*
208  Kerry Hardie / *Rising Waters*
209  Anne Haverty / *Siberia*
211  Rachael Hegarty / *Washing Windows is Out of ...*
212  Niamh Hehir / *The Separation of Mother and Child in a ...*
215  Aideen Henry / *Not Dead, Sleeping*
216  Phyl Herbert / *Taking Steps*
217  Florence Heyhoe / *Full Stop*
218  Rita Ann Higgins / *Unnatural Pleasures*
221  Deirdre Hines / *Disguises*
223  Máire Holmes / *Taibhsí*
224  Eleanor Hooker / *An Gorta Mór*
226  Jennifer Horgan / *Chris, 1993*
227  Liz Houchin / *Love Poem for Tired Women*
228  Holly Hughes / *Erudite*
230  Helen Hutchinson / *A Day's Work in Gammon*
232  Sacha Hutchinson / *The Room*
233  Deirdre Hyland / *Gaillardia*
234  Linda Ibbotson / *Letting Go*
235  Jean James / *Salvation*
236  Rosemary Jenkinson / *Ivy*
237  Maura Johnston / *Places Slip*
238  Tiegan Johnston / *Shadow*
240  Nithy Kasa / *Two Sister-Wives*
241  Virginia Keane Brownlow / *Thyme*
242  Róisín Kelly / *First Photograph of a Black Hole*
244  Anne Marie Kennedy / *Motherly*
246  Hannah Kiely / *In Which the Mother Needs to Dance*

247 Thérèse Kieran / *The Women in Your Family*
248 Bethan Kilfoil / *Found in a Glass Apothecary's Jar* ...
249 Susan Knight / *Portrait of a Lady Restored*
251 Caitríona Lane / *Eochracha an Chúldorais*
252 Ann Leahy / *Everyoung*
253 Donna Leamy / *Poetry Class*
254 Róisín Leggett Bohan / *The Curator*
255 Jessie Lendennie / *What If*
256 Susan Lindsay / *The Dreamtime Memory Machine*
259 Mary Lockhart / *Poppy Purett's Woodland Party*
261 Aoife Lyall / *Painting my Husband as the Forth Rail Bridge*
262 Jackie Lynam / *Gutted*
263 Noelle Lynskey / *Returning*
264 Aifric Mac Aodha / *Tá d'Athair ag Adú Tine, a Chroí*
265 Siobhán Mac Mahon / *Magdalene Laundry for Sale*
266 Colette McAndrew / *Dying Fall*
267 Joan McBreen / *One Another*
268 Catherine McCabe / *All Our Houses*
269 Aoibheann McCann / *Trifle*
270 Felicia McCarthy / *Loss and Gain*
271 Mary McCarthy / *The Sun Also Rises*
273 Helen McClements / *The Day Medusa Washed Up to* ...
275 Clare McCotter / *The Swing*
276 Karen J McDonnell / *I'm Reading* Ulysses *During* ...
277 Afric McGlinchey / *On Learning what Not to Talk About* ...
278 Medbh McGuckian / *On Either Side of Windows*
279 Ann McKay / *Super Moon*
280 Ellie Rose McKee / *Downsizing*
281 Raquel McKee / *Her Laughter Still*
282 Maeve McKenna / *Yellow is Not Alive*
283 Emma McKervey / *Krakow, 1988*
284 E.V. McLoughlin / *Why are you Like This?*
285 Liz McManus / *Muezzin*
286 Triona Mc Murrow / *The Back Garden*
287 Winifred Mc Nulty / *Hiraeth*
288 Liz McSkeane / *How to Make a Woman Disappear*
289 Mary Madec / *Moon Festival on Chung Yin Street* ...
290 Patricia Maguire / *The Knock Girl*

291 Ruth Marshall / *Mermaids*
292 Katie Martin / *Letters in Autumn*
293 Orla Martin / *Daughters of Ireland*
294 Mari Maxwell / *Atop Mount Gable*
295 Máighréad Medbh / *One Night Stand*
297 Victoria Melkovska / *This Year Her Present*
299 Mary Melvin Geoghegan / *In Some Sheltered Spot*
300 Geraldine Mills / *Rhyming the Horizontal*
301 Drucilla Mims Wall / *Galway Plain*
302 Geraldine Mitchell / *Lessons from the Clothesline*
303 Audrey Molloy / *Night Visit*
304 Amanda Moloney / *Endurance*
305 K.S. Moore / *The Shadow when we Kiss*
306 Sadhbh Moriarty / *Nia*
307 Joan Morrissey / *When I Knew*
308 Sinéad Morrissey / *Allery Banks*
310 Julie Morrissy / *The French for Moon*
312 Katie Moynagh / *Look Out*
313 Sara Mullen / *The Haunt*
315 Mitzie Murphy / *Fields*
316 Anne Murray / *Confession*
318 Chris Murray / *Enmesh*
319 Joan Newmann / *How Much Do You Need?*
322 Kate Newmann / *California, Oh California, I'm Coming ...*
324 Róise Ní Bhaoill / *Hibakusha*
325 Ceaití Ní Bheildiúin / *Ospís na Leamhan*
327 Úna Ní Cheallaigh / *In Wilton Park*
328 Dairena Ní Chinnéide / *Aois*
329 Caitríona Ní Chléirchín / *Suantraí na Píbe Uilleann*
330 Laoighseach Ní Choistealbha / *Bánfhilíocht*
333 Bríd Ní Chomáin / *If I Die, Publish My Notes App*
334 Mairéad Ní Chonaola / *Freagra agus Freagracht*
335 Eiléan Ní Chuilleanáin / *What It's Like*
336 Annemarie Ní Churreáin / *The Other Daughter*
337 Ciara Ní É / *An Béal Beo Seo*
338 Éire Ní Fhaoláin / *Níl Ann Ach Scáth*
339 Eithne Ní Ghallchobhair / *Ceol Crotaigh, Caoineadh ...*
343 Colette Ní Ghallchóir / *Ag Leanúint*

344 Ailbhe Ní Ghearbhuigh / *Fear Iomaire ag Taibhreamh*
345 Áine Ní Ghlinn / *Cad d'Imigh ar Mo Dhá Chos*
347 Orlaith Ní Icí / *Teanga mo Mháthar*
348 Réaltán Ní Leannáin / *Bag for Life*
350 Bríd Ní Mhóráin / *Caoineadh*
351 Gormfhlaith Ní Shiochain Ní Bheolain / *Cur Amú*
352 Colette Nic Aodha / *Turas go Deisceart Bhéal Feirste*
353 Gearóidín Nic Cárthaigh / *An Foclóir Nua Béarla-Gaeilge*
354 Pauline Nic Chonaonaigh / *Faoi Ghob an Phréacháin*
356 Eibhlín Nic Eochaidh / *Staying Alive*
357 Margaret Nohilly / *Her Core Belief*
358 Helena Nolan / *A Poem about Hens*
360 Maria Noonan-McDermott / *The Empty Chair*
361 Mary Noonan / *Sunflower, Sparrows*
362 Catherine O'Brien / *Mo Mháthair, Mo Chroí*
363 Jean O'Brien / *As If, Absence*
364 Margaret O'Brien / *Witness*
365 Mary O'Brien / *Tiarna na dTonn*
368 Clairr O'Connor / *Gone*
369 Jessamine O'Connor / *Witness Box*
370 Karen O'Connor / *Cleaning Bricks*
371 Nuala O'Connor / *An tIasc ~ The Fish*
372 Sarah O'Connor / *I'm Not Your Type*
373 Grace O'Doherty / *Miradouro*
374 Mary O'Donnell / *Family Christmas*
377 Liz O'Donoghue / *Entering Eden*
378 Lauren O'Donovan / *Gospel of Birth*
380 Margaret O'Driscoll / *Watchkeeper of the Dreamspace*
381 Orlagh O'Farrell / *Some Days I Want to Be Cillian Murphy*
382 Lani O'Hanlon / *Soothsayer*
384 Helen O'Leary / *Shoe Shopping*
385 Nessa O'Mahony / *Compression*
386 Mary O'Malley / *The Writing Lesson*
387 Síofra O'Meara / *The Boy Band*
388 Bláithín O'Reilly Murphy / *Mná an Domhain*
389 Maeve O'Sullivan / *Five-a-Day*
390 Katherine Orr / *Home*
391 Saakshi Patel / *Chhaya*

| | |
|---|---|
| 392 | Cáit Pléimionn / *Iontráil Dialainne* |
| 393 | Ruth Quinlan / *The Feeding of an Irishwoman in Kuala ...* |
| 394 | Leeanne Quinn / *First Part of the Night* |
| 395 | Liz Quirke / *Here I am Broken into Small Acts* |
| 397 | Saoirse Rafferty / *The Day You Died* |
| 399 | Anne Rath / *Won't You Celebrate With Me* |
| 400 | Nell Regan / *School Visit, Gaza* |
| 401 | Mary Ringland / *Fold* |
| 403 | Connie Roberts / *Mrs Coady's Turnips* |
| 405 | Moya Roddy / *An Bhfuil Cead Agam* |
| 406 | Orna Ross / *Lost and Found* |
| 410 | Robyn Rowland / *Voyeur* |
| 412 | Carol Rumens / *The Call Home* |
| 413 | D'or Seifer / *Sinai* |
| 415 | Sree Sen / *Invocation* |
| 416 | Mary Shannon / *Dereliction* |
| 417 | Lorna Shaughnessy / *Un-Tiling the Roof* |
| 418 | Katie Sheehan / *Offering* |
| 419 | Róisín Sheehy / *Dúil* |
| 420 | Jo Slade / *The Leaving 1914* |
| 422 | Cassie Smith-Christmas / *An Traein Dheireanach go dtí ...* |
| 423 | Fiona Smith / *Maria Luisa Ferrara* |
| 424 | Amy Smyth / *Untold Stories* |
| 425 | Cherry Smyth / *Its Nightly Story* |
| 426 | Eilis Stanley / *A Year of Longing* |
| 428 | Dolores Stewart / *As Alt* |
| 429 | Sarah Strong / *The Female Organs of the Crocus* |
| 430 | Lila Stuart / *As They Were* |
| 431 | Anne Tannam / *Ode to a First Grandchild* |
| 433 | Lynda Tavakoli / *I Couldn't Save Any of You* |
| 434 | Alice Taylor / *The Cobweb of Old Age* |
| 435 | Lisa C Taylor / *At the Seven Sisters' Café* |
| 437 | Gráinne Tobin / *Des Res* |
| 438 | Csilla Toldy / *Photo on the Brick Wall* |
| 439 | Shelley Tracey / *Making a Mark* |
| 441 | Jessica Traynor / *During the Genocide* |
| 442 | Jean Tuomey / *Freedom near Café Branquinto* |
| 443 | Mary Turley-McGrath / *Sealed* |

| | |
|---|---|
| 444 | Niamh Twomey / *Egg Money* |
| 445 | Áine Uí Fhoghlú / *Ag Ullmhú Mála don Siopa Carthanais* |
| 447 | Carmel Uí Cheallaigh / *Marthanóirí* |
| 448 | Máire Uí Ráinne / *Uacht an Uafáis* |
| 449 | Morgan L. Ventura / *Unlock Your Trauma* |
| 450 | Mia Vance / *Birthright* |
| 452 | Monica Whelan / *September* |
| 453 | Grace Wilentz / from *Snow Cats and Me* |
| 454 | Máiríde Woods / *Robes d'Antan* |
| 455 | N.K. Woods / *Never Call a Man* |
| 456 | Máire Dinny Wren / *Caoineadh Shinéad* |
| 457 | Amy Louise Wyatt / *Perimenopause* |
| | |
| 459 | *Writer's Block* |
| | Edna O'Brien |
| | |
| 461 | AFTERWORD |
| | *A Knife Edge Under the Toes* |
| | Nuala O'Connor |
| | |
| 473 | *Book Highlights 2000–2025* |
| | |
| 500 | Nanci Griffith / from *Sing* |

Eavan Boland, 1978

'The trouble with women writers ... We've got to get to the point where the point isn't just that women write, but how well we do it. At the moment we are freaks just for writing'

*from* Lucille Redmond, 'The problems of women who write – a minority in a minor market,' *Irish Press*, 25 December 1978, p. 9

## Writing Women
### Power, Politics, Patronage, Privilege and Pricks

Alan Hayes

I

How fast things change; how fast things are made to change: all it takes is a handful of determined and energetic women; big women not little women.
– Fay Weldon, *Big Women* (Flamingo, 1997)

The *Washing Windows* anthologies over the past decade have been an unexpected and unprecedented success. In this celebratory year for Arlen House – the 50th – I am delighted to produce the final volume of this series, which once again gives us great hope for the future of Irish poetry.

Selected from over 2000 poems submitted by women from the widest spectrum of contemporary Irish writing, this volume is particularly special – being the most comprehensive collection compiled to date. It contains over 300 new and unpublished poems, and is the most representative anthology of poetry by Irish women ever to be published.

Reading all the poems submitted presented me with challenging choices. So, while many poets didn't make it in, it is heartening to know that the poetic talent out there by women authors is immense. The pool of women writers working in Ireland now has grown into a vast lake.

For this project I invited a huge number of poets to contribute; some women had stopped writing, a small number had no new and unpublished work available, some didn't reply. Others I chose not to invite. This being said, the anthology could have been doubled in size.

When I relaunched Arlen House at the turn of the millenium the literary world was vastly different to now. It was a time and a space that was not as open and welcoming to women. There were few opportunities for writers who were female. I remember one young poet saying she was told, patronisingly and condescendingly by a too-powerful broker, that there was not one line of poetry in her manuscript – an opinion that awards judges, media reviewers and a large audience utterly disagreed with. That poet has now made quite an impact.

One of the first manuscripts I received was by Nuala Ní Chonchúir/Nuala O'Connor; like me, a Dubliner also living in Galway at that time. And we both worked in the same university, in the same department, yet didn't know each other. After I read Nuala's work, I knew what a privilege it would be to introduce one of the most original and important voices of twenty-first century Irish literature. In the intervening decades it has been wonderful to see Nuala's work generate huge international acclaim. And it is a joy to continue working with her almost 25 years later – with her new Arlen House poetry collection, *Menagerie*, being one of my favourite books out of the over 300 I have published to date.

After sending Nuala the 300 *Washing Windows* poems I had chosen, I anxiously and impatiently awaited her response. My choices are, of course, subjective, thus I was relieved by her overwhelming, enthusiastic endorsement of the power of the poetry in this volume, as you will read in her beautiful Afterword.

In this anthology are the voices who represent and shape our poetry world. These writers come from all parts of the island and beyond. They span in age over eight decades, and, as with all Arlen House anthologies, diversity is integrated throughout, in all its glory and in all its honesty. There are strong familial and community ties here. Many of these women have contributed to Ireland's cultural life for decades as prose writers, playwrights and visual artists. All have an interest in poetry, often from the days when an interest was not encouraged or welcomed. Thus, this anthology is representative of a new society and a new way of accepting and honouring the talent all around us.

Though it has not always been so.

Women who are poets have not always been accepted or welcomed on equal terms. Talent has not always been the key factor. Power structures operate in dark corners.

There certainly have been better eras for female poets in Ireland's literary history. The nineteenth century was, relatively, a golden time for Irish women writers. American critic Anne Colman, in truly groundbreaking research undertaken in pre-internet days, discovered over 700 women writing poetry during the 1800s. In ongoing research, I have discovered over 100 Irish women who published poetry during the twentieth century who have not yet been 'reclaimed'. However, it is clear from the 1950s onwards that conservative powerbrokers (publishers and funding organisations, in particular) chose to champion their male peers and, in most instances, female voices were silenced. I believe there were always female voices who could be silenced.

However, in 1975, a young Cork woman with a publishing background decided to challenge that imbalance. She is Ireland's first feminist publisher. Her name is Catherine Rose, and she changed the literary, publishing and arts worlds for the better. Catherine's work deserves to be recorded in detail – otherwise it will be lost to posterity, as so much of the creative work of Irish women has already been. The history of Arlen House in the 1970s and 1980s demands to be remembered. And celebrated.

Catherine Rose, 1980s
Ireland's first feminist publisher

Galway, 1975: Arlen House – Ireland's pioneering first feminist press – was established by Catherine Rose. After publishing 2 books in Galway, she then moved to Dublin and there she gathered together a small group of other extraordinary women, including journalist and editor, Janet Martin, communications expert and writer, Terry

Prone, emerging poet Eavan Boland, who brought visionary ideas and practical help, and feminist activist and seer, Dr Margaret Mac Curtain, one of the leading voices campaigning for equality in Irish society.

I believe all women writing today owe a debt of gratitude to these trailblazers who were the first to open doors, at a time when it was difficult and dangerous to do so. They started a new creative movement, demanding a space, a voice and a vision for women. Thus commenced a new flowering, which we witness today in an ongoing renaissance of renowned female voices.

Though it may not always be so.

Unless systemic changes are made and enforced, progressive improvements in equality and diversity can always be dismantled. Power systems operate by twisted untruths. Recent ministers for arts have successfully delivered large increases in arts funding; thus many projects centered on the current 'diversity' buzzword have rightfully been supported. But what will happen when budget cuts come again? Will the decision-makers revert back to prioritising the old power structures – which traditionally had a poor record of equality and diversity? Many artistic organisations existed with specialisms in equality and diversity, but then had their funding either cut, or completely abolished, when funding bodies made poor choices.

The Arts Council/An Chomhairle Ealaíon, in particular, needs to be monitored closely. How many artistic organisations who embraced diversity and equality were destroyed by Arts Council funding choices? How many organisations with questionable track records have been championed by the Arts Council? In 2025, some of the Arts Council's misuse of public funding has finally been revealed, in particular the incompetent and inept loss of at least five million euro of public funding in a mismanaged technology project. I welcome the new arts minister's multiple investigations, and hope we are on the cusp of a new beginning of fair and equitable support for the arts. While Arlen House has the longest track record in equality, I do not feel that the Arts Council is a safe space creatively or culturally. Indeed, the Arts Council has been the biggest obstacle in Arlen House's journey over the past quarter century.

Diversity was not even a buzzword in the artistic lexicon then, despite the fact that equality legislation had recently been enacted by the government, and equality and diversity measures should have been implemented by all powerbrokers and decision-makers. It is inexplicable why it took so long, and disturbing when at times it is done so ineptly now. Often, Jessie Lendennie at Salmon Poetry remained a lone beacon advocating for progress and change in the poetry world. And sometimes a price had to be paid for doing so. Powerful publishers in the western world continued their long-standing exclusionary practices, often with public support and the approval of funding bodies; in Ireland the output of poetry presses, generally, was not reflective of modern society.

But the growing body of women writers, many of whom emerged from Arlen House/Eavan Boland's pioneering WEB workshops in the 1980s and 1990s, demanded opportunities; they refused to be silenced or sidelined. Thus came a new beginning for poetry in both the English and Irish languages. With the right supports, independent management, and honest engagement by the entire arts world, this is the perfect time to create opportunities for growth and blossoming.

Will that happen? Power structures remain stubbornly resistant to real change. We have been told 'change takes time' – though nobody explains *why* that is so. And why do *we* allow it to be so? Over recent decades the Irish literary world has become increasingly younger, female and more diverse; a fact not represented adequately by powerbrokers and decision-makers. Tokenism is no longer acceptable.

The rise of women in the Irish literary and arts world since the 1970s has truly been a revolution – a revolution created by a small group of women, Fay Weldon's big women, not little women. Arlen House women. Later joined by brilliant women in Irish Feminist Information, Women's Community Press and Attic Press. Thankfully so much has changed for the better. Truly, we must not let that progress regress.

This final *Washing Windows* anthology honours all women who have contributed to make Irish writing a safe and thriving space for writers and readers. In particular I acknowledge trailblazing librarians, Jane Alger (Dublin City), Marian Keyes (Dún Laoghaire) and Josephine Vahey (Galway), and dynamic booksellers, Caitríona Bennett (Argosy), Mary Fallon (Alan Hanna's) and Ruth Webster (Books Upstairs) who all have made tremendous contributions over the decades. Leaders in their fields, they are deeply respected throughout the industry.

And remembering those who have passed; from Kenny's Bookshop in Galway, Mrs Kenny was a fountain of knowledge and wisdom, while gentle Anne Brennan was at the heart and soul of the shop. In Limerick, that tremendous and visionary force Bertha McCullough is much missed, as is literary critic, the passionate and energetic Eileen Battersby, while I particularly acknowledge my two aunts, Carol Fitzpatrick and Judy Dorian. Carol was a breathless force of energy and strength who did such good in her too short life. I remember her describing Maeve Binchy's work as the art of a master craftswoman. (How fortuitous it is that decades later I am privileged to publish some of Maeve's groundbreaking work). And Aunt Judy (really my Nana's cousin) who was the chief bookbuyer in Dublin City Public

Libraries for decades, working in Pearse Street Library where she remembered Grace Plunkett visiting in the 1940s and 1950s. Judy encouraged my love of literature; in 1982 gifting me one of my earliest books, a proof copy of Edna O'Brien's short story collection, *Returning*. How amazed she would be that decades later I am privileged to publish Edna's poetry and worked with her many times. And I had the honour of working in that same library for many years on the Dublin UNESCO City of Literature project with the incomparable Jane Alger, who herself worked closely with 'Miss Julia Dorian' back in the 1980s.

In compiling *Washing Windows V* I thank Donal Ryan, Siobhán Hutson and Carmel Kelly for recommendations, wisdom and practical support.

And for now, and for ever, let us raise our voices to celebrate these 300 poetic voices, help them on their continuing journeys and watch as they bring new vitality into Irish and international creative life.

And let it always be so.

Gura fada buan ag cumadh filíochta iad.

## II

*The Publishing Game*
Publishing is implicitly a political activity and experience. In Ireland a small number of book publishers and funding organisations have traditionally held the power of veto – and the power of enabling – over what is published, how it is published, when it is published. And who is published. 'Women', as a general category, have been particularly marginalised by this unofficial (at times unwitting) censorship.

The quest for equality, diversity and inclusion in Irish literature commenced with a small group of women in

1970s and 1980s Ireland. They addressed inequality head on, thus changing the face of Irish literature and publishing forever. While the past fifty years has seen an impressive amount of progress and change, much more work remains to be done in order to integrate and embed equality and diversity lastingly. And new challenges and obstacles present themselves. This section of the essay contains a rapid survey of the past century and seeks to address some of the current challenges, alongside a history of the early groundbreaking work at Arlen House and of its activists who made such an impact. As the *Examiner* stated in 1986: Arlen House in the 1970s and 1980s was more than a publishing house, it became a movement.

*A Snapshot of Women and Publishing*
During the twentieth century hundreds of Irish women writers worked with prestigious publishers, both in Ireland but more importantly and lucratively in Britain and the USA. It was not unusual if a young writer signed her book deal with Longmans or Heinemann or Hutchinson in London, or Houghton Mifflin in Boston or Doubleday in New York. In Dublin, Talbot Press was particularly responsive to women writers, publishing over 100 from the 1910s to the 1940s. The biggest selling writer in Ireland from the 1920s to the 1940s was a woman – the criminally under-rated Annie Smithson, who wrote well crafted literary feminist novels that were hugely inspiring to women.

Post-independence, though, Ireland became increasingly a conservative society, and the position of women disimproved. From the 1930s, the Censorship of Publications Acts caused much damage to the careers and livelihoods of numerous Irish writers, including Norah Hoult, Kate O'Brien, Maura Laverty and Edna O'Brien. Publishing itself became more conservative, less risk-taking, more boring, with fewer opportunities for new writers, and especially for women writers. The power and authority of the Censorship Board waned later in the century, though I would argue that the Arts Council/An Chomhairle Ealaíon, in its judgement of what books and authors they chose to support, has acted as a gatekeeper of contemporary Irish writing and publishing, and not always for the good.

The feminist presses founded in the 1970s and 1980s – Arlen House (1975), Irish Feminist Information (1978), Women's Community Press (1983), Attic Press (1984) and Women's Education Bureau (1984) – broke new ground, challenged authorities and power structures, established new audiences and markets, and created a new vision of Irish publishing. The repercussions of this continue to be felt today. Though I wonder now how many of the current recipients and beneficiaries know the names of the women responsible for changing the literary world in their favour?

The publishing scene of the 2010s and the 2020s is vastly different from that of the late twentieth century. It appears so much easier now for women to get agents and to be published. However, the landscape is not an equal one for everyone. Gender, age, sexuality, ethnicity remain stubborn obstacles for those who don't fit the ideal publishing model. And there are other challenges.

'Diversity' is the biggest buzzword in the arts in recent years. Government, organisations and businesses have publicly announced their commitment to diversity, introducing impressive new schemes, opportunities and events. These are all to be welcomed, encouraged and supported, as indeed are all initiatives which aim to create a more representative and equal cultural world.

But why has it taken so long?

The original Equal Status Act was introduced in 2000 and covers nine discriminatory grounds – gender, race, sexual orientation, age, disability, marital status, family status, religion and membership of the Traveller community. It prohibits discrimination in the provision of goods and services under these grounds; it respects, values, accommodates and encourages diversity. The 2000 Act, with its subsequent amendments, was envisaged to actually welcome and encourage more diversity in Irish society. Why did the Irish arts world not embrace the equality legislation then and incorporate diversity at its core and in its funding models and decisions? Why was it impossible, then, to address power and privilege? Particularly so when members of the arts world have been, and still are, especially susceptible to discrimination.

We are in a cultural world of buzzwords now. Social media, which lack nuance, have become increasingly powerful, potent and poisonous. The so-called 'cancel culture' can act as a noose in attempts to destroy people's careers and lives, based on weak evidence and dubious interpretations bayed by a mob mentality.

Another term used problematically at times is 'privileged white male'. Attempts to call out power and privilege are brave and are to be welcomed, though it is disturbing when done by those who fail to name *their* own power and privilege. And it would be naïve to assume that some women have not supported the patriarchy in the discrimination of other women, while it is also true that some men have worked towards equality and justice in the arts world.

Wise woman Edna O'Brien, who more than well-earned her legendary status, said in a powerful speech on 8 March 2021:

> In this troubled, berserk world of ours there are women all over the world who cannot write ... We as writers have an obligation to those women to write their stories ... We are the mere messengers, and what we have to do is research, follow, investigate, as far as we can, into the minds of those girls so that their feelings, their intensities, comes as though by a current to us, to understand, or at least understand as much as any human being can understand the other. And also I would

suggest that we forget as writers, or rather omit, the current incendiary gripe about cultural appropriation. There is no such thing. There are no borders to the imagination. Writing at its best is a testament to our shared humanity.

Most books do not have long lives, and many writers are forgotten, even in their own lifetimes. Those writers who are brave, take on challenges and become part of the living canon of literature are few, and unique.

Publishing is increasingly now about marketing and numbers, rather than artistic talent and quality work. The marketing budgets authorised by power brokers indicate what they want prioritised, ranging from bookshop buyers and allocation of shelf space, to the media and the reading public. Books can be marketed as the 'first', the 'original', the 'ground-breaking', even when their content clearly isn't. Books can be declared 'bestsellers' before they are even published. Books can be shortlisted for, and win, awards they are not even eligible for. These problems, sadly, are not gender neutral. They need to be called out through vigorous and rigorous scholarship, rather than jumping on bandwagons with the masses whooping praise.

Poor practices in the arts world were (and still are) tackled by brave people – mainly women. In the 1980s it was incredibly difficult for women to receive bursaries, get published, be reviewed, or to be elected into the artistic organisation Aosdána and receive annual financial support for their art. Some organisations worked then with passion, integrity and a genuine commitment to diversity, yet their work was ignored in favour of other agenda-driven ideologies. There was a lack of an overall vision for equality in the arts. Would or could an anthology of literary work by Traveller women have been refused funding, then, yet the same anthology be met with substantial funding and rapturous praise, now? Can the Arts Council answer this question? The reasons why?

Simplistic presumptions, and problematic use of

language and buzzwords, need to be called out. It appears that the mistakes of the past – created and utilised by some 'privileged white males' – can also be adopted by others now, thus perpetuating inequalities rather than stamping out bad practices. Equality is a two-way street. As the 'woke' agenda is becoming increasingly more judgemental and toxic, we need to find a way to create a new common ground where all can start on an equal footing. Diversity policies will work best if integration is key. Quality must be at the core of all endeavours. Tokenism is no longer acceptable. One set of power and privilege cannot be substituted for another. Re-inventing the wheel is no longer an option. Sustainable solutions must be found.

Sustainable solutions *were* found from the 1970s onwards to create opportunities for a large proportion of the literary public then denied access to the published word – women.

Ailbhe Smyth, in a 1987 US feature article, stated that Arlen House and Attic Press have played 'a central part in the process of reclaiming women's history and identity'. She interviewed Arlen House founder Catherine Rose in a 'sophisticated but miniscule space they now occupy in a brand-new Dublin office block ... a far cry from the livingroom in Galway where it all began'. In the early 1970s Rose had been commissioned to write a book on feminism in Ireland but the:

> publisher let her down very badly, leaving her with a broken contract, no money and the conviction that if women's knowledge, ideas and dreams were to be recorded, women would have to do it themselves.

And so she did. Arlen House thrived and survived because 'so many women gave so much of their time for nothing'. Editorial meetings took place in each others' houses, around kitchen tables, 'with small children under the table and sticky fingers in the proofs'. A photo survives from a national newspaper of one 1970s editorial meeting with directors Catherine Rose, Janet Martin, Terry Prone, and editor Eavan Boland making history.

They did make history.

The most famous feminist press in the world is Virago Press, founded in London in 1973 by Carmen Callil, although it was to be September 1975 before the first Virago book appeared, published in association with a mainstream press (due to capital and resource issues). That same month, September 1975, Arlen House published its first book, in Galway, from an independent publishing house established as a limited company owned by a woman. *The Female Experience: The Story of the Woman Movement in Ireland* was advertised as:

> an informative and entertaining book of social comment in which the author charts the course of the women's movement in Ireland. Giving reasons for Irish women's apathy and for the lack of a vigorous women's movement, Catherine Rose sets the Irish situation in the context of international women's liberation.

From the *Books Ireland* review:

> summing up helpfully and critically the multiple entrapments and role-casting of women ... using snappy quotations to get our interest – for one of the problems is a disinclination by both men and women to do more than adopt a stance without much reading or thought – she roves in a free-thinking way over the history and sociology, but without making much effort to argue in the language (or on the level) of the Catholic traditionalist whose attitude is mostly expressed in such different terms that no real dialogue is possible. One feels that the author could have come to grips with her entrenched opponents better ... she angrily shoots down the idea that women must change to fulfil themselves better in existing society. No, she says, it is society that must change to allow them room for fulfilment, but after that her conclusion seems rather lame: that we can only concentrate on research, information and education.

The second book published was *The Essential Guide for Women in Ireland*, originally entitled *What Every Woman Needs to Know*, written by Belfast journalist Janet Martin, former women's editor of the *Irish Independent*. This, the first practical handbook for women in Ireland, was launched in 1977 at Listowel Writers' Week:

> Janet Martin guides women through the bureaucratic maze of legal rights and social welfare entitlements. She deals with education, retraining, going back to work, equal pay as well as giving advice on problems concerning sex, marriage, children, health, pregnancy. Concise and comprehensive, this is an essential guide for women in Northern Ireland as well as the Republic.

In an interview with the *Clare Champion* in 1977, Catherine Rose stated that:

> it was her duty to make information available to women, not just about their history, but about how women's bodies work and how 'we can control them'. She said that in making factual information available to women, she was not a purveyor of pornography and asked for a radical reform of existing legislation.

Rose remembered in 1987:

> It's hard now to understand just how radical that *Guide* was. As well as dealing with the standard sorts of information – which no one in fact had ever dealt with before – it broached the taboo subjects of contraception and abortion.

Both author and publisher, young women with young children, took the risk of imprisonment under the terms of the Censorship Act when they published the book. In 1978 a supplement was released, providing updates and additional information.

Arlen House worker-directors, 1978

In 1978 the press was renamed Arlen House: The Women's Press, with Janet Martin, Terry Prone and Margaret Mac Curtain joining as worker-directors. Early feminist publishing output was focused on political and social affairs, health, children's rights and childcare, family status, education, inspiring biographies and history, new and classic literature and art. Arlen House also distributed feminist material from other publishers, including a biography of Constance Markievicz, and a pamphlet, *Make Sure You Get Equal Pay* (1977) compiled by the Trade Union Women's Forum.

The first huge seller was Margaret Mac Curtain's *Women in Irish Society: The Historical Dimension* (1978) which is widely regarded as beginning the coherent writing of Irish women's history. It sold over 10,000 copies, with the international rights being acquired by an American publisher. The next hit was the very first book ever published in Ireland on the menopause. Mollie Lloyd's *The Change of Life* (1979/1981), sold over 20,000 copies in multiple editions.

They also published men. *Children First: A Source Book for Parents and Other Professionals* (1979) by Charles Mollan was commissioned for International Year of the Child. Women's history continued with two biographies of strong-willed Victorian women; *Margaret Anna Cusack: One Woman's Campaign for Women's Rights* (1979) was a biography of the famous Nun of Kenmare, written by Irene ffrench-Eagar. Vera Colebrook's *Ellen* (1980) was a biography of a distant relative living in nineteenth-century Britain who emigrated to New Zealand, recounting her fascinating life in diaries. Other bestsellers included two books in a Help Yourself series: Ronit Lentin and Geraldine Niland's *Who's Minding the Children* (1981) and *Coping Alone* (1982) by Clara Clark.

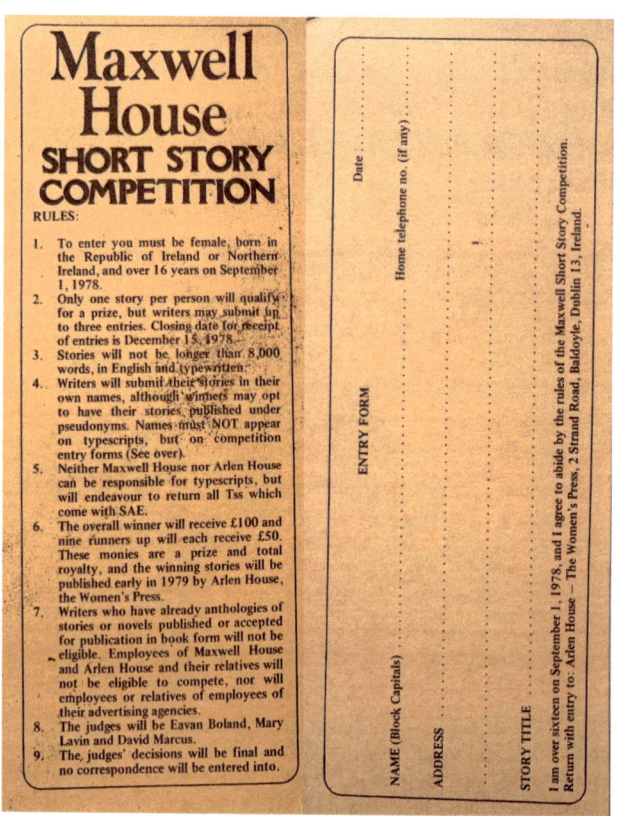

In 1978 they announced a major new initiative. This would be the beginning of literary feminism in Ireland – giving priority to focus on women's literary and creative output.

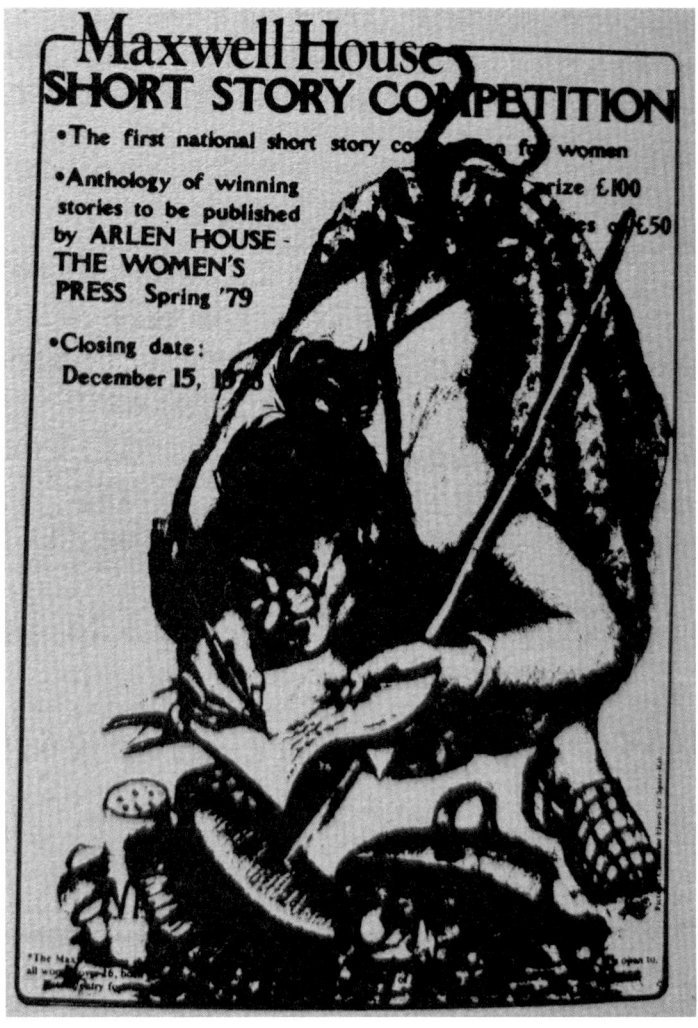

In 1978 poet Eavan Boland contacted Arlen House to offer her support. She became an associate editor and enthusiastically got involved in projects of new writing and reclamation. Terry Prone had come up with the idea of a literary competition to discover new women writers and found a willing funder in Maxwell House. In October 1978 Arlen House: The Women's Press, in a reception held in Marsh's Library, announced the first ever short story competition for emerging women writers, sponsored by Maxwell House and judged by Eavan Boland, Mary Lavin and David Marcus. Over 1000 women, all previously unpublished, responded. Eavan promoted the initiative in the media and addressed the backlash against the need for a women-only competition and book. She also wrote the foreword to the collection of winning stories, *The Wall Reader and Other Stories* (1979), the first fiction anthology by Irish women to ever be published. As Boland says in her introduction: 'These ten accounts of disappointment, adventure, self-realization have tones and colours that could hardly have been projected twenty years ago in Ireland'. *The Wall Reader* was an unexpected success – reaching No 1 in the bestseller charts for many weeks in summer 1979, displacing Marilyn French's *The Women's Room* from the top spot.

From *Books Ireland*, August 1979:

> Arlen House, the Women's Press, did things in style on 21 June when they launched their first anthology of short stories in Dublin's Berkeley Court Hotel. The Arts Council and Maxwell House were the generous sponsors and the vibrant, mainly youthful, gathering was fêted with, among other goodies, lashings of coffee, iced and coffee braced and coffee cake ... Fiona Barr, imminently expecting her second child, went up to receive her cheque for £100 as overall winner ... Cheques for £50 were awarded to the other winners and it was remarkable how many had Northern Ireland backgrounds and teaching as a profession ... The County Cork printers were criticized for poor performance and production issues. Dr Margaret Mac Curtain stated that Irish printers are, on the whole, so unreliable and such messers and how could they be otherwise when women are still excluded from their union!

In March 1980 *Books Ireland* reported they:

> received over a thousand entries for this year's Maxwell House sponsored competition to discover new feminine writing talent, for which the prize money will run to nine awards of £100. Fifty per cent of the entries were gunge, Catherine Rose told us ruefully, but to us that sounds a remarkably low proportion, especially when you consider that poetry as well as short stories are eligible this year.

Ireland's earliest short fiction anthologies by women writers published by Arlen House: *The Wall Reader* (1979); *A Dream Recurring* (1981); *The Adultery* (1982)

The 2nd competition, now open to poets also, was judged by Eavan Boland, Richard Llewellyn, Máire Mhac an tSaoi and Wolf Mankowitz, while the 3rd was judged by Benedict Kiely, Máire Mhac an tSaoi and Jennifer

Johnston. Winners of these competitions, published in the anthologies, include Mary Rose Callaghan, Ann McKay, Ivy Bannister and Fiona Barr (who was then published in Blackstaff's *Sisters* anthology in 1980).

In June 1981 they announced a Women's Literary Competition bursary of £500 for women writers 'who could best benefit from a subvention to buy writing materials and books or attend courses'. At this time it was incredibly difficult for a woman to receive a bursary from any funding agency. One of the beneficiaries was a woman in prison. Another was Ruth Hooley (now Ruth Carr), who was awarded £100 which was presented to her at a ceremony in Dublin by writer Beryl Bainbridge, pictured below with Catherine Rose in October 1981.

Ruth Hooley, Belfast, receiving her share of the Maxwell House bursary from the celebrated novelist Beryl Bainbridge, at the Projects Arts Centre.

Catherine Rose commented in 1987 that the literary competitions revealed the 'store of stifled imagination, wit and ability of women' writing throughout the island.

One of the winners of the first Maxwell House competition was Mary Rose Callaghan, who then got a book deal with Arlen House for her debut novel, *Mothers*

(1982). It was enthusiastically received, but was unofficially banned from publicity by RTÉ because of the fear that abortion would be discussed. The book sold 2500 copies in Ireland, and went into hardback editions in 1982 and 1984 with Marion Boyars publishers in London and New York. In 1985, her second novel, *Confessions of a Prodigal Daughter*, was published collaboratively by Marion Boyars and Arlen House.

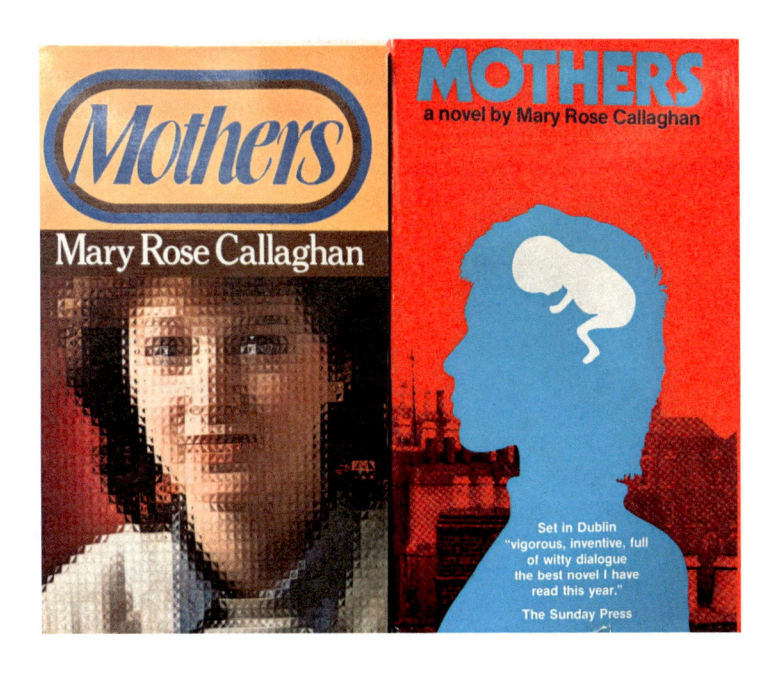

Another Maxwell House winner to receive a book deal was Rita Kelly whose debut short story collection, *The Whispering Arch*, was published in 1986, as was Terry Prone's *The Scattering of Mrs Blake and Related Matters*.

A fine balance was created between publishing works of literary fiction and poetry, and non-fiction feminist polemics and history. In 1983, Arlen House published an American feminist nun, who came to Ireland for a whirlwind tour, including an appearance on the *Late Late Show*. Madonna Kolbenschlag's *Goodbye Sleeping Beauty:*

*Breaking the Spell of Feminine Myths and Models* (1983) was a provocative and timely study of the situation contemporary women were in, arguing that a feminist vision is not only a fundamental basis for personal wholeness but also for a just society and that the empowerment of women will be a crucial factor in the spiritual and social transformation of the world.

That same year saw Máire Mullarney's *Anything School Can Do, You Can Do Better: The Story of a Family who Learned at Home*, a book advocating home schooling which was an enormous success, selling over 10,000 copies in Ireland, with international mass market rights being acquired by a London publisher.

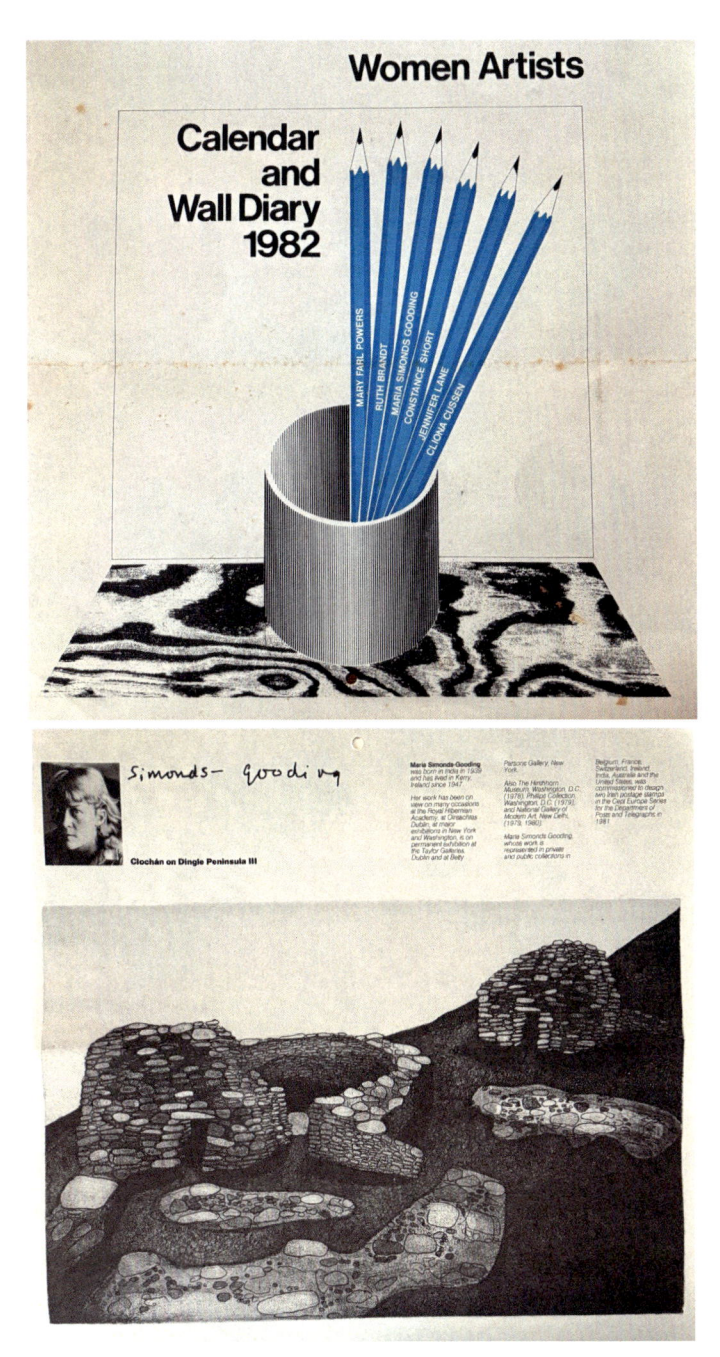

In 1981 Arlen House published a wall calendar, devised by Constance Short, promoting Irish women artists.

some 1970s/1980s catalogues and newsletters

Feminism, as an inclusive politics of equality, was at the heart of all that they planned and wished to achieve.

# Dr Margaret Mac Curtain OP (1929–2020)

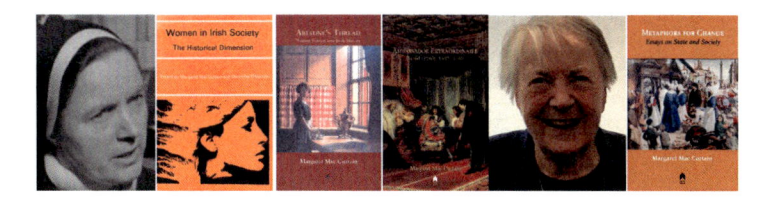

Margaret Mac Curtain is the only author who published with Arlen House, Women's Community Press and Attic Press, and worked with Irish Feminist Information and Women's Education Bureau.

Born in Cork in 1929, she was a student activist in UCC in the 1940s before entering the Dominican order in 1950, where she took the name Sister Benvenuta. A life of teaching and religious work lay ahead, but she was granted permission to enrol for a MA (1958) and a Ph.D (1963), necessitating travel around Europe for research, giving tremendous freedom to a young, inquisitive nun. Back teaching in Dublin, social justice was at the heart of her beliefs. She took public stands on key issues such as feminism, equality, domestic violence, apartheid, corporal punishment, the right to remarry. She was a political activist, with a public profile and reputation, even before the Irish Women's Liberation Movement started in 1970. She mentored generations of activists, including some Irish Presidents. One newspaper referred to her as the most famous woman in Ireland. *Women in Irish Society* (1978), the first Irish women's history text, sold over 10,000 copies. On her deathbed she said that founding Ballyfermot College of Further Education was her proudest achievement.

Intellectually razor-sharp, she wore her genius lightly, using her gifts to impart knowledge and inspiration to vast numbers of people over her 60-year-long career. It would be unwise to underestimate the influence of Margaret Mac Curtain on Irish society.

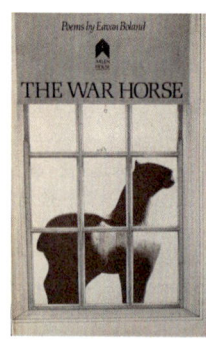

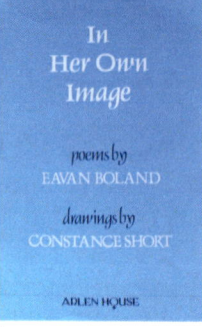

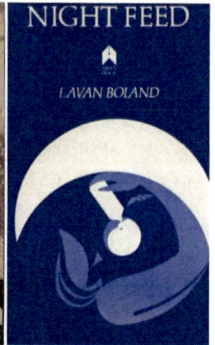

THIS IS NUMBER FOURTEEN
OF A LIMITED EDITION OF
FIFTY COPIES.

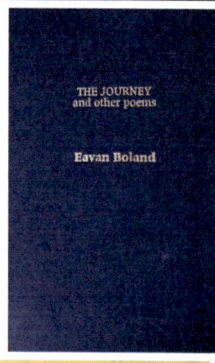

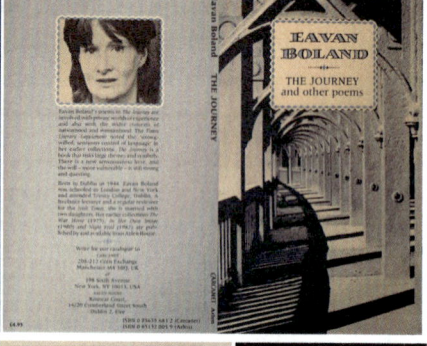

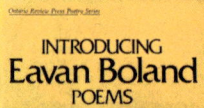

Arlen House published Eavan Boland's poetry collections *In Her Own Image* (1980), illustrated by Constance Short; *The War Horse* (1980); *Night Feed* (1982); *The Journey and Other Poems* (Arlen House, 1986 in association with Carcanet, 1987) and *Selected Poems* (WEB/Carcanet, 1989).

> Arlen House the Women's Press can thank the male chauvenism of Coolock car thieves when their *In Her Own Image* by Eavan Boland and Constance Short appears ... When the Gardaí finally ran their stolen car to earth everything of value was missing from it, except the typesetting and artwork for the book (*Books Ireland*, March 1980).

In a 1993 interview with Jody-Allen Randolph, Boland stated:

> The early eighties were a time when some of the very stubborn resistances to women writing the Irish poem surfaced. Those resistances need to be analysed more carefully than I've ever done to be sure what they consisted of. But there's a fair argument to be made that the male poetic community sensed that women poets would disrupt a privileged vantage point ... male poets spoke about the limitation of women's themes, and the mediocrity of women's writing. There was a sort of condescension in the air, and occasionally something more raw and exclusive ... power has operated in the making of canons, the making of taste, the nominating of what poems should represent the age and so on ... I was incredibly lucky during those years to have Arlen House to publish me. They were a feminist publisher and Catherine Rose, who ran it, was a wonderfully steady presence. She was very committed to women participating in the levels of decision-making in the arts (*Irish University Review*, 1993).

In 2016 at the launch of *Eavan Boland: Inside History* at Poetry Ireland (with Mary Robinson, Catherine Rose and Colm Tóibín as special guests), Boland stated that Arlen House was her favourite publisher over her 55 year career.

Eavan Boland's poetry will be read for centuries. Many people will not know that she was a founder member of the Irish Women's Liberation Movement in 1970. Later in the 1970s and 1980s, working with Arlen House, she was the first to create safe literary spaces – physical, emotional, financial, practical – for women, both fiction writers and poets, in the days when they were not always welcome in the Irish literary world.

In 1979, Arlen House, inspired by Carmen Callil's recent launch of Virago Modern Classics, announced a new series of classic literature by Irish women writers whose books were out of print and forgotten. This was Eavan Boland's suggestion and she was the first editor of the series. Boland championed Kate O'Brien, writing the preface to *The Ante Room* (1980). Boland also wrote an introduction to a planned edition of Mary Lavin's *The Becker Wives*. The project progressed enthusiastically, with Lavin even visiting the National Gallery of Ireland to view the painting chosen for the front cover, but for some unknown reason the book was not republished.

In 1984 Arlen House founded The Kate O'Brien Weekend to commemorate the life and work of one of the twentieth century's most important writers; this event was organised by staff member Louise Barry (aka Louise C Callaghan), and included a reading by Maeve Kelly. This was the first festival in Ireland to be named after a woman; sadly in recent years the festival has been renamed, with Kate O'Brien now reduced to a subtitle in the name of her festival that had brought great pride to Limerick, restoring the author to her rightful place at the height of the literary world.

Janet Madden-Simpson's *Woman's Part: An Anthology of Short Fiction By and About Irish Women 1890–1960* (1984) was the first reclamation anthology of short fiction by Irish women writers, with stories by Norah Hoult, Dorothy Macardle, Maura Laverty, Jane Barlow, Mary Lavin, Erminda Esler, Mary Beckett, Geraldine Cummins, George Egerton, M.E. Francis, Elizabeth Bowen, Katharine Tynan, Edith Somerville, Violet Martin (Martin Ross) and Elizabeth Connor (Una Troy). Many of these authors had been completely forgotten by this time; some were still living. The book was published in hardback and paperback editions, and was distributed internationally by Marion Boyars publishers, London and New York.

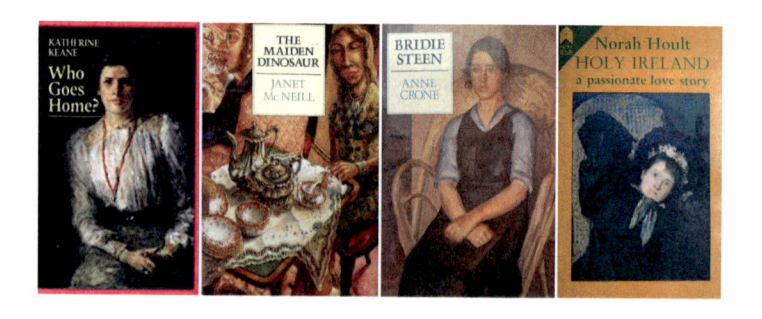

Other authors championed in the Classic Literature series included Norah Hoult, Anne Crone, Janet McNeill and Katherine Keane (grandmother of Madeleine Keane, now *Sunday Independent* literary editor). For Norah Hoult, the financial support given and interest shown in her work must have been helpful in her final years. Many other titles were planned and announced – with inspired suggestions by later series editor Janet Madden-Simpson – but they fell foul of the vagaries of publishing and funding agencies. The titles that were published were critically acclaimed and large sellers. They demonstrated that Irish women had a distinctive literary heritage worth exploring, commemorating and celebrating.

Celebrating the tenth birthday of Arlen House in 1985 are directors Louise Barry and Catherine Rose with Audrey Dixon of the Council for the Status of Women.

In 1985 Arlen House celebrated its 10th birthday with receptions held in Dublin by the Council for the Status of

Women, and in Cork City Library to celebrate the publication of *Irish Women: Image and Achievement*, edited by Eiléan Ní Chuilleanáin. Catherine Rose later recalled that the Cork event was particularly special to her because her mother was able to attend the reception just months before she passed away.

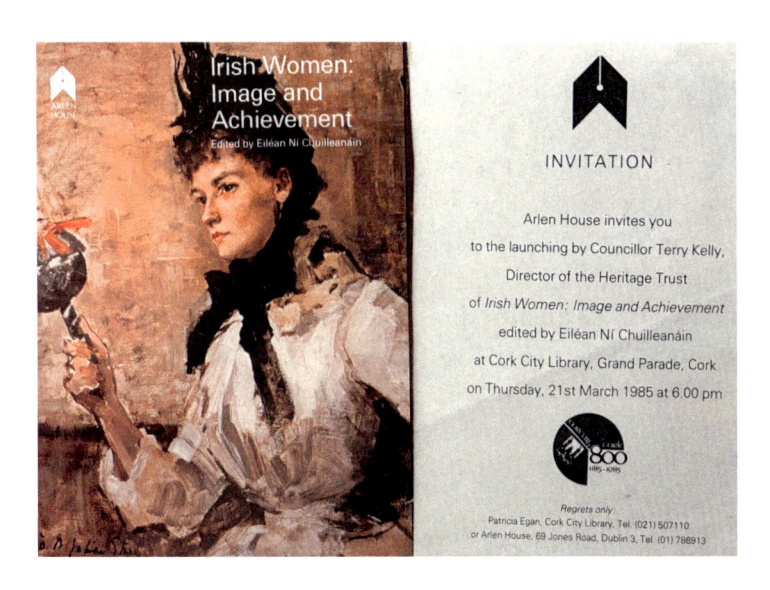

*Irish Women: Image and Achievement* (Arlen House, 1985) was the first book to explore the place women have occupied in the development of the Irish imagination, tracing images of women found in art, folklore, religion and law, and documenting women's artistic achievements. Contributors included Margaret Mac Curtain, Nuala O'Faolain, Nóirín Ní Riain, Helen Lanigan Wood and Miriam Daly (who, in 1980, had been assassinated in Belfast). The book was based on a US lecture tour undertaken in 1979 by a number of prominent Irish women.

Also published in 1985 was Stanislaus Kennedy's *But Where Can I Go? Homeless Women in Dublin* (1985), the first study ever carried out on homeless women in Ireland, revealing the plight of women who were surviving without homes, and detailing their own stories of family violence and rejection by society. Would they think the situation would continue forty years later?

In 1986, at the National Gallery of Ireland, they organised the first ever Writers and Readers Day, with speakers including Maeve Binchy, Jennifer Johnston, Mary Lavin, Eavan Boland, Clare Boylan, Medbh McGuckian and Maeve Kelly. A woman journalist wrote a scathing review, commenting that a 10-year-old boy and 2 (famous) men, Derek Mahon and Kevin Barry, were bored and only 'stayed the course' out of duty. She said Maeve Binchy was 'booming' platitudes, while 'we all wondered what [Jennifer Johnston] was doing there' and she reduced Maeve Kelly to a senseless (without context) line from her reading. Suffice to say, there was outrage at the inaccurate and condencending reporting. The event generated over £2000 in ticket prices and book sales. Another Writers and Readers Day was scheduled for 1987, but other factors intervened.

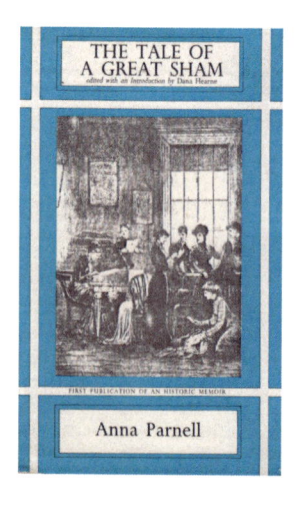

Pioneering women's history continued in 1986 with the historic first publication of *The Tale of a Great Sham* by Anna Parnell.

A new journal was launched in 1987. *The Web: New Writing by Women*, Vol. 1 (Arlen House/Women's Education Bureau, 1987). General Editor: Eavan Boland. Guest Editors: Evelyn Conlon, Mary Rose Callaghan. Boland wrote in her introduction that *The Web* is 'part of the search for different, more sensitive structures which might be more responsive to the needs and growth of emerging women writers in Ireland'. Contributors include Liz McManus, Máiríde Woods, Joan McBreen, Louise Barry, Jean O'Brien, Christine Michael, Frances Molloy, Joni Crone, Eithne Strong, Joan O'Neill among others. The Arts Council refused to financially support any further issues.

Quoting again from that 1987 US interview, Ailbhe Smyth declared that Arlen House have:

> a plethora of plans and are clearly full of optimism and enthusiasm ... They would like to expand into contemporary American and European fiction by women, and translations are a dream Catherine Rose is determined to realise. She is emphatic that Arlen House has to become self-supporting – It's not only a service – you have to trade. Publishing is super-

capital-intensive. We need to raise the print run, keep ahead all the time. Editorial policy has suffered in the past because of our precarious finances – that has got to change ... we have got to move outside and beyond ourselves. We can't afford to be isolated. It's very important for Arlen to bring the diverse experiences and creativity of women elsewhere into Ireland – we need an enriching, nurturing exchange.

Rose admitted to having been idealistic:

> ... quite simply I wanted to change the world. I'm not disillusioned, but feminist publishing is a difficult business, and although I've lost the naïveté, I get immense pleasure from working with women who have their own ideals and visions. The thrill is still there, the books are so exciting, the potential is vast ... Isn't all feminist publishing, in fact any feminist project, a risk? Which doesn't mean the gamble isn't worth it.

Arlen House was bought by two female investors and a substantial new publishing programme was developed for spring 1987. Shortly before the books were to go to print, the investors decided to close down the press.

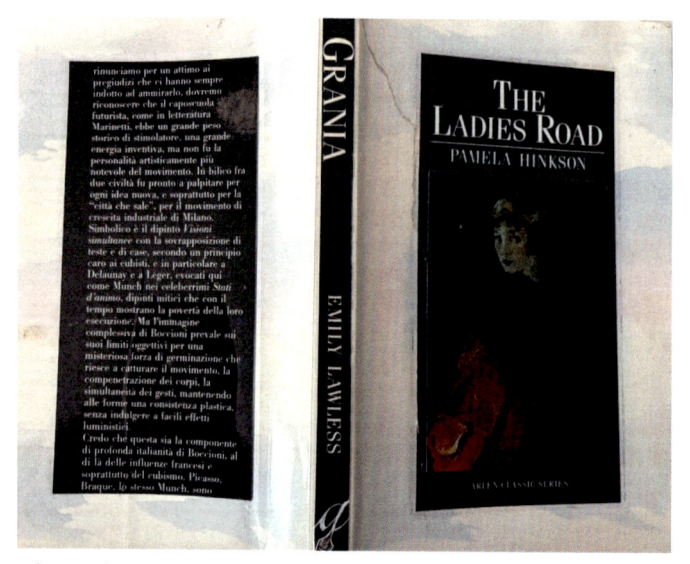

mockup of design template for scheduled Classic Literature titles, *Grania* by Emily Lawless and *The Ladies Road* by Pamela Hinkson, 1987

In 1988 *Books Ireland* commissioned a special feature on feminist publishing with guest editor June Levine. They announced an upcoming revival of Arlen House:

> The pioneer of women's publishing in Ireland and a name justifiably respected by the trade, Arlen House launched many women writers on their writing careers and did much to redress the unbalanced representation of women in publishing.

That revival didn't happen. Catherine Rose had just completed a 20 week stint as director of the first 'Women into Writing' course jointly organised by AnCO/FÁS and WEB, with former Arlen House/WEB staff member Eleanor Murphy working as the administrator. The course, with 27 women students, was strongly orientated towards the practicalities of marketing and presenting work to editors and publishers. Rose was 'delighted to have been part of the course, but disappointed by the lack of employment opportunities for such an immensely talented group'.

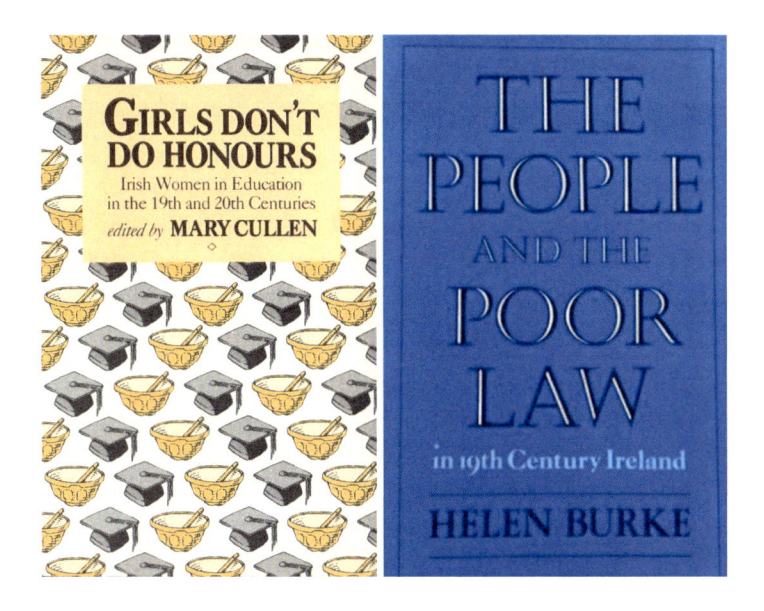

With Arlen House closed, WEB completed some of its publishing plans, such as important publications by Mary

Cullen (*Girls Don't Do Honours: Irish Women in Education in the 19th and 20th Centuries*) and Helen Burke (*The People and the Poor Law in Nineteenth-Century Ireland*). The final book was a co-publication with Carcanet Press in Manchester of Eavan Boland's *Selected Poems* (1989). WEB, the Women's Education Bureau, had been founded by Catherine Rose in 1984 as the national organisation for women writers, to develop workshops, mentorship and supportive and safe creative spaces for women, with Eavan Boland as Creative Director and Eleanor Murphy as administrator.

WEB logos, 1987 and 1989

The WEB workshops continued into the 1990s, some being day-long courses, others full weekends. An array of prestigious writers conducted the workshops, including Clare Boylan, John McGahern, Seamus Heaney, Jennifer Johnston, Nuala Ní Dhomhnaill, Mary Elizabeth Burke Kennedy, Terry Prone, Mary Rose Callaghan and, most importantly, Eavan Boland. She wrote: 'it struck me too often and too forcibly that women had to struggle at a physical and metaphysical level to be writers in this country'. WEB, as the national representative organisation for women writers in Ireland, was a membership body, and it had over 600 members. During the early 1990s, the WEB board of directors continued to meet, trying to find a way to relaunch the press, but no solution appeared then.

In 1998, the Women's Studies Centre at NUI Galway hosted an exhibition on Irish feminist publishing, co-ordinated by this writer, gathering together an expansive collection of books and archival material. From this research project and launch event came the idea of relaunching Arlen House, with encouragement from original directors, Catherine Rose, Margaret Mac Curtain, Mary Cullen and Eavan Boland. Some of the fruits of that story are shown in the final section of this book.

A WEB writing group still exists in Dublin to the present day, which includes many of the writers featured in this anthology. In 2023 Nessa O'Mahony edited a fascinating anthology of WEB writing, *Tearing Stripes off Zebras: Forty Years of Women Writing in Ireland*.

The vast array of Irish women writers today, reaching international heights, owe a debt of gratitude to these trailblazing, brave women for their radical work revolutionising Irish writing and the literary scene. Now Irish writing is a more diverse and open space, for both women and men, because of the truly groundbreaking and perilous work started by visionaries like Catherine Rose, Eavan Boland, Mary Cullen and Margaret Mac Curtain. Let us never forget. Let us never write their work out of history.

Catherine Rose and Mary Cullen, Maynooth, 2023

Eavan Boland's workshops have achieved quite a degree of legendary status, and they have inspired these five bestselling *Washing Windows* anthologies.

To her credit must go the determination to develop workshops for women countrywide, to give up substantial amounts of her time, particularly when her girls were so young, to travel the long windy broken 1980s roads to Tuam, Cork and numerous other places. Poet Áine Ní Ghlinn recalls participanting in Eavan's first workshop held in Kilkenny in 1982.

But Eavan persevered in her mentoring of emerging women writers. She wanted to help make change. At one workshop a talented woman told Eavan she was reluctant to 'go public' with her creative work; she said she couldn't tell her neighbours she was a poet because they would think that she didn't wash her windows.

This is the space and the culture which Eavan Boland, Catherine Rose and their sister feminists subverted and exploded. How lucky we are they did so.

Many thanks and wishing much luck to all the *Washing Windows* women. This is the finale. Well, for now, anyway.

Eavan Boland

## In Her Own Image

It is her eyes:
the irises are gold
and round they go
like the ring on my wedding finger,
round and round

and I can't touch
their histories or tears.
To think they were once my satellites!
They shut me out now.
Such light years!

She is not myself
anymore, she is not
even in my sky
anymore and I
am not myself.

I will not disfigure
her pretty face.
Let her wear amethyst thumbprints,
a family heirloom,
a sort of burial necklace

and I know just the place:
Where the wall glooms,
where the lettuce seeds,
where the jasmine springs
no surprises

I will bed her.
She will bloom there,
second nature to me,

the one perfection
among compromises.

*1980 first edition, illustrated by Constance Short,*

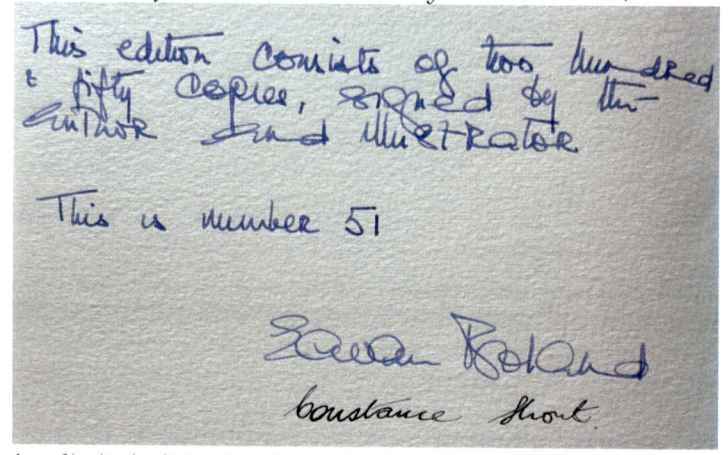

*in a limited edition hardback of 250 copies, plus 3000 paperbacks*

## NIGHT FEED

This is dawn.
Believe me
This is your season, little daughter.
The moment daisies open,
The hour mercurial rainwater
Makes a mirror for sparrows.
It's time we drowned our sorrows.

I tiptoe in.
I lift you up
Wriggling
In your rosy, zipped sleeper.
Yes, this is the hour
For the early bird and me
When finder is keeper.

I crook the bottle.
How you suckle!
This is the best I can be,
Housewife
To this nursery
Where you hold on,
Dear life.

A silt of milk
The last suck.
And now your eyes are open,
birth-coloured and offended.
Earth wakes.
You go back to sleep.
The feed is ended.

Worms turn.
Stars go in.
Even the moon is losing face.

Poplars stilt for dawn
And we begin
The long fall from grace.
I tuck you in.

'In Her Own Image' and 'Night Feed' from Eavan Boland's
*New Collected Poems* are reproduced courtesy of Carcanet Press

*Eavan Boland with her daughters, Eavan and Sarah Casey, Dublin 1982*

# WASHING WINDOWS V

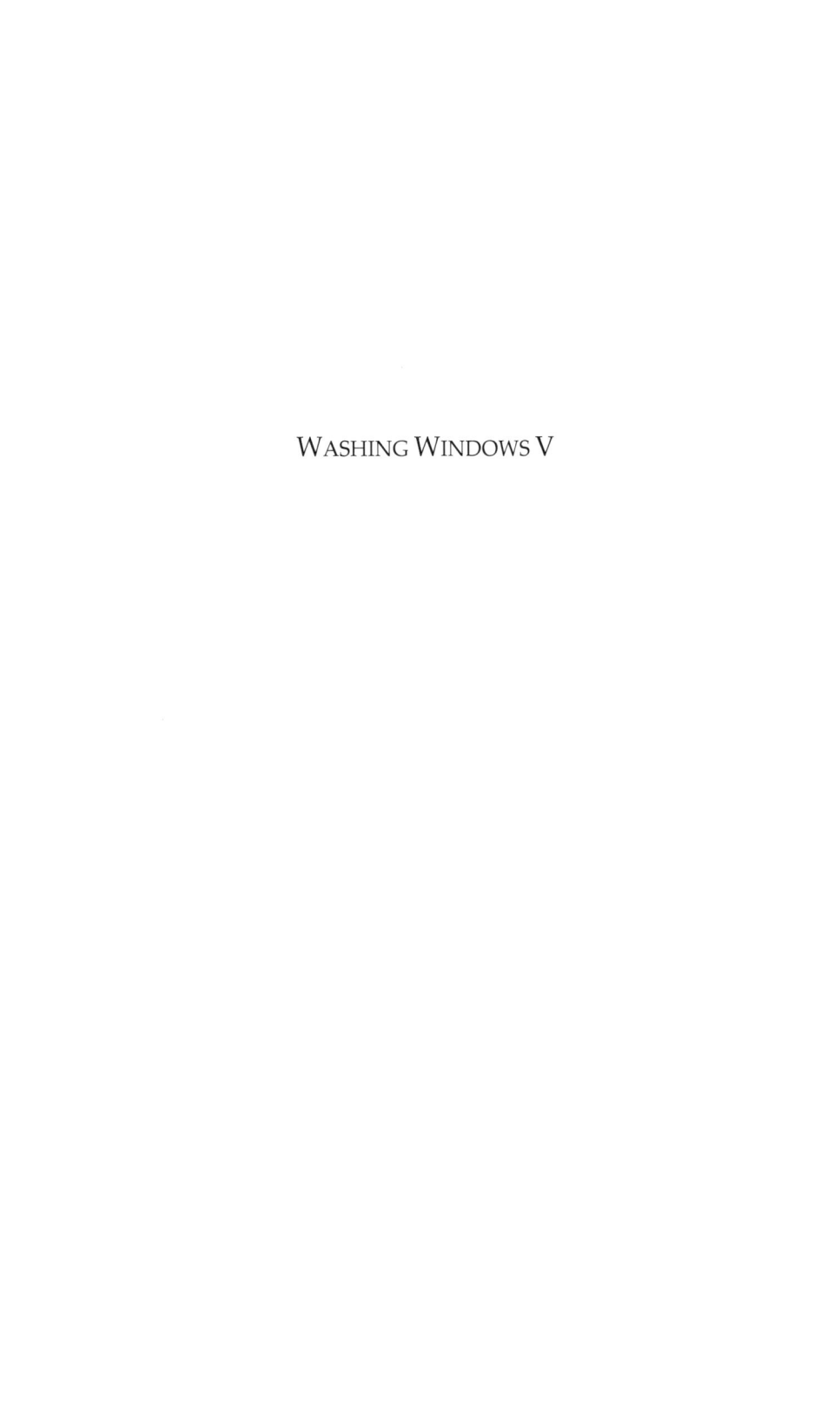

Amy Abdullah Barry

### Times of War
*for Peg Broderick Nicholson*

I am a girl of eighteen
dragged from my home to the inky night.
I remember a crackling roof,
grey coils of smoke,
a blaze the colour of raspberry.
My hair hacked with blunt scissors,
soon to be shaved to the scalp.
Cutting, I say, is the best way to stir growth.

Sonia Abercrombie

## The Singer

### I

These first stitches made are the smallest steps
by this machine with a name that sounds like love.
Its motor noise is the rush of a lift in its shaft,
the glory of playgrounds, and our red car
rattling through the brambles on a country lane.
Its little light canopies the flowered cloth.
It spottles my hand, anchoring it old as another's,
flushed pink from vegetables and soap suds.
She is here in my hands, teaching through memory,
prodigal summers returned, with field rose and daisy.

### II

The young women are making ready for The Plaza.
Bridie raises her eyes to upstairs where laughter tumbles.
In the dressing room I am lifted and cradled
because I've crawled over the handmade dresses
which lie like shadow puppets on the Belfast quilt.
Our Breige and our Margaret paint their eyes like Cleopatra.
Breige dons her ocelot coat and they run out into the night,
past the rosebuds, along our garden path, in their stiletto
heels towards the bus, through a street that is amber with
gaslight. At the window I draw them dancing, and look
back to the parlour where Nan listens to the wireless,
in the old world.

Síle Agnew

## Murty Magic
*In memory of Murty Herbert, who died 9 November 2024*

Autumn is here
the orchard is bare
Murty has flown.
His superman cape swishes
in the November wind
before the cherry red of Christmas.

His happy soul will always
make us pause
when we hear his laughter
echo across a crowd.
A lump in our throats
when we hear his favourite song.

Wrapped in his loving ways
cheerfulness his nature
laughter his blessing.
Moments of gladness
surrounding him always.
The draught board awaits.
'Who's next?'

Michelle Ivy Alwedo

## TK Maxx Christmas Temp

Winter in Limerick city – half past five.
Night clocks in quicker than day shifts can end.
304 Parkway Retail to UL; Stables is empty,
Scholars closed for holidays since kids flocked
to their families for festivities, leaving campus
and international student residents desolate.

I plod my tired feet home through frost and fog.
Awaiting my company is a Bordeaux glass
of white wine, a warm shower, and pesto
pork pizza leftover from solo date night
last Saturday, my only weekend off work.
Time away I should have spent more wisely,
writing poetry instead of wistfully bingeing
Netflix K-dramas for a quick serotonin boost.

Nathalie Anderson

MAGPIES

*One for sorrow* I was then, mirrorless
among the nuns, and glad of my small cell
in their hostel, grey though it was and chary,
their lamps so few and their waters chill.

Not that I met them – intuited rather
from cell and bath and bed, imagining
a sister there, tucking her smalls where
there was no cupboard, drying herself

without seeing her skin, kneeling where
there was no floor for kneeling, thinking
*sorrow mirth, death birth, boy girl, heaven hell,*
and all of it *secret, never to be told.* Summer

in Dublin, my first time there, and stifling
in narrowness, the bed no wider
than my hips, no table for my baggage
to settle on or open itself. I slept

with my bookbag for a pillow, my suitcase
under my knees. Nights, I'd open the casement
on *faery lands forlorn,* wake to bird shit
streaking the glass, and no clear way

to clean it: magpies – that hacking laugh
at my window, that crack in my dream.
Mornings, I'd see them circling the gardens
in their blue-black and white – stark, geometric –

stalking after the meditating sisters, each neat nun
smaller by comparison. *Two for joy* eluded me then,

the verges thick with birds, too many futures to count,
and me distracted, wondering how those nuns

came out so starched, where they found space to press
their habits, launder their black and white decisions, while
ever behind them, those mocking cries. Who, taking thought,
would change her feathers? Oh, wouldn't I, wouldn't I!

Nuala Archer

## Memoir

1
I lied.

2
This genderless deliquescence
the size of a nearly newborn
astronaut falling

is no fawn

3
& I am no longer four.

4
So I can look
& see my own staring eyes
staring back at me

5
from the glass
jar, a jarring
mirror etching

6
my retinas, fathoms
deep with what lies
before me & is

7
in my face. Always
now, always forever
I am still looking
at this form floating

8
in my nervous system
like flotsam, like a flux
of roots feeding
on my living light.

9
Forever floating
in formaldehyde
this fetus

10
is what my fundamentalist
father, a Dublin Quaker,
who does not believe in Darwin,

is showing me:
a birthday present
for my seventh year.

11
Still,
I do not blink.

I keep a careful watch
as he pivots the jar,
tightly sealed,

12
to point out
a tail growing directly
from the tiny human spine.

13
*Is this why
the baby died?*
I ask.

14
*No, it isn't
because of the tail,*
my father answers.

15
*The Mama
couldn't stay alive,
homeless, in the winter's
cold lightning
her baby*

16
Sixty two years later
I ask myself
*why the effingever did you never
ask him why this show-&-tell.*

17
I know
why.

18
He meant no fright-fest.
No reckless rout.
No nonchalance.

19
He revels in mysteries.

20
Life-changing,
dangerous mysteries.

21
Risk

22
He did not want
his daughter to be
locked out the way he was
on that day in 1930
when he was told , *No, you
are too young to attend
Granny's funeral.*

23
His fundamentalism
is oppressive, but
he is not oppressive

24
Amazingly, there is room
left inside of me to walk
around. To breathe.

25
Slowly, I understand
that there is another me
inside of me gazing quietly.

26
She is my advocate,
my sympathizer, my friend.

27
I could send out
a Doppler whoop of sirens.
I have a choice.

28
Struck alive by lightning
I see that human beings are
born strangely,

best unfastened
from freeze-dried smiles.

29
This is no
portrait of love.

30
You ask me where
are my children?

31
I have none.

32
I've long learned to make
my home
myself.

33
Alone?

34
Every grief
requires its grief.

35
Beauty's terror
is no error.

36
I'm just beginning
to understand
your kindness

37
Where my blood is

& where it has been
is the opening

38
to true night
truing me:

39
(It's hard to believe
that it will ever be better)

40
I enter:

41
(It's hard to believe
that it was ever any better)

42
A gem, an ice-cube, a tear

43
A puddle in the sun,

44
its yolk oozing into everywhere.

t c arkle

## The Parable of the Green-Eyed Monster

Peter was a little bitch. *Why should we listen to her?* he moaned. *She's a girl – why did the Lord like her more than us?* He clearly had a stick up his ass. All the others understood that Mary was the first to witness Jesus's resurrection, *even a blind man could see he preferred her because he used to kiss her on the lips*, said John. Some people can't read the writing on the temple wall, or in the sandstorm coming towards them. Peter was one of them. He thought Mary's words idle ramblings – women's *blah-blah-blah*. All he could see was the devil in a blue dress dancing like a thousand Jezebels, goading him on. He couldn't hide his hard-on and yet he couldn't bear the fact that he had one. Who wouldn't – Jesus was a total hottie. Who wouldn't love a long-haired surfer that can make bread and wine appear out of nowhere? *Hot is in the eye of the beholder,* says Zac on *Quora,* a Forensic Astronomer and Theoretical Cosmetologist. *The long shadow of hot Jesus (Vox). We need to talk about how hot Jesus is (WW News). Hot AI Jesus is Huge on Facebook (The Atlantic).* Peter had his heart set on Jesus riding in on a flaming stallion bringing justice in a hailstorm of jism and joy. He couldn't understand why *a woman* should have the greatest secrets revealed to her above him – it drove him nuts! In the desert one night, as the moon climbed into the sky, he lay his head down, cheek to the moving sands, and cried. He'd never had any luck with the ladies, in fact *he would flee at the sight of a woman's face (Leloup)*; even his own daughter, who was more beautiful than the sun coming up over a grove of cedar trees, caught his unappetising eye. He prayed and prayed till Petronilla – that was her name – became paralysed; he was happy to see her die a virgin, a saint and a martyr. Peter tossed and turned that night on his pallet, he saw Mary laughing at him, taking Jesus by the hand, pressing his hand to her breast, to the warmth between her legs; he saw them rise like nymphs into the cantering stars and Jesus' naked chest oiled by Mary's alabaster jar, as she dipped again and again, her hand raising myrrh and Frankincense to his hair, his feet ... Peter awoke with the smell in his flared nostrils. He got up off his pallet, and knelt, as he did every morning to pray the same prayer, but this morning, more than any other, he felt a latch catch like an internal metronome, as the weight of his words swung wildly – fantasising – perhaps? *Thank you, Lord, for not having made me an invalid, poor – or a woman ...?*

Bebe Ashley

CHLOE, ON CHESIL BEACH

I come away from Whiterock Road with two small loaves
of San Francisco sourdough and half a dozen white roses.

I thumb over the sticky strip of the post-it note
folded in my fleece pocket. thank you, it says.

I ignore the cars reversing in and out of the driveway,
and the toddlers, their wild fists squirming against car seats.

I walk the short distance red-faced in clothes that could
do with an iron, hair that could be better brushed.

I make it past the postbox with the last of the light.
It will rain again now and I should lock the back gate.

It is Mother's Day and I'm growing more comfortable
with the notion of never becoming a mother.

Home, with the cats, I arrange the flowers in the jug
on the kitchen table. I don't know why I'm crying.

Ivy Bannister

## WALKING WITH THE SAINT

I am walking with St Francis
but I'm old and ill, and can't keep pace.

Cast away your shoes, he says.
But the stones, they'd pierce my feet.

Cast away your shoes, he repeats, so I obey
and the way grows easier, and I keep pace.

He sings, the saint, a child's song *en français*.
My *maman* was French, he says, now take my arm

and sing with me, as we make our way
past menace and shadows. But I neither sing

nor speak French. Open your mouth,
he insists, as birds do sing so will you.

Then my mouth opens and I sing away
like a *rossignol*, like a French nightingale.

I am singing with St Francis as the city gives way
to hedgerows and fields and a glorious day.

Terry Barrett

## This Morning

On the Isle of Arran
we do morning yoga.
Stretch and strengthen our bodies.
"Only do what is good for your body,
Terry's body is different from Sheila's body".
Stretch out into cow.
Round back into cat.
We finish lying grounded on the warm carpet.

Yoga flows into meditation.
I look at the big strong tree.
I notice how the sunlight has spotlighted
patches of bright green and new yellowing.
The light catches Jan's yellow t-shirt
and Julie's white woolly jumper.

The big tree breathes
and the breaths resonate with my breaths.
My chest expands and contracts soothingly,
joins other breathing bodies here.
There is nothing missing from
this morning.

Marie Bashford-Synnott

GARRYKENNEDY FOREST WALK IN THE TIME OF COVID-19

Nervous after so long inside,
afraid at every bend in the road,
her breathing slows as he parks
under the chestnut tree by the harbour –
candle flowers stark
against tender green leaves.

They stroll along the pathway,
the lake silver and pewter
in the weak spring sunshine –
quickly pull on face masks
at the sound of laughter,
of a voice calling.

The young woman rushing past
shakes her head, points
towards the disappearing children
and, amused, they nod and wave –
remembering.

Suddenly sad,
she reaches for his hand
as they stand – listening
for the fading voices.

Amanda Bell

## LIGHT YEARS
*for Malcolm*

One night sticks in the mind:
my little brother and I, with
our parents and grandparents,
standing in the blackness of a field
at the foot of Nephin mountain,
our faces raised to the Milky Way
hoping to glimpse Kohoutek.

Halley's, Hale Bop, Neowise –
no comet since has flared so bright,
nor matched the wonder
of that distant night in winter coats
and blankets, little knowing
we were basking in the light
of stars that had long ago died.

Trish Bennett

ON THE TURN

The door's unlocked. I pray no one comes in
while I'm standing there with it all hanging out.
A nurse called Pamela Anderson tells me what to do
and where to look, and me not knowing where to look.
Pamela says to, *stand still – turn and face the corner.*
Something I haven't done since primary school
when I got into trouble for talking nonstop
about our cat's new kittens, and our dog
who insisted on carrying the butter home from the shop
un-pierced by his soft mouth.
I stood in the corner in front of the class,
turned to face the blackboard wall,
watched the chalk dust float in a pencil of sun
till it reached my closed throat.

On the turn again I face the corner.
An air freshener tries to disguise the smell of must
from black mould that clings to the ceiling.
I want to say, *bleach on a cloth would wipe that right off.*
Pamela says to keep my mouth shut or I'll upset the image.
Pamela wants everything clear – in black and white.
I do as I'm told for I want everything clear too.
On the other side of the unlocked door
a row of women sit in hard plastic chairs.
One white knuckle grips her bag to her chest.
I want to stop to comfort her
but I'm ushered out
for Pamela has a queue to do before her lunch.

Clodagh Beresford Dunne

STABILISERS

You cycled a bike when you were five –
a blue bike with metal stabilisers,
black handlebar grips
and a white padded saddle.

You cycled a bike outside each evening
to wait for your father,

a bike on which you'd sit
and ask your father how people were able
to cycle without stabilisers.

A bike from which your father,
one twilight, removed the right stabiliser
and told you to lean left.

A bike from which your father,
the next evening, removed the second stabiliser.

He placed his right hand
on the back of the saddle,
his left on the handlebar grip.

With his face against yours
you cycled with your back straight,
your eyes fixed ahead,

a bike from which your father
carefully removed his hands
and clapped them together.

Sara Berkeley

## Where We Are Going

In the grand hall of today
everything is breaking
and mending.
I cross the river in the morning
on my way to the dying, the Hudson
is tranquil and heavy
bearing its weight in weather,
rain blurs the Catskills.
I can't take all the sadness in
and give it a home,
there isn't room. The day
takes wing, filled with the old concerns:
here we all are at the edge
peering over together.
What's going to happen?
Victory, defeat, victory.

This part of life –
I know in my bones how to live it
but I keep getting turned around
by the change, the acceleration,
summer intensifies as it fails,
I want to hold it close
but the leaves are turning
and curling, thunder rolls
across our home in the afternoons,
the light gets blotted out,
saturated.
I'm going to burn things,
make my intentions known
to myself, get into the ceremony,
celebratory.

In the Port Ewen cemetery
the stones lean forward
against time, against expectations.
I'm lighting candles for the living,
their hearts that stretch and fill
and spill over, breaking
and mending.

Clíodhna Bhreatnach

JOHNNY DEPP V. AMBER HEARD: A DUBLIN SESTINA

At the table sit Karl's wife & daughters, his father & mother,
so he eats standing up. *OK kiddos!* he says. *Come on you girls in green!*
First, school; then, too soon, he's at the warehouse, that fag-butts-in-the-gutter
hole – shooting finger-guns of *Heya* – but it's only Zoë here, who smiles,
then puts earphones in again. Silence gets him. He plays Newstalk
on the radio, starts chuckling, waving his hand to say he's on one side

of things & earphones out. Zoë hears it is the man's side
because who leaves a shit in someone's bed but the most vile? *Mother
of god.* Zoë's hands hover over her laptop, missing her podcast's talk
of murder now continuing far away, staring out at the algae whose green
consumes the cooling pond on the estate; her *absolutely* & nod & smile
meaning *shut the fuck up, boomer.* Karl stands up. Crows move in the gutters

of the roof. *Just checking.* He does his rounds, first stuffing his guts
with biscuits, more coffee, before attempting to hike the mountainside
of deliveries and packages, his phone bleeping adverts of smiley
emojis for cheap flights as his trolley fills with boxes. A friend's mother

is dying. Boxes labelled, stacked, then with the departure
   of the green
van they're gone. Another weekend funeral. When did life
   give up on talk

& laughter, people & noise? When he returns to the office
   talk
explodes from him as heavy rainfall down a gutter
pours out twigs & dislodged earth – he says, his thoughts
   green
& yearning for sun – *a SHIT in the BED? How could anyone
   side
with such a liar?* Zoë freezes. Her peace interrupted. No
   mothering
of a grown man now – mollycoddling over, done – she
   hates Karl's smiling

enjoyment of this, his fun, his childlike faith in the
   sidelong smile
of a famous scumbag who said he'd rape a corpse – please.
   *Let's talk
of nothing but the facts: bruises, split lip, torn hair, attempts to
   smother
her with a pillow.* Karl rolls his eyes & grins. Her voice
   guttural
with stupid emotion, she trembles. Why does he assume
   she's outside
the story? That such acts aren't as real & terrible to her life
   as the green

labels she puts on green boxes that go into the green van?
   No green
valley but a flashing sea of memory. Karl says, *Yikes.* Then
   smiles
once more, says *See ya.* Evening comes. Zoë's friends sit in
   a pub beside

the Liffey where with competing monologues of their own
   talk
everyone is crying out. Zoë tells her boyfriend to have the
   guts
to just stay over. They try their best not to wake her father
   & mother.

Claire Blennerhassett

### Reverse Progress

They are murdering the hedges,
flailing the outstretched praise of summer branches
and cutting off the hands that feed you blackberries.

Spraying
verges deathly brown
with soil-polluting sickness
so nothing wild may grow.

Obey. We must tame your wilderness.

They are hiding the meandering stream in a culvert.
Ironing out the twists and turns of ancient stories spoken.
Burying its treasures lest it reflect the sun,
caress the fronds and ferns
or cause a rush to grow where
zest of kingfisher might seek to land.

Forgetting that the air we breathe is borrowed,
gifted, every breath connected to the "desperate" green,
this verdant "curse" of moss and leaf
sustaining us, each pair of lungs –
robin, raven, you.

And wondering why,
when the floods come
and the crops fail
and the earth is chemical and slurry choked,
dead and bereft of worms,
why the birds don't fly
nor the bees pollinate,
why the dragonfly's fire is still and wan,
why it all feels – somehow – wrong.

Then, they'll call it progress
and count the winter days in silence,
eager to begin once more.

And they'll rise, and strike a match
as they head away to burn new growth
on the upland furze of spring.

Roslyn Blyn-LaDrew

## Seothín Seó d'Oklahoma (19 Aibreán 1995)

Nóta: *dhá rud a spreag an dán seo, an suantraí traidisiúnta 'A bhean úd thíos ag bruach an tsrutháin' agus an grianghraf clúiteach a glacadh ar 19 Aibreán 1995 a thaispeáin comhraiceoir tine ag iompar linbh amach as smionagar an Fhoirgnimh Murrah, i gCathair Oklahoma.*

A linbh úd thall i mbacla 'n fhir bhrónaigh,
*Seoithín seó, lú ló ló,*
Mar leanbh ina codladh i ngnáthucht a máthar,
*Seoithín seó, lú ló ló,*
Ach fiafraím díom cad é an táimhe sin ort?
*Seoithín seó, lú ló ló,*
Ní taithimhín é ach fíor-mharbhshuan,
*Seoithín seó, lú ló ló.*

Na coisíní beaga a bhí ag lapadán siúil,
*Seoithín seó, lú ló ló,*
Ina luí anois, gan bhrí gan bhogadh,
*Seoithín seó, lú ló ló,*
'S na stocaí beaga bána atá fós a gcumhdach,
*Seoithín seó, lú ló ló,*
Mar a bheidís réidh do na bróga nach gcaithfear.
*Seoithín seó, lú ló ló.*

Do shúile a bhí ar leathadh ar maidin,
*Seoithín seó, lú ló ló,*
Iad cruinn mór mar shúil an nóinín,
*Seoithín seó, lú ló ló,*
Ar dhún siad go tobann nó ar dhún siad go fadálach?
*Seoithín seó, lú ló ló,*
Táid dúnta anois go deo na ndeoiríní,
*Seoithín seó, lú ló ló.*

Ba mhinic do mháthair a bhí do d'iompar,
*Seoithín seó, lú ló ló,*
'S do lámha thar a muineál mar bhláthanna na féithleoige,
*Seoithín seó, lú ló ló,*
Anois chomh faon tú mar bhabóg éadaigh,
*Seoithín seó, lú ló ló,*
Gan úinéir girsí a chuirfeadh an bhrí inti.
*Seoithín seó, lú ló ló.*

Ba mhinic tú ag éisteacht le suantraí istoíche,
*Seoithín seó, lú ló ló,*
Gan bharúil ar bith faoina leithéid agus goltraí,
*Seoithín seó, lú ló ló,*
Ach mar 'tá sé anois, 's iad an t-aon rud amháin iad,
*Seoithín seó, lú ló ló,*
Marbh-shuantraí don chodladh buan,
*Seoithín seó, lú ló ló.*

Ocht naíonán déag atá mar a gcéanna,
*Seoithín seó, lú ló ló,*
Ocht n-ucht déag na máithreacha eile,
*Seoithín seó, lú ló ló,*
Naoi gcathaoir déag i bPáirc na gCathaoireach Folamh,
*Seoithín seó, lú ló ló,*
Gan ann ach cuimhne ar an muirniú a bhí ann,
*Seoithín seó, lú ló ló.*
*Seoithín, seoithín, seoithín, seoithín,*
*Seoithín seó, lú ló ló.*

Fióna Bolger

CANAL BANK POEM 2024

Crowded with camps, but footpath left clear,
the calm waters of the canal, despite those who
would draw us to hate. The will of all people
to move freely instead here fenced between railings

erected to keep tents away instead of homing
people – go move shift. There's been a rift –
never expected, leafy here, site of a deadly shootout.
Mount Street Bridge has seen blood before

then too some neighbours came
and helped the dying men – and now
the women come and offer hot food.
The nightly suffering we see on TV

is coming close and we
must choose how to be human.

Eva Bourke

### STARLINGS OVER NIMMO'S PIER

*Nightingales sing not for pay or glory,*
*but for the joy of rivalling each other in song,*
*and because they cherish the beautiful* – Plutarch

Arriving at dusk, singly, in threes,
in their dozens, hundreds, landing on aerials, atop
the fire station, the cables strung up like riggings
to transmission masts, poles,
and more and more of them collect mid-air, magnetically
drawn to each other and headed in the same direction,
and scores waft in on a gust, salute and join
the growing flock that fans out across the blue grey sky,
rises, sinks, contracts and unravels;

and still more gather, scatter and spill across the landfill,
flowing fluid black as Indian ink, a lengthening pixellated
shadow above the playing fields, turning
the air dark, contract into a ribbon, thin
as a knife edge, a fluttering necklace, the next moment

uncoil like a lasso whipped across the sky,
turn, reverse and wheel around as one,
wing it back to the church spire, swoop and loop –
the sheer joy and artistry of it – and fall fast,
a shower of soot-coloured rain,
their hearts beating in unison,
and again and again:

berry gourmands, crumb stealers,
winged Cassandras, fortune tellers,
pour from behind a cloud like dark smoke,
and slide down, down, back
to their green roosts in the willows,

their vespertine palaver meeting by the canal
to exchange gossip and chatter till nightfall
swaying on thin branches among twitter, flap
and whoosh of wings, while the locals
look on from doors and balconies.

The dog and I stand for a while and watch,
each in our own way:
he lifts his snout and sniffs the air,
and I, taken by their high spirits, the swiftness
and unfailing choreography of the dance, know
no man-made algorithm could ever match this show.

    II

I'd seen one in a painting long ago
(*Lady with Squirrel and Starling*,
by Hans Holbein the Younger) twittering
prophecies of love into a young woman's ear,

and once on a Vienna Market as Mozart strolled past,
a starling in a cage seized its chance
and whistled the sweetest
tune it knew, so Mozart took pity, paid
a pittance and brought it home.

Did the singer know Mozart would steal
its song for the allegretto
of his Piano Concerto No. 17?

Lucky beggars casually pecking at nothing
in particular. Rip-off artists, fly- by-nights,
curtain raisers for sunset dramas.
Nimble quick pickers, mimicry tricksters,
brave hearts – I love them, their starry night
plumage, their mischievous faces,
these winged city-slum Moirae.

What centre holds them? Is it desire
around which they dance so jubilantly?
If only I could read the signs!
What momentous thing is waiting in the wings?

Niamh Boyce

## The Trinity

*We're sick of your sort around here,*
men shout from a gate as she walks by.
She hears them still, despite the years.

Three old dudes in ash-coloured suits
coming alive for a young mother and her child.
*Hey you! We're sick of your sort.*

Going to the shops is complicated enough
(blankets, nappies, changing mat, wipes)
without the roars from across the road.

They want her hands unpeeled from the pram,
want her shorn, numbered, confined.
*We're sick of your sort, go home.*

They fling words like *slut* as she kneels
to button the rain cover over his toes.
Hearing them from across the years

she imagines instead a smile, a *lovely child*.
She holds that, and holds them a while,
those so sick of her sort,
their swan song can still be heard.

Sara Boyce

BLACK SAND

I

When home was no longer safe,
Hassan saved one picture from their wall,
its glass smothered in brick dust.
Swaddled in the softest of headscarves,
he cradled it across two oceans.

That photo sat above the counter
of his Belfast grocery shop
that sold everything
the people wanted –
drinks and snacks,
hair and beauty,
poultry, cheese,
cleaning products.

Hasaan's customers were curious
about the picture of his wife and girls,
smiling faces flecked with black sand
from the Wadi Quandil beach, taken
on a day trip from Damascus
when they'd fished off rocks and swam.
Adults, incredulous:
*Here mate, is there really a beach in Syria?*
Kids quizzing him about the dangers:
*Are there jellyfish?*

II

Hassan sits on a fold-up camping chair.
At his feet – mounds of fire sand
flecked with the black ash of his shop.
An early morning sun reveals
rainbows of petrol on the pavement.
Hassan aches for that black sand.

Maureen Boyle

TRINITY, CHRISTMAS 1980
*for John*

*December 4th*

Crossing Front Square after our morning lecture
you tell me you are going to Mass. It is the final
week of term and we have all survived.
There is a sense of having changed
from the first lonely weeks of October, when
we'd go for walks along the canal and wonder
as we looked into windows lit for dusk
if we would ever know anyone in this city
or have somewhere to go on a Sunday.

Now there is the excitement of going home,
of bringing some of this world back;
Grafton Street full of lights and Switzer's window
entrancing children. It's the end of the term
we've learned to call 'Michaelmas' and when we return
the place won't be strange anymore.

And then you tell me you are going to Mass.
It is so unexpected that I'm sure I say the wrong thing
like the day on the Green when there was a huge thrush
on the lawn and you said, in your best Belfast accent, that
you didn't know what it was! City boy, I slagged you but
laughed hysterically when you protested, in the same accent,
that as a little boy you had been sent to elocution lessons.

And now, on this sleety day on the cobbles, you tell me
you are going to Mass and I realise you are serious.
All that I remember of your answer when I ask why
was the phrase you used for the anniversary you are
marking,

'It was a 'boom boom job!' – a child's phrase – as though
you are ten again in that upper room waiting for your
mother
and sister to come back from another Mass, lying on the
floor
with your brother playing table football just before
that world ends and everything goes topsy turvy.

I should have gone to Mass with you that day
but what you said made no sense to me then.
Until it did.

    *December 8th*

Heading home, the day all the sweeter
for having stayed in Dublin all weekends in between,
managing to resist the lure of family and comfort.
Now, a pile of books from the Lecky to lug to Busáras
for the Letterkenny bus and a new friend helps me there.
Dublin is dark at four and we schlep
through the Christmassy streets,
carols blaring out of shops, crowds of country people
who have travelled to the city to do their Christmas
shopping on this, the Feast of the Immaculate Conception.
When we get to the bus he helps me on, handing in
the pile of earnest hardbacks, and beside the bus
an old-fashioned newsboard says that John Lennon
has been shot.

Did the bus play his music all the way to the north
or was I just singing it in my head
looking out on the dark winter night?

Yvonne Boyle

### Swimming with my Cousin in the Lake
*for Marjorie*

There were times in childhood when life
seemed to fill out all the spaces.

We are walking down through the willow
and black walnut trees to Lake Ontario
by my cousin's white slated wooden house.
I have just had a photo taken in the doorway
like many relatives before. *Your father
and aunt swam here,* she said. *My family and I
have swum here every day we could.*

Swimming with my cousin in the lake,
I feel I could not be living life more fully.
Everything complete, nothing wasted,
freedom reaching out to the edges.

Caroline Bracken

## Amygdala

This is not about citronella ants
so called because of the lemon verbena scent
they exude when crushed.

This is not about the colour of tears
which are not clear
but cloudy white.

This is not about an irrational fear
of the word *merge*
entirely unrelated to motorway driving.

This is not about the disembodied recording
in an elevator with a proper English accent
announcing *Doors opening … Doors closing.*

This is not about the pins and needles
in your arms when you hear the crack
in a man's voice as he speaks of the dead

or how an electric shock
goes through you
every time your intercom buzzes.

This is about someone else's children
learning to paddleboard
in the bay outside your apartment

their feral joy
lifeboat-orange
rescuing you.

Julie Breathnach-Banwait

COMHAIRLE

sa seomra codlata, lastall den halla, is í ag clupaideach na mbraillíní nite os coinn na leapa, chuir sí comhairle ar a híníon maidir le guaiseacht a grá nua, á rá léi go meallfadh sé í leis na focla milse úd, is í ag filleadh isteach na gcúinní, go ndéanfadh sé alpadh uirthi, is í ag slíocadh le cúl a boise, ag iarnáil na bhfilltíní amach go coirnéil na leapa. Go sínfeadh sí a croí chuige ar leac óir, go bhféadfadh sé é a roinnt is a dháileadh mar a thogródh sé. Mar sin a bhí sí, ar sí. Ró-oscailte, ró-ghoilliúnach. Seafóideach. Go mbeadh sí ag tógáil a cuid gasúir léi féin, is go mbeadh seisean amú ag fiach, ag sáinniú is ag caitheamh uaidh, is í ag plimpíl na bpiliúr, á ndíriú go réidh in aghaidh chlár cinn na leapa. Bheadh sí coganta le buairt aigne chráite, a lean sí, ar foluain is amú i saol gan aithne, ag streachailt na mbraillíní thar leithead na leapa. Is cé a chuirfeadh suim inti ansin?

déanann sí seabhrán uaithi, dóite is ag púscadh, a gúna breac le spotaí fola, smionagar srapnail sáite ina craiceann. Giorranálaithe ag focla.

chuirfeadh sí féin suim inti féin, ar sí. Is d'alpfadh sí í féin. Léi féin.

Marie Breen-Smyth

PAINTING MY FATHER
*Henry William (Harry) Smyth*
*19 February 1920–18 September 2013*

Because I refuse to let you disappear
I picture you as you were,
poised to speak, hands folded on your stick.
You are silent now.
I picture you in this place.
You built the hut beside the chapel,
the road climbs the hill to the house
you bought for a home.

I picture you below the chapel
at the bottom of the hill, in this land
where you were famous for poetry,
for making things and telling stories;
this country where you built and mended
byres and motorbikes, invented wheelbarrows
with sides to win turf, and kennels
for the sows and piglets in the muck of fields.

Where I picture you now is where you remain
below the chapel, at the bottom of the hill;
your gravestone, black and jewelled with tears
of rain. And I will paint you, write you.
You will not disappear. For our lives
are all heroic in their own way.
So I picture you,
I will not let you disappear.

H W Smyth wrote *As I Recall: The Life Story of a North Derry Man who was in Turn a Pantry-Boy, Farm-Hand, Joiner, Motor Mechanic and Bus Driver* (2011).

Clodagh Brennan Harvey

## THE CALL TO MASS

Do they talk of us still
in that far country –
that night before Christmas
you chanced me away
to the craggy fastness
from the revellers
on the hilltops
and the night's din
of cows' horns and pipers?

We made a pact then
and we kept it;
not a regret since,
only that longing
for beckoning horns
sounding from hill to hill
on a Christmas morning.

Deirdre Brennan

## Na Cailleacha Ghána

Tugann siad leo a mbaintreachas
go campa na gcailleach,
a nguagacht giúmair is sos miastrathe,
a ndíchuimhne is néaltrú seanaoise,
a neamhbhailbhe is a gcallaireacht,
greim na hainspride ina mbéil;
thug an taoiseach is an fear feasa breith
gurb iad foinse chuile tinnis, chuile bás linbh
is an tír smíste go deannach leis an triomacht.

Seo é a ngéilleadh deireanach chun iad féin
a shabháil ó chéasadh is linseáil
óna graibeáilí talúin a chuir dúil ina dtithe,
a ngairdíní le guabhaí is mangónna,
a mhóidíonn go rabhadar ina idircheap
do mhallachtaI a d'fhág ina luí faon
sa leaba iad le tinneas droma, is maláire.
is a dhallaigh iad le cith saghead
caite ón tsúil nimneach mhillte.

Is mór an mí-ádh é ar mhná ag dul in aois,
gan ball éadaí ach iad ar a ndroma
seilbh a dtithe bainte díobh,
díbeartha go botháin i gcampa na gcailleach,
uaigneach, gan chuairt chlainne is an pobal anuas orthu,
buartha ar eagla go raghadh an t-aon chaidéal i ndísc
is lá i ndiaidh lae ag faireadh ar an spéir ag rothlú
le badhbha is le titim na hoíche na héigrití
ag filleadh ar a bhfara sna crainn.

Heather Brett

SIGNINGS

I

The solicitor offers her the pen.
It is a blunt knife, sawing at the already frayed rope
of her marriage, how, how, she asks herself,
has it come to this, tears and ink lubricate serrated steel,
and it is almost through, strands now forever apart,
recoiling, gravitational pull, collapsed.
He never fought for me, mantra from turning
the point on herself. Bitter lesson.
When the decree is absolute, she thinks,
there will be no hesitancy, a strong gold nib
severing: machete cleave.

II

In the registry you imbue a sense of gaiety,
the audience retreats to the wings, forced chirrups.
All the lackadaisical years. Hold an opal to the light,
look for fire: panhandle the residue, but sift the rich earth,
better a devil you know.
Both hands splayed towards the spotlight,
a vaudeville stance,
grin. You did it. There are always conditions.
No one will go there, no one will
finish the sentences. Shoved under the starched tablecloth
of a Shelbourne breakfast.
You write with a flourish. Legal, and all that jazz.

III

Your sisters have to agree, they'll, hopefully, be the ones
left. Your corpse making its way to UCD for storage,
for cutting up
years later, allowing students their way with your flesh.
No funeral, no clergy, a poem perhaps, a drink to the days.
When they cremate you, your granddaughter
will collect ashes in a mason jar. You've left her a note
to open for fireflies, bound to be one or two hovering,
and to scrutinise the dust for crystals, quartz, carbon,
labradorite, Alaskan gold, pyrite.
The sisters validate; the granddaughter is left a map.

Lynn Caldwell

BUTTON NECKLACE

I can show you the necklace, ribs of colour that fit just so around my neck, buttons on a bright yellow string. It was in Dublin, in the only house my children had ever lived in, the one I've spent more years than any of the others: a draughty flat 80 steps up in Brussels, the basement suite in Victoria – I loved that place on Jennifer Road – Hardwick Street with its giant hill that grew small in later years, the farm on Cedar Road where the wind in the Douglas firs and Western Red cedars whistled into my dreams, a trail of homes in Nanaimo.

I could go on, but it was there, I remember, in that Dublin house where I sat at my sewing machine on the round oak table from the grandparents' home in Chapelizod, a pedestal, not too fancy, gorgeous grain, but always too low. That table is long gone. I still have the sewing machine. Who knows what I was sewing? Those were the years that crocheting, making jam, doing anything with my hands helped soothe the creative storm. Anything but writing. I couldn't. I sewed by the window with the rippled glass, beside me on the floor my three-year-old son, silent with the button jar, choosing – how: Colour? Size? The next one in his hand? He remembers nothing now.

I remember. The light, the machine whirring its vagaries in starts and stops, his silence. The buttons I planned to unstring, put back in the jar where someday I would find a use for them. Someday. That day, an afternoon so ordinary I have just one picture and he has none. You'll find us there, at that table in the back of the Dublin house, me and my three-year-old, lit by burgundies and sage, cobalt and sienna, smooth plastic, dark wood, under our fingers. I'll show you the necklace.

Louise C Callaghan

### Winter Morning Run
*i.m. Ashling Murphy*

Run, keep running sister,
keep running, women and girls.
In the morning, before work,
during your lunch break,
after work. Never give up.

By the Canal, or the Boyne,
along narrow mud paths ...
in mild or freezing weather.
Listen as you go, to birds,
see them skirt the water.

Should a malevolent person,
a predator come after you,
you'll never be strong enough.
But use your voice, scream,
for your cries will carry –

echo a promise to us forever.

Mary Rose Callaghan

## The Green Tin House

The summer I was eleven,
a time before things changed,
we stayed in a green tin house
a stone's throw from the sea.
We were six kids then with
a Mother's Help and the usual
parents who liked their G&Ts.
It meant nine of us had to fit.

A French Madame was landlady
who lived next door to us.
What did she make of our fridge
brought all the way in a trailer?
We didn't know it then
how the days of sun and sand
were the last of childhood for us
as our father's tumour grew.

I pictured it over the years,
that green tin house by the sea.
How *did* we all fit in? I asked
the brother who doesn't forget.
We never stayed there, he said.
We must have, are you sure?
No, Madame used it herself
and rented us her bungalow.

My green tin house was a dream.
What matter if I was wrong?
Memory's said to be invention,
how we create ourselves.

Rosaline Callaghan

GRANITE

*The silence of his absence is deafening –*
lettered in gold
below a guitar carving
on a granite slab.
The cold inscription
of his date of birth
and date of death
brackets the span of his life –
hardly a man when felled.

Life is caught
in the whistle of a breeze
through lamenting trees.
Life is caught
in the rustle of my footsteps
over mourning grass.
Life is caught
in my breathing as I move on
to another grave.

Glistening gold on granite gathers
my sister's twenty-seven years
into an arrow shaft.
Formless fletching guides
grief's barb to its mark –
cleaves a heart.
Another life so short.
Too short.

This one felled
by *féinmharú* –
death by one's own hands.

Siobhán Campbell

## BLUSH

Here is a rose to shatter roses
stiff in the frozen dawn of flowers.
Pinked like no pink of fleshed creatures,
this rose undoes even as it charms.

This bud forgot about winter,
felt the fey sun suck on its cells.
Turned in the yearn of the unwilling,
petals edged from unlapped folds.

Found itself out upward and amazed.
Pushed as though it were not pulled.
Pattern halts and day shortens
tightening in that bed of calls –

stalls the blush china rose
leaves an imprint crisp and thinning.
What is hawed beyond this rose –
what is winning?

Moya Cannon

SOUP

A plastic container
of frozen vegetable soup
has been warming in the sink
since this morning.

When I slip the block
into a saucepan
it breaks up
and melts quickly.

Often when I see this
I think of A74,
a shelf of ice
bigger than greater Paris,

which has broken
off Antarctica
to float in the Weddell Sea,
and I wonder
if all the king's horses

and all the king's men
and all our technologies
and all of us
will ever be able

to put Antarctica
together again.

Caitríona Caomhánach

## CADHAIN AONAIR

Laethanta ag tiomáint thart i m'aonar
ar bhóithre na cathrach is amuigh faoin tuath
béile i ndiaidh béile ag ithe i m'aonar
gan aghaidh os mo chomhair, nó comhrá a dhéanamh

Maidineacha ag múscailt sa leaba i m'aonar,
leaba mo thí nó leaba thar lear
bianglóidí ag cur m'intinn trí chéile
is ní dhiúltaím gloine fíona meadhránach

Caithim mo shaol anois i m'aonar
an bród tógtha uaim leis an uaigneas domhain
dóchas, misneach, 's cumhacht ar eitilt
mo ghuth ina thost, mo rúnta faoi cheilt.

Eibhlís Carcione

## INÍON

An iníon sona,
í ina gearrchaile,
gléasta i ngúna dearg
le bláthanna oráiste,
a dhein a máthair di
ar an ineall fuála,
an ghrian ag scoilteadh
tríd na crainn ghiúise.

An iníon
fásta suas
glao teilefóin borb,
sneachta crua
ar fud na cathrach.

An iníon
i ngrá,
máthair suaite
ag ní is ag triomú éadaí,
bainis thar lear.

An iníon
sona suairc
le beirt pháiste is fear,
cuairt thapa
comhrá giorraisc.

An iníon
croíbhriste,
páiste a cailleadh
tost na huaighe sa tigh,
sreang imleacáin
ar sileadh,

linnte fola
ar urlár na cistine.

Ruth Carr

HERE WE ARE

As with Gaia
so with her inhabitants,
things are hotting up.

We strip and dump,
pollute by word and deed
the ground between us.

We tarmac and frack
while flood levels rise,
fiddle while forests burn,

have goldfish-recall
of *the War to end all Wars*
of mutual destruction.

Here we are
deleting human rights
instead of toxic habits,

bloated with consumption,
riddled with cancers,
lapped by mermaids' tears

while Gaia cracks up
at our antics,
her ice caps melting.

Alvy Carragher

## The Neighbour's Voice at Night

His words are low at first,
growing high enough to seep
through plumbing, wires.
I don't hear her.

Perhaps she presses her thumb
to the inside of her wrist,
the point where the river
runs closest to the surface.

I, too, have been stone-like,
clean of bald emotion.
Motionless as any heron
poised at the edge of existence.

Passers admired my stillness,
how nothing touched me,
not love, not sorrow, not
the tailend of wonder, flicking.

I stood in the morning
unable to ask myself
any serious questions.
I was waiting

for something to happen –
the flicker of an opening,
so I might leave
in one sudden movement.

Deirdre Cartmill

## War Wound

It's not the moment when I clean the blood
and mud from your chest,
cauterise the wound,
pull the edges of the fault line in your flesh
back together and stitch skin to skin
as the bombs fall around us,

but the moment when your blood spills
over the edge of the stretcher
and you scream for your mum
and I take your hand
and you squeeze back hard
and you know for as long as you're breathing

I won't let go.

Anne Casey

WAR CABINET

My father waged war for years
on chairs and tables,
miscellaneous shelves,
a potted plant stand
and one bulky dark armoire –
all handed down from my mother's
family. Grumbling for anyone to hear,
he would sand and shave and oil
and sand again then lacquer
and leave,
only to find
some months later,
the offending wormholes
and small piles of timber sand
had reappeared. Year upon year
the marital heirlooms continued
to incur his DIY fury and yet

his furniturely sensibilities neglected
entirely infestations incumbent
in his own inherited relics:
the walnut wardrobe,
for instance,
from whose dusky
smoky surface my
dead grandfather watched us.
Inside, his grease-cuffed suits still hung,
limply mimicking his standing form –
here an elbow bulge, there a knee crease –
grimy pennies suspended in their grit-lined pockets.

Eileen Casey

## Posting Home

My daughter wakes to crimson rosellas
or a red-tailed cockatoo's kurr kurr on the wing,
strange to her Irish ears. Aborigines use its scarlet
and black feathers worn in hair for rain making
ceremonies – 'Tears from the sky'.
Six months gone, three less than the nine spent
safe inside my body, she rises early. Breathes
a new city's rhythms. On the edge of Sydney,
travel time eats into her sleeping
as worry eats into mine.

Rents are high, her room's scarce big enough
to hoard hope. Seasonal as flowering Eucalyptus.

Photographs are filled with bright flashes.
Honeyeaters, lorikeets. Common as crow.
Today, another image *WhatsApps* in.
A circle of white cockatoos,
jaunty sulphur crests swept upwards.

There is solace in their story; generations of birds
bonded together in one strong flock.

Pratibha Castle

## RECALLING KELLS

potato mashed with/scallions called *colcannon* that she/couldn't eat/bacon/boiled/cabbage with a look of sick/caterpillar on her/leg an auld soak's/sneak herself/a *mammy's/trophy* in her Sunday/best buckle sandals/pink smocked dress/traipsing along country lanes/after cousins who/grabbed sticks thrashed/hedgerows squelched/ through swampy fields/squished a frog/*raucous/rowdy*/like marauding rooks

they could well/afford to be in bagged-out/ganzies patched short pants/herself a hopeless/cause/*like yer Uncle Alfie/* well before the fence/and though she hadn't/crouched to watch the tadpoles/lest her dress get/splashed yet she'd/slipped/himself who'd/grabbed her/hoiked her up to standing/that lad knew the heft of it to/get a punch be/yelled at

a woman grown she'd/shipped the mammy back that/boy-grown-man cheeks/scourged by gales a/lifetime/tending sows and memories/as he shovelled/dirt into the/grave had a look that spoke he/saw her ache

Sarah Clancy

## ANOIS TEACHT AN EARRAIGH
*after Antoine Ó Raifteiri*

Last night in Stoneybatter
I hung a Keffiyeh out for Brigid
and as luck would have it
late that evening she came upon it
and said her words above it
and of what little magic
the world has left in it, I know
Brigid took a handful of the strongest
the most love filled and resilient
and she gathered it and sent it
to those picking through the rubble of their lives
in Khan Younis, in Deir al Balah,
in Rafah, in Jabalia, in Beit Hanoun
and Beit Lahaya, and in Gaza City's
Shuja'iyya where another poet caught it
and in the face of his own death, defied it
and sent the magic skywards
and watched it almost imperceptibly
descend on every living entity and caress
the hearts of those departed
and those who lost them
and I hope against hope that every person felt it
and they raise their sails
and never settle
until their land is free.

Jane Clarke

## Cherry Trees, Charente

After dinner my friend and I stroll
past cherry trees to the terrace

> where we spent long afternoons
> in the shade, moving in and out

of the swimming pool,
chatting like chiffchaff in the woods.

> She didn't mention her illness
> all week, only that she wished

she'd seen Kyoto in full bloom.
Tonight we lie on sun loungers,

> gaze up to the sky and play
> at naming the constellations

while cherries drop on dry ground
in the lingering heat of the day.

Marion Clarke

## Capricorn Child

Milky Way ...
your appearance at the end
of the year

So tiny when you arrived, it took a month for you to get
back up to your birth weight. You had problems latching
on when feeding, you see. I was in such pain and
was certain you could feel me wincing, although I tried my
best not to. But thankfully we got there after a few weeks
and enjoyed those special moments together so much that
your night feeds continued for two years.

midnight movement
a vixen on the kerb
coaxes her cub to cross

And look at you now, a fine young man preparing to leave
this small island to follow your dreams on a much, much
larger one.

soft light
your animal alphabet book
lies open at *wallaby*

Catríona Clutterbuck

### The River in Fethard

On the narrow road between the town and the river,
a woman stands alone. How often,
having lost their place in this world,

did others like her, wimpled in grief,
stare at an empty stretch of grass and stream
under high stone walls that Cromwell spared?

No one else is here this early May evening
but three smartly-dressed office workers
who glance at an older woman in passing.

Who can know how, one festival day on this spot,
three children by her side had stroked an Irish wolfhound
at their own eye height, then minted coins at the stall?

How, down on the bank, stones skimmed free
from their hands, or how, still buried in the air
is their song in the back as she drove home –

*row, row, row your boat* in a round,
never dreaming that one amongst them
so soon must embark;

that it would be for her own fair daughter
that the Clashawley River that sunlit evening
spilled its endless cups of silver into the dark.

Louise G Cole

### Eating Yoghurt with a Fork

This day has not gone as it should.
No one in the right place at the right time.
Things misplaced, displaced, broken,
unavailable, unattainable, unnecessary,
a lexicon of failure similes, then:
no clean teaspoons in the drawer.
A lifetime's mismatched metaphors
glint in the sunlight of awareness:
it's not about the right cutlery,
not even about the way it is used –
it's about having someone to eat with.

Susan Condon

## Heated Words

The January wind bites the island air.
Bare trees sway, their lifeless branches
reaching out across swollen fields.

A raven perches on a broken gate,
cold, beady eyes staring at me.

My breath plumes before me.
Gravelled footsteps, the only sound,
as I search for you through tangled briars.

It's over forty years since I left,
when heated words, flush with anger
and resentment bubbled to the surface.

After Kath arrived, I mellowed.
I wrote. Wrote often. Bared my soul,
my regrets, my remorse. But no reply.

"I've found her," she whispers.
Her long fingers caress the cold,
engraved letters on the grey marble.

Making the sign of the cross
I shout scribbled words in my head,
loud enough for you to hear.

Your namesake appears by my side,
kisses my wet cheek. "Kathleen,"
she breathes, linking her arm in mine.

Áine Rose Connell

## A Double-Volted Antigen Test

You are a moustachioed man, an Einstein of sorts,
travelling through the cacti sands of New Mexico
with a sheepdog and your partner, Michael,
a thriving ten year old. You will happen across
a city, an infinite stretch of trimmed housing rows
cast in public art moulds. Pink paint fading
in the parched sun. Olive clay benches, bug-trap
doors, dollhouse lace curtains. A stiff clothesline
that never felt the slightest of breeze. Indoors
you sense a grey-haired woman watching.

After you solve your own theory of relativity
in the shower in one oddly-placed home,
the front door slightly ajar:
everyone left long ago and you are alone.
It's you in the hall, a stopped grandfather clock,
sandy work boots by the door, the laces untied,
a calendar on the wall with half a month of ticks.
You expect to hear a finger dialling the reel
from an old telephone but
it's just your wet feet on the kitchen linoleum.

You wake up to find yourself
without facial hair, nibble
a cuticle, Google *what does it mean
to dream of your partner as a child*. It will tell you,
*he or she is financially or emotionally dependent
on you*. Dang. You text your pal and she replies,
*it's the abandonment of your unconscious masculine child*.

Dang-er. Later that morning the antigen test beholds
two little lightsabers: the contemporary two fingers.
You fall back onto the bed, *Sleeping Beauty* awaiting

her big kiss. Instead you'll watch Michael pinch his nose,
slipper-slide over the floorboards, fly out
the door like he's just got word of the Nobel Prize.

It's funny how some old things just keep on:
all those times that toothy boyish part of you left
out in the rain, like the time you believed butterflies
in your belly would steer the way, harvest the nation,
little *el hijo*, inner Miguel: hung up his hat,
his spikes, to be trampled on by cacti
even now amidst the Sudafed, the Spanish Flu,

everyone left long ago, you are alone.

Monica Corish

## LOVE RISES LIKE BREAD, EACH DAY BAKED FRESH

Elephants grazed in my past,
wildebeest, zebra, Thompson's gazelle.
Once, near Nairobi, I saw a lioness up close,
drowsily digesting her dinner, bored at the sight
of me leaning out the window, thumping
the side of the van. Despite my ardent desire
she granted me no closer audience. I loved
adventure then, kindly strangers, strange lands.

Now I stay late in bed, snug
beneath my golden duvet, discovering
new lines tucked inside a line of poetry.
Today it's Richard Snyder: *Let true thanksgiving
bruise our lips.* You swig coffee in your room,
browse *The Marginalian, The Writers' Almanac,*
email me juicy poems. Eleven or thereabouts
we meet in the kitchen for Earl Grey tea,
wholemeal toast, rhubarb jam with cloves.

My younger self saw no wonder
in the everyday, left no novel stone unturned.
In middle age, I'm pleased to say,
I'm sweetly bored.

Polina Cosgrave

## Fireworks 2025

How carefully the sun
is rising over Hiroshima,
blue light tiptoeing around our bare spirits.
The golden eagle in the sky
unfolds like a modernist novel.

I can't focus on facts.
The eternity is shaking
its crooked badge before my eyes,
having found out that I am the addict
of the good old times.

I don't have a single gram on me,
but you have to be responsible.
Here we go again,
another junkie got into trouble.
And the patrol wagon is driving us

through the slow planet
hooked like a hungry fish.

Enda Coyle-Greene

### INSTEAD OF THE SNIPER
*Dublin, 1916*

After she had run from man to man
there was nothing left to do
except surrender;

and there was so little of her
to be taken out – an inch or two of skirt,
her *sensible* shoes –

but instead of the sniper she expected
all the way down Moore Street,
in that final eyeful,

man to man, while she stood quietly, at attention,
the lens of history's aftergaze
erased her.

Bernie Crawford

## Looking for my Grandmother in Ireland's Fight for Independence

There is a story in our family that you eloped,
that yours and his was a big love story.
In your wedding photo from nineteen hundred
you are beautiful, your eyes round and wide,
your stylish silhouette in a high-collared dress
molded by a corset that squeezed away your belly, a belly
that swelled thirteen times (miscarriages weren't counted).

I like to think you wanted votes for women,
that you might have smashed a pane or two.
Did you wonder at the likes of Hanna Sheehy
who kept her own name after marrying?
Did you want to keep Donoghue?
What did you think of your husband's two nieces,
Cathy and Lena, learning to shoot?
Did you adjust their leather belts,
tilt their Cumann na mBan felt berets to a jaunty angle?
You were, after all, the fashionable one.
And was it awkward with your husband's other niece,
whose dad was in the RIC, or did all the cousins
sit around your kitchen table chatting?

Or were you too bogged down by pregnancies and
housework to follow the trajectory of Ireland's
independence? When your husband filled the 1911 census,
was the baby (my father) sitting on his knee?
Were you preparing supper for your other children
... you had seven under ten by then. And did you
say a silent prayer for the little one who died?
Did you tell them goodnight stories?
Did you ever get time to sit and read
the *Irish Citizen*, which Cathy bought each month?

You were forty-two
when you passed away on Valentine's Day
during Ireland's bloody civil war.
In your mortuary card you are still beautiful,
a cameo brooch on the bow at your throat,
but there is sadness in your eyes:
*dearly loved and deeply mourned.*
In April 1923 the anti-treaty IRA
ordered its forces to stand down.

Catherine Ann Cullen

## My Bones Sing
*i.m. Breda Wall Ryan*

The weather has turned
but I cradle my mug on the threshold,
hands warm, bare feet cold on the paving.

A robin flings himself at his rival in the window.
A blackbird gorges furtively on the ivy berries.
The *Scarlet River* lily blooms like fire.

Our one tree is an extravagance of apples.
Every morning I pluck windfalls from wet grass,
every evening, peel, core, excise bruises.

I stew until the house is dizzy with sweetness.

Neighbours have all been gifted.
I have run out of containers.
Still, they fall.

When the screen found three stones
in the seedless fruits of my breasts,
you sent me your number.

I keep your poems by me
to remind me to hear
my bones singing.

I send you the warmth of my cupped hands,
the fragrance of a glut of apples,
two birds, and a river of fire.

Majella Cullinane

PINCH

My mother stands outside a shop. I'm six or seven,
I could be eight or nine. She's talking to someone.
It strikes me then – she always has something to say.

She seems so big to me, her eyes smiling,
her face animated as she talks about this and that.
No sooner does she meet one woman
than another comes along. Then another.

Impatient, I pull at her sleeve, tug at her skirt.
When she continues to ignore me
I bring out my final weapon. With my thumb
and index finger I snatch a fold of flesh
around her waist, first – a warning nip,
then a full-on, insistent pinch.

She squirms, glares at me, grits her teeth.
Mortified, she probably says something like:
Well, we'd better go, this one can never wait.

Not five minutes later she bumps into another woman
and the whole thing starts again. I fidget,
twist and turn, roll my eyes, sigh extravagantly.
This time I pinch so hard she winces.

I wonder what she said to all those women –
if there were things she could have said but didn't,
if she said things she shouldn't have? If any of them
would remember? I wonder too – did she suspect
the child pinching and pulling away from her
would rarely, if ever, know what it is to stand still?

Denise Curtin

## Margo: The Love Pattern

I will never forget you on that crowded train,
waving me into the vacant seat beside you
with a knitting needle,
leaning into the warm chat
the way we Irish often do.
You, a Cork woman, brimming over
with the pride of your recent prize.
*Have you seen Oppenheimer?* you beamed,
a perfect opener for me, a movie fan. I was home.

You were knitting some multi-coloured little thing,
a thousand balls of wool streaming from your leather bag.
*It's a wrap*, you told me, *for newborn babies in conflict zones.
I've knitted three of these this week.*
I immediately wanted to hug you, but didn't.

In between the fast and fluffy loops of *plain* and *purl*,
you told me you were 83,
slowing down the pace
to tell me of your husband's recent death
and that you'd also lost a son.
I could see how you worked through all of this.

*It's always, always, always,* about love,
as I watched your wild and lovely pattern
come together, in the language of wool,
a love letter, in stitch after stitch
to the newborns
and to those who were gone.

Martina Dalton

## The Return

Three godwits standing there, at the water's
edge. Breasts – gold they've borrowed
from tomorrow's sun.

Did not know (how could they?) how things
had changed between us:
how when they had left I could not bear

to look at it – the place they used
to settle when evening came, when our work
was done. How contaminated

it now seemed. The cuttlefish: perfect
till I held it in my hand. The hairline crack
remembering their wings.

The white of it, unmelted ice. Its bone existing
in the earth among the faded thrift, self-heal,
the skeletons of birds.

Old hurts buried
underneath the clod: not vanished at all –
but preserved, with yesterday's headlines.

No longer the thing itself, but a bank of words
remembering. The page – mute
as the last remaining swan.

Maureen Daly

## How We Do Things Now

We get up, shower the devil out of ourselves,
put oils back with a super rejuvenating cream.

Have a bowl of coffee, the offer of half price for the 2$^{nd}$,
guzzle pain au chocolat in every airport in Europe.

We drink water out of carcinogenic plastic bottles,
eat Chicken Korma reheated in the microwave.

Run with extra bouncy heavenly runners,
endure sweaty mates in the gym up the road.

We sit goggle-eyed surfing the web sending emails,
Google is our companion 24/7.

No need to read papers, deaths are on rip.ie,
delicious meals on *Best Recipes for the Day*.

Never put thread in the eye of a needle,
throw the holey socks and whatever in the bin.

Some day it will catch up with us,
a heat age or an ice age will dam us to smithereens.

'Ah go on ... have that second cup of coffee.'

Ailbhe Darcy

Fear

I never used to be afraid of cows or spiders.
Or men. Or having one day to rely on another
person's care. Or disposable barbecues
on sandy beaches. Or campers who
don't know you mustn't cook beneath
the canvas. Or raw sewage released
all along the Gower. Or jumping feet-
first into a stilly pool of ice-cold water beneath
a waterfall, fully dressed and fully braced. Or
solitude. Or too much routine, or not enough.
Or walking home from town at night. Or walking
with my hips and not my glutes. Or ending up
without a place to live. Or cooking
with the window closed. Or leaving
the window open when I leave. Or forgetting
my hair straighteners, roused and steaming.
Or ironing in bare feet. Or flour mites.
Or driving on Bank Holiday weekends in
Britain. Or sitting in the passenger seat
with my feet up on the dashboard, doing
the mess around. Or being taken to
a second location. Or passing through
a series of heavy doors, soon after the wedding.
Or being arrested for protesting. Or being
in pain and not offered relief, despite
relief being an option. Or giving birth in Britain.
Or getting sick in Britain, again. Or losing
my job. Or keeping my job. Or growing
old. Or recognising the child who came to our door
in lockdown, and we let him go,
we let them take him back to his foster father,
in a photograph on *Wales Online*. Or forever particles

entering our bodies and staying there
every time I open the door of our new log burner.

Eilín de Paor

## Pishogue

Early in the last century, Guendolen,
daughter of Sir Neville Wilkinson, saw fairies
in the woods of their home, Mount Merrion House.
Concerned for their shelter she convinced her father
to have an elaborate dolls' house built for them.
In time the estate fell to ruin
but the dolls' house, Titania's Palace, survived.
In 1978 it was bought by Legoland.
The dislodged fairies stayed on,
satisfied with the rare and special glimpses
of Aurora Borealis visible from their vantage.
We used to perch long hours on the old house ruins,
a stable mound for climbing with a bunker under –
all earwigs, beer cans, cigarette ends.
Pocket money welting our denimed hips,
the fairies pinned us there with tether spells
then napped their days away.
Hearing our breath catch
they'd crawl from their leaf beds,
remove miniature designer shades just in time
to see green light daub across the bay.

Celia de Fréine

## The Wasteland

On a summer's night a tour bus was abandoned on the wasteland north of the estate. The driver had had enough and, when he ran out of petrol, made the passengers disembark and walk back to town with only thin pashminas as protection against the chill air.

Or that was what the girl thought when she came upon the bus. And, as more junk was abandoned around it, she made up stories about each item: the pram that had carried fourteen children and was now too battered to hold a sack of coal; the bookcase that had caved in under the weight of words; mattresses whose springs had taken so much fucking they burst through their covers.

She and her friends could shelter in the bus when it rained and, on sunny days, rearrange the junk to create the world they'd like to live in – one where they didn't have to steal when hungry or go to bed when their mothers had to leave for work.

It was a place where there was no way of comparing what they did or said with the lives of those who lived on leafy avenues. It was where they could lay down their own laws. While summer lasted. Before returning to school where they would be put sitting at the back – too far away to see the blackboard – where the teacher could ignore them and they could harbour their disappointment.

## An Fásach

Ar oíche shamhraidh tréigeadh bus camchuairte ar an bhfásach ó thuaidh den eastát. Bhí a dhóthain ag an tiománaí agus, an peitreal ídithe, chuir sé iachall ar na paisinéirí tuirlingt agus siúl ar ais chuig an mbaile gan ach *pashminas* tanaí orthu mar chosaint ón aer goimhiúil.

Nó b'in a cheap an ghirseach nuair a tháinig sí ar an mbus. Agus, de réir mar a tréigeadh tuilleadh dramhaíola thart air, chum sí scéalta faoi gach ní: an pram a d'iompair ceathrar déag, a bhí róbhatráilte mála guail a sheasamh; an leabhragán a ghéill faoi mheáchan focal; tochtanna a d'fhulaing an oiread focála gur phléasc a spriongaí as a gclúdaigh.

Bhí sí féin is a cairde in ann dul ar foscadh ón mbáisteach sa bhus agus, ar laethanta brothallacha, an dramhaíl a athchóiriú leis an domhan ar mhaith leo maireachtáil ann a chruthú – ceann nach raibh orthu a bheith ag goid ann agus ocras orthu, nó dul a luí am a raibh ar a máithreacha dul ag obair.

B'áit é nárbh fhéidir an méid a rinne nó a dúirt siad ann a chur i gcomparáid le saolta iad siúd a raibh cónaí orthu ar ascaillí duilleacha. Áit a raibh siad in ann a rialacha féin a leagan síos. Fad a mhair an samhradh. Sular fhill siad ar an scoil, áit a gcuirfí ina suí ar chúl iad – rófhada leis an gclár dubh a fheiceáil – áit a bhféadfadh an múinteoir neamhaird a thabhairt orthu is a bhféadfadh siadsan a ndíomá a chaomhnú.

Helen Dempsey

## TURNING

For now, there is inertia. Curtains,
in a green subterranean glow,
hang limp.

The fabric bulges and ripples
when bodiless voices
muffle sentences.

Crocs and casters shuffle-squeak
under the hem near the floor.

Behind, in the wall,
oxygen gushes a downpour
of noise.

There will be a turning,
a shift from supine to upright;

a reveal when the drapes swish
around corners and the dregs
of a wintry sky shadow play
on the familiar.

There will be bustling corridor
activity, uniforms, equipment
and arrows for an egress to wellness.

It will be different,
quadruped of metal and flesh
scarred, slower, measured.

The after-path curious, expectant,
open to encounter.

Annie Deppe

## THE MUSIC OF THE NAILS

It was the summer of the big move,
the summer dedicated to reclaiming
a rundown New England farmhouse.

As my mother and older sister
stripped wallpaper, my father and brothers
fenced in acres, raised the post-hole digger

high above their heads
then drove it down deep into rocky soil,
setting the posts and cross rails in place.

At six I was too young to help so I practiced
pounding row after row of nails into a board.
Sometimes I balanced my way

across the top rails of the new fence
climbing from there into the apple tree
which became my kingdom.

As my family moved walls
and added doors and windows to the house
I dragged dusty planks from the barn.

The short wooden ladder rose to where
crooked branches spread and my red metal tin
sang with the music of the nails.

That summer of the move
I built and rebuilt. Each house
higher than the last. By August a trap door

opened into an expanse like a sea.
Everything I did seemed to reach
for the sky until the day

of my father's heart attack.
The heavy work of fencing
nearly claimed him. I thought

somehow his hospital room
was his new home. Far above me.
A place no child was allowed to go.

Deirdre Devally

### Dressed to Kill
*Inspired by an article/photo in the* New York Times, *11 April 2022*

Detailed to Bucha, the company rounds up
suspicious persons who *militarily pose a threat.*
The Commandant bellows at the belligerent prisoner,
*Put it on – skin beneath.* Face inches
from his, she smells onions on his breath.

Of the twenty-five women, young, weeping,
the pretty brunette reminds him of his Liliya.
*Put it on,* he says again, slapping her
with a matted, filthy, fur coat – spoils
of the past hour's looting.

She shakes her head. Whispers, *Never.*
He strains to hear her. *I'd rather be dead.*
Then strikes her harder. *Skin beneath.*
A memory ambushes him; first gift to his wife –
a coat of blue-hued Barguzin sable.

Later, newly-conscripted Ukrainian soldiers,
battling exhaustion, retrieve her body
from a bombed-out house cellar.
Naked, blood-smeared, pummelled.
Reputable sources estimate she'd endured

a month of 'visits'. In the wait for medics to tag
her a young recruit thinks of his mother.
Fighting tears, he gags, vomits. *She is someone's daughter.*
He searches through rubble, finds a stinking,
mink coat, and gently tucks it round her.

Zoë Devlin

### Two Hearts
*for Nik, 1963–2020*

The day you were born, the October sun
shed a long, golden ray across the Rotunda,
lighting your passage into my young arms.
I thought I would never love you more
but found that I could.

When those old arms held you tightly
for the last time, fifty-six years later,
our two hearts never beat as close.
How were we to know that one heart
would be stilled by the plague?

Now those arms are empty of you,
memories are all I have to hold close.
One heart has gone, one heart condemned to stay.
I thought I would never love you more
but found that I could.

Déirdre D. Dodds

### Bearáilte

bíonn tusa fós ag *creep*áil timpeall an tí seo
ar nós gadaí oíche
ag foluain os mo chionn sa seomra leapan
ag déanamh trua duit féin sa seomra folcadh
ag dul i bhfolach orm ar chúl an dorais sa halla
reidh le mé a scanrú.

Reidh le léimt amach romham ar an staighre
is mé a bhascadh arís is arís is arís eile.

Bíonn orm tú a chíoradh amach as mo chuid gruaige
chuile mhaidin, chuile oíche
ach ar nós sial chnis
nach scuabann mo leathlámh chun siúil
fanann tú ina bhruscar ar mo ghuaillí.

Agus fiú dá scuabfadh
bheidh tú ar ais arís amárach, beidh muis
tá do bholadh fós sa vardús greamaithe de mo ghúna
is do ghuth sa seomra suite ag caint os cionn na teilifíse.

Sea, tá tú ann ann ann
agus tú bearáilte.

Leag an teach seo
óir teastaíonn teach nua
uaimse.

Moyra Donaldson

## Where Was I Looking

I looked at the small black creature
scuttling across my vision.

I looked behind me, fearing
what might be coming forward.

I looked at the tulips, half mad with grief
in the Hotel Opera, Budapest;

they opened their black throats
and filled the corridors with absences.

I looked at the blue lights, the monster
in the cupboard, the broken things;

I looked for a mystery,
as if a mystery was ever to be found.

I looked at the scattering of shadows
but could not see the pattern,

saw consequence
but not the thing itself.

Rosemary Donnelly

## Nighttime

He lies awake and thinks
of how she might be
and what has happened,
how everything has changed
but on the surface seems
the same. He is at sea
and wants to be supportive
but doesn't know how.

The ghost of
a hole is in his chest,
absence nibbling
at the edges, an ache
inside of the loss of joy
and ease of get togethers,
of the time they all met
to be with her, not each other.

Silent tears grieve
in the darkness
for that which has not happened
yet inside he feels it has.

Out of nowhere comes comfort,
a presence enters,
spreading soporific peace
throughout the room
so exquisite
he tries to stay awake,
but sleep envelops him.

Katie Donovan

## The Midnight Baker
*for Bertha*

After hours of rest
to soothe the pain,
she rises
to crack eggs,
mix butter, sugar,
layer the baking dish
with coconut, pecans.
The kitchen fills
with warm scent
as the hurricane cake
firms its fissures
in the alchemy of heat.
Fragrant, her offering,
next morning.
She wraps it
for my long journey:
she knows about upheaval,
how to sweeten the cracks.

Mary Dorcey

## Our Heart-Stricken Earth

Outside my window –
once golden, lovely,
heart-shaped leaves
fall yellowed –
perfectly dead,
from the outstretched
limbs of grieving
trees;
mothers, once young

In spring –
proud life-givers
dancing, lissom –
on warm earth,
now, stripped of joy
of hope, of light.
Outside my window
elm and beech,
corpse-grey arms

Outstretched,
reaching for solace
finding none.
No comfort, no rescue
beyond my gaze –
these leaves of
brilliant amber, drop
like tears on the heart-
stricken earth –

Our earth –
where we bury
our children.

Alive.
Our golden
heart-shaped,
perfect children –
who die in season
screaming.

Their hands open
pleading for mercy –
finding none,
from helpless
women,
their mothers –
howling.
The name of each
child they call

Searing their tongue –
their perfect,
laughing, children,
flower-bright infants,
now burnt to bone,
scattered ash
on soil and sky –
in this year's
classic staging of

The slaughter season.

Doreen Duffy

## I Watch You Dance

Through bars on the stairs
laths of dark across
a carpet of light

Bare feet
strained, tired,
shush as you cross the rug,
turn as you circle
into stroking arms

A remembered hand warms your lower back
while you twirl, your eyes close,
seeing everything, touching
creases beside his eyes,
bringing colour to his lips, a kiss

You smile into the mirror above the fire,
eyes flutter open again, in time
to see your reflection
dancing
alone

Ger Duffy

## Anchorite

After Mother's funeral, Father rowed me
across the bay. My fingers threaded glass

water, little minnows, little stones, wind
flecked, last rays of sunshine. A horse-drawn

cart jigged us, its wheels pierced puddles,
splitting my shadow into two. Black tea

and bread in the parlour with Mother Superior,
her face brickstiff. Clack of beads, feet shuffle,

somewhere a choir, organ music, my shift grates
my skin. I breathe in, I breathe out, I sit, I stand,

I am, I was. My flaking skin tastes of ash.
I witness damp walls, moss frothing between stones,

the slow descent of dust, a drop of water shatter.
I crouch, root, rub, moan, lick.

Katherine Duffy

APPARITION

She keeps her old self pressed
close, a flower

on her skin, her hair
in the sun a statement
not entirely true.

She walks with care as if
wearing a wedding dress
(I'm sure her own still fits), or as if

a sound only she can hear
draws her, step by numbered
step, deep into the trees.

We pass. I nod. Perhaps
we are sisters. Then again,
maybe not. Not a dimple, not

a furrow, nothing
shy of immaculate. Her feet hold
tight to the rope. And what

after all are the years
but shoes kicked off a touch
too close to the tide?

I keep to the river.
I like how it bubbles
and slides. I like to sit and read

by the sound of it. In my book
people have choices to make.
Among leaf shadows they pick

a path. I stop to reflect:
we must be about the same age.

Ann Marie Dunne

## ANNIE MORLEY

Granny sticks a Silk Cut
in her mouth and lights it,
the signal there is work to be done,
washing up after feeding
the gang of grandkids.
She wrings out the wet dish towel,
her knobbly knuckles
and bumpy blue veins
stand out with the strain.
Not a drop of water
now drips. How? we ask –
"years of practice" she says.
She smokes hands free,
the ash dangles dangerously.

Mother lights a Woodbine,
sticks it in her mouth,
rolls up her sleeves and puts
the big black pot to heat over
the turf fire. It's Monday,
washing the clothes day.
She pours hot water into
the galvanised bath and pummels
and rubs out the dirt of a husband
and eleven scruffy children.
She scrubs shirt collars with
carbolic on the washboard,
scraping the knuckles off herself.
She hears the rain arrive and sighs.

Annie lets the blue-eyed gentleman
light her Lucky Strike,
one of her many acolytes.

Her and her girlfriend leave
the smoky speakeasy,
giddy after three gin rickeys.
They hail a yellow cab to Highbridge.
Annie hangs up her slinky flapper dress,
her good coat, her black cloche hat
and slips off her silk stockings.
She washes them carefully
in the bathroom sink. Then she wrings
them out, her slender fingers
squeeze out every last drop.

Áine Durkin

## Forainm

É?
Í?
Iad?

Sé?
Sí?
Siad?

Tusa?
Sibhse?

Linn mo ghrá.

I love *you*!

Micheline Egan

### She Shaped our Faith

It was her toes that did it ...
these slim toes grounded
this mighty woman for 84 years.

They carried nine children.
They stood their ground.
They walked through 45 years of marriage,
and in her younger days
they cycled a bike with a pig stretched on the back.
Those toes cycled revolutions to Edgeworthstown.

And now, they walk her in a tiny circle
from home to mass,
home to around the Mall on her daily walk,
home to downtown on her messages.

That those toes once belonged to a woman
who worked all the hours God gave her,
who, en route to her monthly pilgrimage in Knock,
would crack a hard-boiled sweet between her teeth
so that her three young ones
all had something to suck on.

May those tiny calloused toes walk her to purgatory
and hold her there
until it's time.

Orla Egan

## Stand Strong Together

We joke that we have the same name,
Orla and Rola,
same letters, jumbled up differently,
Irish roots, Palestinian roots,
two Cork women standing strong,
entwined in our commonalities, connections
feminists, parents, writers, activists

But they only see our differences
one taller, one shorter
one white, one brown
one queer, one straight

'Do you know in Palestine they'd stone you
for being queer' they warn me
as if homophobia, transphobia, biphobia
do not exist in Israel, Ireland, UK and USA

They warn me when I share photos
of striding proudly with my rainbow Keffiyeh
behind the Cork Queers for Palestine banner
Free Free Palestine
Stop Genocide Now
IDF and USA – how many kids have you killed today?

How many kids have you killed today?

They sow seeds of division and hate
attempt to divide us
pitch us against each other
shift focus from their atrocities

How many kids have you killed today?

But we continue
to stand entwined
with love and respect
for our differences
our commonalities
our shared humanity

Queer Rights Now
Free Free Palestine

Attracta Fahy

INISHBOFIN

The sea was choppy. I clung to my son on the early
ferry, our last day before his return to Los Angeles.
An islander said 'it's not the worst,' and we smiled.

As the boat crested, heaved on waves, we rocked,
water sloshed over the bow, surged against plexiglas,
foam drenching our hair, sea a sheet of liquid steel.

As passengers sheltered downstairs I waited up deck,
salt air sting on my skin, spray sousing my face. I kept
my eye on the island, a hummock in the distance.

The skyline plunged, reared, fumed against boundless
grey cloud. Seats bolted to the floor, we swayed
between mainland and island. Four cormorants

emerged from the water, glided, then taking speed
from the wind, left us behind, as we'd left Cleggan
at the end of a surf path. We were slicing water,

coasting the tip of a deep gateway. On the horizon
the faint blue whale shaped Mayo hills, Clare Island,
the cone peak of Croagh Patrick.

I thought of Cliodna, Celtic goddess of sea,
looked down into the black melancholy, blood
and bones of her dead. Out of nowhere the music

of birds who snatch apples from her mystical tree,
their songs a balm to a mother's lament. I made a
wish on her waves and the waters calmed.

We sailed around the tower's wild rugged landscape
into the harbour, left of Cromwell's fort.
Stepping onto the pier the wind and Inishshark

at our back, we climbed past sea pink blossom
growing out from the long schist and shale walls.
Out over the bay fishing boats arrived with lobster,

others leaving, rounded Dún Gráinne, and through
a mild mist I imagined her at the helm of her ship.
Taking strength from her perseverance, a cotillion

of terns flying overhead. I linked my son's arm.
Although I couldn't recall what we said
I remember how we laughed that day on the island.

Emer Fallon

## Gardening with my Mother

My mother is conjuring ghosts
under a grey June sky
in the vegetable garden behind the house
where she's perched on a hardwood chair.

First Uncle Jim, dapper and moustached,
a bunch of flowers in his hand,
followed by Uncle Michael
with his upright officer's back,
fresh off the 65 bus from town,
a bag of homegrown fruit on his arm.
And here he is again
at the foot of a hotel staircase
comforting my mother's
bridesmaid while she weeps –
there there, he murmurs, don't cry.

Why was she crying, I ask my mother –
because she was losing me, she replies.

Auntie Abbie is lip-sticked and jolly.
I mention her moustache
and my mother says yes, I'd forgotten that.
We watch the bristles appear.

The dark cloud of my father's grandmother
waits in the wings – a tiny figure
dressed in black,
she shadows the patch I've cleared.

I say to my mother
you could probably
hoe this sitting down.

She asks
is that really all
I'm capable of? Later
when I'm reading in bed
Great Uncle Corry appears.
What do you want with me? he asks.
Nothing, I tell him, nothing at all. My mother
was digging through her memories and found you.
He slips from the room like water leaving
a whiff of the Grand Canal in his wake.

Helen Fallon

OUR COUNTRY
*for P.O.*

Back then, you showed me how to cook groundnut stew.
We took turns thumping peanuts in the cracked pestle.
You laughed, as tears from scarlet chillies,
streamed down my freckled face.

You brought me to the market, showed me how to haggle.
*You go less me,* I echoed you, bought cloth
tie-dyed in swirls of apple pink, ocean blue,
mango yellow and lime green.

We clattered along potholed roads in a rust-eaten poda-poda,
*Fear Judgement Day* splashed in bright red paint
across the bonnet. Your mother welcomed me
with sliced papaya, sweet and buttery.

Now, your children live in Ireland. Evenings, they marvel
at bruised pink sunsets. On days when seasons merge,
showers catch them unprepared. Then the sun,
a feeble relative of their sun, smiles again.

In winter we trudge in boots and duffle coats
through ice-crusted snow in fading light.
Ice pearls drop from pine trees huddled in snow shawls,
dissolve, splash our skin. We laugh.

Carole Farnan

## Women, Life, Freedom

*Gave birth to you with love and pain*
*Gave you back to the motherland.*
(On Nika Shakarami's tombstone)

You gave them your resistance
your burning hijab
your teenage rebellion
your street protests

They took your flailing limbs
tried to take your virtue
they took your kicks
they took your broken body

dumped it on Yadegar-E-Emam Highway

They took away your funeral
they took away your blood and bruises
they took away the truth
burying it

with the hundreds who had gone before

You gave them a chant at your graveside
– all your champions of courage –
*"We are all Nika*
– Fight and we will fight back"

Tanya Farrelly

CANVASSING

On the doorsteps they all wanted something.
On darkening evenings she stood
listening to their needs
as the lamps kicked in up and down the street,
flickering before settling to a steady stream.
And beyond their doors life went on:
sautéed onions, toddlers' tears,
some crank on a TV game show
who promised a shot at the jackpot
as the old woman in the bed upstairs
pounded on the floor for attention.

Orla Fay

### Mil na Fianna
*for Sarah*

Is tú mo chailín,
mo aoibh gháire ar oíche Vailintín,
dearg mo chochaill,
corcair dorcha an rós,
lár veilbhit na cruinne.
Is tusa an tost láithreach
idir patrúin báistí,
tusa a bhfuil aithne mhaith agam
agus ní ar chor ar bith, rúndiamhair.
Is cailín thú a thit mé i ngrá le
ag tóraíocht fianna sléibhe.
Tá do chroí cosúil leis an conch
fuair mé i óige
ag coinneáil na farraige i mbraighdeanas.
Is lullaby thú.
An cuimhin leat nuair a d'fhág tú do lipstick
ar an pillowcase?
Nuair a bhí tú milis agus deataithe?
An cuimhin leat nuair a, trí deora,
brúite mé do bhéal le póga?
Is mil thú,
timpeallaithe ag solas.
Is aingeal thú, a stór.
Is cuimhin liom spéir lán le bláthanna.

### The Honey of the Deer

*You are my sweetheart,*
*my smile on Valentine's eve,*
*the red of my hoodie,*
*the dark crimson of the rose,*

*the velvet centre of the universe.*
*You are the present silence*
*between pitter patters of rain,*
*you whom I know so well*
*and not at all, a mystery.*
*You are a girl I fell in love with*
*chasing mountain deer.*
*Your heart is like the conch*
*I found in childhood*
*holding the sea captive.*
*You are a lullaby.*
*Do you remember when you left your lipstick*
*on the pillowcase?*
*When you were sweet and smoky?*
*Do you remember when, through tears,*
*I crushed your mouth with kisses?*
*You are honey*
*surrounded by light.*
*You are an angel, treasure.*
*I recall a sky full of flowers.*

Pauline Fayne

LUAS LASS

The girl facing me on the tram
speaks to everyone who gets on,
teasing youths and tousling toddlers curls

Halfway to the terminus
she grows quiet,
eases face wipes from her bag

Removes all trace
of the unneeded mascara
from her luminous eyes

Four stops away
she smooths and pins the shining hair
that flatters her face

Three stops away
checks cheeks and lips
with the tiny handbag mirror

Two stops away
runs black cloth
through reluctant fingers

Last stop
niquab in place
only her smiling eyes are visible

Felispeaks

## Green Lady

Madness is only a misunderstanding of scenery.
Like buttering toast on the bus with a plate on your lap.
An inside performance in the open.
The rest of us are much too afraid to pack our Kerrygold.
So we watch thoughtfully. Envy morph into shame.

Audacity is scarce in Dublin right now.
Home is a tight fist no one can breathe in, deeply.

I want to clothe the green lady with a name. She is St Brigid.

She is delicately expelling out of her springtime midsummer.
It is a devastation nobody joined her in prayer.
We are all desperately behind.

Blooms are an awkward thing to do in concrete.
We are blossoming slower than ever before.

There aren't enough gardens and picket fences for all of us.
St Brigid is at least making pavement into grass.

Shouldn't we all stretch as much as we can?

There is not enough space to dance unless it is outside.
It is where they have left us all.
Out of sync.

She is dancing for her life. Her feet tapping on the rain the sky yawned.
Me and you are coat crouched umbrella-less heading into all directions unsure.

St Brigid is stationary and soft moving.
The season will change someday, in one of these tomorrows,
and her ceremony would have been complete.

Anne Fitzgerald

## Heatwave 1976

What of the day
your Father left

the print of his hand
on your thigh.

His five fingers burned
bright as a starfish for three

whole weeks that summer.
He would not let you swim till

redness died down a touch.
By week four, at the beach

in jeans and woollen sweater
before heat demands you strip

to swim. Noonday sun hits
ripples beyond water wings

and swimming rings. Meteorologists
record unprecedented high pressures.

Afterwards swimmers will
remark, not where he left

his mark, but of a cold
you could not shake

that year of the bank strike.
Gulls cry out as you walk

from waves. Sunlight traces
his hand, brine holds like a bas-relief

for all the world to see, but
not the sting which still sears.

Deirdre Flaherty Brady

## Circadian Rhythms

The ache is like no other,
there is no pain, or nervous shudder,
it requires no attention
nor medical intervention,
it renders deep into primaeval spaces
where empty cradles lay,
swinging silently to the circadian rhythms
of the decaying day.

Deirdre Flannery

## Son

You lie there, all limber, long-limbed
like a lamb. Infant child
of mine. Your downy head is a light
bulb in shape, the bedroom lamp dimmed
to lull you into slumber. But you will

hardly sleep. I live a zombie life now
but it's worth every moment. I lie
down beside you, watching your chest rise
and fall faster than mine, lullabies lilt low
in the background. My room is now filled

with nappies, lotions and potions. The sweet smell
of you after your wash, in water like vanilla
milkshake. The teardrop bottles – shampoos yellow,
moisturisers white, bath blue. Shadows fall
through the wooden slats, thrown on a wall

I see the new life, I weep
and now I too may sleep

Siobhán Flynn

## How to Find the Witch

Take the path through the cornfield,
squint your eyes against the sun
until you feel the shadow of the trees.

Whether you bless the leafy coolness
or fear the whispering darkness depends
on which side of the witch you are.

In the dark depths of the woods
you discover her house, not made
of gingerbread but solid stone.

She comes to the door, her cats gather
in her footsteps. You stand and hope,
relieved by the nod of her welcome.

You know she will do what no one else will;
she will take away what's left of love,
the pain, and other unwanted effects.

She will give you vengeance if you pay
but there's no going back – now
you have found her she's yours forever.

Catherine Foley

SÍOS LE FÁNA

Tharla sé ag breacadh an lae,
go mall ar dtúis.
Seanduine ag dul in aois a bhí inti,
tá mé cinnte de.
Ní fhéadfá stop a chur leis an ruaig a d'éirigh fúithi,
i ndiaidh na fearthainne agus an fhliuchta
a tharla
i rith na hoíche
ar bharr na haille.

Shleamhnaigh gach rud
in aon ghluaiseacht amháin
go dtí go raibh sí ina cnap ag bun na haille.
Máthair treascartha,
sciorradh talún lena ghéaga ardaithe in achrann,
éadaí iompaithe amach ar chladach na trá.

D'imigh sí síos le fána
go dtí go raibh sí ar a glúine,
leacaithe and íslithe.

Níor scréach sí
ach chloisfeá a cneadach,
fiú dá mbeifeá i do sheasamh ansan
taobh thiar den ché.

Chonaiceamar í,
spréite amach ar chlocha na trá,
a seansciorta stróicthe,
sceacha taobh léi
ag tairngreacht an mhúchta.

## Downhill

It happened at the break of day,
slowly at first.
An old woman already frail,
I'm sure of it.
You couldn't stop the rush that carried her down
after the rain and the soaking
that had happened
during the night
at the top of the cliff.

Everything slipped down
in one easy movement
until she was in a heap at the foot of the cliff.
A mother vanquished,
a landslipe with its arms raised in anguish,
clothes strewn across the shoreline.

She went downhill
until she was on her knees,
flattened and levelled.

She didn't screech
but you'd hear her panting,
even if you were standing there
behind the pier.

We saw her,
spread out along the stones of the strand,
her old skirt in ribbons,
thorns nearby
foretelling the end.

Bernadette Fox

## Habit

She enters the white distempered room
where an iron bed stands
covered in virgin blue candlewick.
Overhead, the crimson Sacred Heart
beats on the wall.

Beside the long-paned window
a chest of drawers lacquered
in lavender polish
contains everything she needs:

Black leather-bound *Office*,
rope of Rosary beads,
oversized crucifix
nails her bridegroom's bloody hands and feet.

Bundled together
a shapeless serge tunic
hem sweeps the ground,
white wimple veil
to adorn her cropped brown hair.

Outside, giddy children
horse playing on the street
are drowned out by Angelus bells
knelling them home for tea.

She stands silent,
listens.

Anne-Marie Fyfe

## WISHBONE

The day we come home with bramble scratches

is the day the lofty pines start to brush against
the door's architrave, push hard on bedroom panes,
curl their fronds around our chimney stack.

They come to brood increasingly over our growing up.
One August afternoon our English cousin climbs,
falls to the ground, branch and all; we hear a limb snap,

see his arm as an ungainly wishbone.
The following Christmas we wish for an absence
of trees, the throttle of a chainsaw.

I become obsessed with calculating distances
between sturdy somnolent trunks.
They remain resolutely unchanged.

Daily I check, tally figures in a notebook,
long for the millimetre that will confirm
to three decimal places that I was right all along.

The whisper of leaves becomes deafening
on this elmed avenue: they steal the last of our light.
In time we acclimate to the semi-dark.

Nights now I dream of a child in a Trondheim forest
who wakes to row upon row of bone-white birch,
to her very own post-nuclear January.

Amy Gaffney

HOLY TRINITY

The last day of April brought the heaviest storm.
It bruised the tulips, bent them double under the strain.
It pounded the mud sending splatters into the air.
The pond overflowed till it streamed into the grass.
I worried for the gelatinous black-eyed mess of spawn.
I'd never seen such rain. Seen such bluster.

A crumbling statue, draped in stone, took quite a battering
where she stood in the centre of the garden
where the paths cross. She didn't topple,
even if there was a moment where she might have.
Later, the cherry petals stopped falling, leaving
a carpet of pink under the stars.

And I exhaled, for in the dark, I'd found the trinity
of myself: The Maiden, The Mother, The Crone.

Bernadette Gallagher

## Dancing in the Dark
*for Maureen Gallagher*

*I won't dance again,* you said,
then I reached out my arms –
we danced and laughed and danced.
I know you've already forgotten
our dance
our jigsaw making
you listening as I read poems to you.
It happened
it's real
and I will recall for you
retell our time together
as you repeat
*it's a fine day*
*well, it was lovely having you stay.*

Peggie Gallagher

## The Gift
*for Eibhlín Ní Eochaigh*

Your Glencar poem came in the post.
It brought with it a bright May day, hedges
veiled in hawthorn, a landscape of hard-won
fields, and the many-windowed house
you rented that year.

Though what I remember most was
the call of the cuckoo,
the big blue bird high in the sycamore
and you waiting
to scold me for losing my way again.

But we were not lost; a truth so large and simple,
I want to tell you now as we stand at the side
of our lives in these days of lockdown.

What we shared:
Words laid like a room in a new house.
Words like *cleft and fissure cut the tongue;*
*the real thing, 'Poll in Aghaidh' deep enough*
*to escape inside and hide.*

Elaine Gaston

ON ROUND THE COAST ROAD

We stopped for a paddle
which became a dunk
which became a
full blown swim
well, you got your head wet but I didn't.
I piled up the black and white stones in
a torma that wobbled but did not topple.

Scotland so near we could touch it, unbelieving
it was another land, ancestors who sailed there,
easier than wading inland, through bogs, midge bites.
Even though it is twelve miles at the nearest point,
even though Finn built a causeway,
it was still a million miles away.
Might as well be a different planet
altogether I said and you concurred.

Scraps of villages came and went
as I threw invisible mandalas out of the moving
car, open window, dedicated them to land
on the scar of the murdered husband, the hill
where two men scratched up through furze
but were hunted down, the bomb that killed,
the shot that narrowly missed,
the shot that didn't miss
the back of the teenager,
the disappeared mother.

And not only the troubled gashes but also
Inge Maria buried late at night under forest pines,
no prosecutions, even now.

Past aqueducts and waterfalls, more mountains,
the outer ledges of extreme – Tievebulliagh, Lurig –
through glens carved by glaciers faded
into the gentler rolls of Trostan, Orra, Knocklayd.
Knocklayd! And bogs, Islandmacallion, Moycraig,
Knockmór.
*You know where you are now*. Once more.

Shauna Gilligan

## Beverly Allitt's Push of Dreams

With each push of each syringe
she whispered, *Look at me:*
with each rise and fall of
tiny lungs beside each tiny heart she
nursed them, until she couldn't.

*Look at me,* she said
to the TV in her prison cell:
in programme after
programme and maybe
a poem or a fantasy.

*Look at me,* she says
the femme fatale you think I am:
the scent of death
on these fingertips until
I fall back into invisibility.

Aimee Godfrey

## Devotee

There's great money in it, apparently,
and I wouldn't even have to do that much.
I watched a documentary on it once.

I have always paid men
to decide what to do with my body,
to know about the greater good,
what's good for me.

But maybe better fetish than patient
than science project.
A rose by any other name.

Either way, just a body,
but this way,
the body can afford to eat.

You'd be surprised what there's a market for.

Trudie Gorman

## Synonyms for Loss

The summer we made lighthouses
from our voice boxes,
I swore everything we touched was possible.
The phone calls signalling your slow
steps home along the Rathmullen cliffs,
my single bed between day shifts.
I only called it desire later.

I remember it now –
your cropped hair and my long
lingering milk teeth.
The day I brought you love notes
on the bus from Dublin and forgot
at the crossroads how to breathe.
The slow potion of it touches me
like a dream.

Your bite, and my lonely.
Everything back then was wet
and holy.
In autumn, I got on the plane alone
and you went back to university,
trained yourself in how to forget me.

The first grief of my young years
was that silence –
how everything lived was forgotten.
Nothing we knew was ever possible,
and I sung myself dulcet lies
for the years I lost you.

Anita Gracey

### The Lonely Passion
*after* Carel Fabritius, *1654*

The goldfinch perches on my heart like a bruise.
Gazing from gilt boughs and empty walls
he watches the shadows creep across disinterested furniture
waiting for the relief of darkness.

He dreams of a banquet of quivering leaves,
picking through discarded chaff for grain,
warm striations surfing his feathers,
ruffling honeysuckle hedgerows with the breeze.

In the young sun he stirs,
everything seems better in the half light,
everything is this room.

Angela Graham

## It Broke my Mother's Heart
*Glenview Gardens, East Belfast, 1972*

A very young tree is a brave thing,
innocent, hopeful, defenceless.
Some people like to break stuff.

A new neighbour across the street.
*Go and tell him what his son's done,*
– my widowed mother, wary her brogue said *Catholic*.

I, at fifteen, East Belfast born and bred,
could – in a crisis – pass for Protestant
so I did what I had to.

Bravery is not a lack of fear.
It's knocking on the door;
it's pointing to the broken sapling;

it's saying, *I saw your son do that*
when you know they could torch the house
and no one would defend you.

Yes, they would find out later what you were
but you'd have had your say
as though you were a normal person.

They stonewalled. The tree died. I grew,
but warped – and many like me – not dead
but darkened, my bark stripped,

my body growing bruises and mysterious pains
– the wounds I felt that they, and others like them,
thought I deserved.

That slender tree – it used to whiplash
when a high wind caught it.
Had anyone got hurt who mattered?

But someone bears the load into the desert;
no blood or bullets mar the street,
nothing shows up in the statistics.

Tryptizol and Librium and Valium
moved in – for good this time –
and kept my mother brittle, hardly calm.

Since the way we act can change a world for worse,
can the way we act change the world for better?
That's what I ask.

Mim Greene

### Beloved
*for Trish*

I have no words, but I will try.

My sister,
mystical dancer,
my teacher,
my fellow warrior woman,
our tribal fire lighter.
The little girl with a cheeky grin
who holds mischief in her belly
and warmth in her blood.
You are a spiritual astronaut.

Thank you for your enthusiastic and loving heart,
a heat-seeking missile that offers mystical joy
and twinkling light.
We have woven a cradle of pure love
as we relay you home.

I hope their awaits the next great adventure
where you get to witness the majesty of your heart,
all the good you have done in this world,
all the hearts you have touched.

Hands you have held
we are here now to hold your hand
and invite bliss into every cell of your body.
Only love is real
and you are beloved.

Anita Greg

## Sweeter than Ashes
*the love song of Takabuti*

I am sweeter than ashes,
a rose in the desert. In chains,
a leopard. In history
a war that never happened
... or went underground.
I am your yesterdays,
over and over,
a memory lodged in the back of your skull.

It is time.

You are a squirrel that buried a seed
in the roots of an oak tree
and never remembered
until it was too late. I am a cat in the dark,
a tumbling star that got caught in the branches
and sitting here, burning,
I've learned how to stare.

I am rain,
a dot on the horizon that grows as you watch it,
a howl from the hill
and a tooth from a crocodile.
Twenty five in the light,
eight hundred in darkness,
a hundred and fifty in something that's neither.

I've been wrapped in my skin for a thousand years.
It is time I was wrapped up in yours.

Nicki Griffin

Another Life

The room was everything she'd known,
set of drawers, table, fireside chair,
newborn safe within her arms,
eyelids fluttering, skin so freshly made
you could see through it.
Wrapped in warmth, in home.
In the distance another thwump,
a tearing sound as though the sky
were being unzipped. Closer today.
Tomorrow they must leave.

Sinéad Griffin

## The Score

Back when we played the field,
my sister played the flute.
Her soft kiss of embouchure
could spring harmony from air.
That tilt of her head, flirtation
with quavers, the rigor
of her practice. But then

I didn't know about the percussionist.
The secret of his meter and beat
she confided only to the cellist,
who set him for herself
with her endpin.
My sister boxed the flute,
married a banker.

Sharon Guard

FOR FEAR

I might move through a life
and leave no trace, hot summers
reduced to flower wisps of memory,
warm whispers for ghosts.

I might hide from winter,
hibernate, the potential
wild winds thwarted
with warm gilded glitter snip.

Autumn and spring might
pass unremarked, the wonders
of nature domesticised
and rendered small in my eye.

I might disturb nothing.
Feel nothing. No pain. No joy.
Swerve festering manifestations
of grief, actively deny them.

This singular adventure
might be left unexplored. My
children too, swaddled so tight
they learn to avoid experience.

And, when the final moment comes,
they, whoever they may be,
might close crinkled flesh over eyeballs
and sigh: sure she did no harm.

Christine Hammond

PERPETUAL MOTION
*Indian Summer*

We came into our own that year.

Somehow, everyone did
but together, more than anyone
we took what the summer gave
and ran with it
trailing clouds of glory
heads up, sunward
wild-eyed
invincible.

I never saw you again.

Life is motion, you said
we sobered up, got real
threw away headiness
and moved with the seasons
slowed down
descendent, separate
free-falling
eager for autumn.

Eithne Hand

## THAT DATSUN WAS OUR FIRST BEDROOM

You easily hopped
over the hand brake;

the cassette player
blaring Meatloaf,
risking a battery drain.

Talking and touching,
we steamed up windows
by the dashboard light.

One night a policeman
knocked on the glass.
*Alright in there?*

In there we were exploring
an entirely new menu –

a hunger for touch, for salt,
for lust, savouring our first
taste of a sweet private life.

Rachel Handley

## A Soft Reckoning

I can sink into
the fresh heart of it
just as you do.
A soft reckoning.
An easy vibration so
small that it takes years
to sing from your body
to mine. For you to
notice that we are
not in the same place.
That when I try to
move, my whole soul flies
up, eating freedom
under wing, feeling
the soft heat of the
sun. Having to say nothing more
than hello. A bone
attempts escape and
your mouth tells me I
am not made well like
you, I am frayed edges
yet you are the one bitten,
and brought, burnt, back to the earth.

Kerry Hardie

## Rising Waters

The sea holly's going,
back into the sea, a white exile once reserved
for those old saints and heroes –
(only a flung glance
over the shoulder before the horizon
dips under the prow) –

bare feet are thankful, but eyes
that have loved its pale spikes,
its spectral blue flowers,
are searching deep water to find its root-tangle
peopled with sidle-of-green-crabs that watch
as the sea takes everything back to itself

yet leaves the wild pansies, otherwise known
as heartsease, a name of such balm,
such a timid daring-of-joy
that those mauve-yellow faces
still spring out of sands
where even the rabbits are squeezed,

their underground tenements
spiralling inwards,
lebensraum taken,
long, tunnelled ghettos drifting to sea.
When I wake in the morning
it will be today's tomorrow.

Anne Haverty

SIBERIA

After
that night
after
you left
I left too.

Was sent away
to this north land
I call Siberia.

This waste
a graveyard
for fools and mad,
for the wilful and the lost

stumbling through the snow
after a chimera.

Tramping
across Siberia
digesting your loss
in raw seal meat
in the congealed blood
of a bear.

And for guardian
only the black fox
restless
by the door.

In this outrage
of a place
at times I see you

as the Tsar;
and I your exile
shambling
across the steppe

eating your absence
in bitter
seal meat.
For drink
the sour
blood of the bear.

Only an ice-light
to guide us
the fox and me.
This cold sun
that glints

with the glassy eye
of the lost
and forsaken.

Rachael Hegarty

## Washing Windows is Out of the Question

I'm not known for me good housekeeping ...
washing windows is out of the question –
it wrecks me head if we wreck spiders' webs.

In the corner of our front room's window frame ...
one spider's been at it for a while now –
spinning a crisscross world of silken threads.

Our eldest, the resident naturalist,
gives me a lesson on the spinneret ...
'Ma, imagine an organ that spits out
and weaves these tangles of deadly snares?'

Our youngest is pure chuffed with less pesky
fruit flies, mozzies or bluebottles – they're trapped
in cocoon coffins in our spider's web ...
meanwhile our crafty huntress waits, unseen.

The husband stands in pure admiration
of the spider's sturdy builds ... not even
a red weather warning of gale force winds
can shift her, she'll stay put – until she won't.

Her spider fractals look best in the morning
when the light lands on cobweb dewdrops
and changes the view from our unwashed windows.

Niamh Hehir

## The Separation of Mother and Child in a Nazi Yard

Flicking through channels
I stumble upon this image
caught on camera –
a mother and her young son,
part of a heaving mass of people
being organised into groups by Nazi guards.

She is told to join one line.
He another.
But he doesn't –
instinct gets the better of him
and he follows his mother,
as he has always done,
not understanding
the sophisticated adult cruelty
that sees him as nothing
and her as nothing that reproduces nothing.

He is marshalled back,
she is forcibly pulled away
by soldiers following orders,
far too efficiently
dividing the line
between mother and child.

You have entered hell here,
young as you are,
this means nothing to them.

    ii

If we can get out of this –
if we can stay alive

I will unravel with you
the tight thread that waists your heart.
The panic in your hands,
the deep undigested fear.

If I can endure this without breaking,
or giving cause for a casual execution –
(that might be sweet release but for you).
If I can stay here ready for you, ready to hold you
and love the horror away.

But it is dark.
And I hope another hand is holding yours
in case mine doesn't make it.

I wish for a woman with floured palms who
scoops you up in her ample arms and fits your body
into hers with no sliver of light between you and promises
again and again, until her words
wash away your fear,
to never ever, ever
let you go again.

   iii

Some images
are enough
to take every grain of faith away,
and once seen
can never be forgotten.

History brings us
such evidence of cruelty
ongoing, unending –
children dead in Gaza, Sudan.

I want to take my son, my daughter,
and find somewhere to hide them
far from the treacherous reaches
of humanity.

But there is no elsewhere here.

Aideen Henry

## Not Dead, Sleeping

At fifty eight I started HRT,
prince's kiss to my sleeping womb,
long finished its lifetime cycle
of ripening, shedding, bleeding
– it reawakened.

My aging brain may have ceased
its monthly dispatch of signals
for the womb to lay down
a lush scarlet bed
where an embryo might bloom.

Now each month HRT promises
the womb that embryo. It does not
reawaken my quiescent ovaries,
so no middle-aged egg appears
rubbing its eyes, looking for its glasses.

Instead, month after month,
the womb ripens and sheds,
forever hopeful, forever ready to cradle a baby,
should that egg appear, should that egg meet sperm,
should the pair merge and flourish.

Phyl Herbert

### Taking Steps

She had made her bed in that holy place
for far too many years
and her morning matin
*The Lord is my shepherd: I shall not want*
now seemed to mock her.
*The Lord is my shepherd,* I want much more.

A furnace of feeling between her and her father.
Her ponytail swinging, still in her school uniform.
'You'll find your feet here,'
were his last words to his daughter.

Captive in that holy place
she learned to walk with mincing grace,
to hide her body and honour
the lord above herself.

Now, lord, let me take my own steps
out of this frozen world.
Let me answer the call of my body.
There is a world elsewhere
and I want to dance in it.

*Lord, is it too late to learn how to dance?*

Florence Heyhoe

## Full Stop

She gets there early, dressed in yellow. Flowers in her hair wafting scent around her. In her hand a small ridged green bottle of her urine ... freshly filled. Going round to the back of the church, the spread of plastic grass identifies his grave. Opened last night to lay down his wife.

Standing at the head end she empties the contents and prays his skeletal mouth is relaxed and open. Returning the bottle to her bag, she washes her hands.

mountain top view
an eagle fully fledged
circling the thermals

Rita Ann Higgins

## Unnatural Pleasures
'Mixed athletics are a social abuse and a moral abuse'
*The Irish Press* letters page, 24 February 1934
Rev. John Charles McQuaid

1

*Christian Modesty*

The sporting places
that women could inhabit
in 'Ireland of the no space for Women'
were few and less between.

One flapping crow
raged against mixed athletics.
It should be about Christian modesty,
he howled, spittle flying from his mouth.
Mixed athletics are an abomination.

These spaces where women compete
in the same sporting spaces as men
are un-Irish and un-Catholic.
Flaunting herself in front of the males –
her breasts dancing with pagan delight.
A smile on her lips –
it can't and it won't be tolerated.

2

*The Moral Dangers of Tampax*

The flapping crow
was worried about
'the internal sanitary tampons'.

The bishops disapproved
of these contraptions,
and the flapping crow
lost sleepus interruptus
about any unnatural pleasures
that might be had.
The disapproval was for unmarried persons mostly.
Could that mean men?
I don't suppose it does.
The unnatural pleasures were a scourge,
they can't and won't be tolerated.

    3

*Hockey Parturition*

It was the twisting movements
in hockey that bothered the flapping crow.
The way they moved
those beautiful bodies –
letting out animal sounds
when they collided.
It wasn't right for crying out loud.
Some of the posher schools were told,
get the hockey stopped
and get it stopped now.
It can't and it won't be tolerated.

    4

*The Souls of Women*

The flapping crow
was worried
for the souls of women.
Mixed athletics
had mortal sin written all over it.

Women and men frolicking
on the same patch of grass,
at times heaving and writhing –
not on my watch.
As for the pommel horse –
it was rumoured
that unnatural pleasures
were to be had thereon.
It can't and won't be tolerated.

Deirdre Hines

## Disguises

We sneaked into the grey backyard
while the babby paddled in the puddles.
Two weeks into the wettest summer
and this our only danger. I wore a disguise
of my mother's best brown jacket over a skirt
held up with a yellow ribbon.
You wore your father's driving cap.
We needed out from chores and chores.
We were looking for some evidence
the stranger with binoculars
was enemy spy. Tiptoeing through
the open back door we crossed
an invisible line in a kitchen
piled high with books and drawers
and drawers of eggs. Except those eggs
were not the brown of Granny's backyard
crawthumpers. But row on row
of blue, yellow, red and cream treasures
laid out on their little cotton shrouds
in row after row after row in stack
on stack of kitchen drawer.
And then a floating feather
bounces in the air, collides with another
and it was as if our entrance
closed the lids on all those tiny
rainbowed coffins
releasing all the spirits of those stolen
chicks chirping and cheeping behind us
as we hotfooted it out that ordinary
kitchen door, down the empty lane
and onto the empty beach
forgetting all about the babby.
But isn't that always the way

for bird or girl? Isn't there always glitter
of light or lure of lair
disguised as life's great adventure
that reveals itself to be Fata Morgana,
or trickster god, that sly old fox
that fools everyone of we little red hens.

Máire Holmes

## TAIBHSÍ

D'éalaigh na blianta,
'Sgan focal scríofa,
Iad sáite in áit doshroiste
I bhfad ó bhaile.

Bhuail clog san intinn,
Phreab na smaointe.
Rith an chéad íomhá trasna
Deora na mblianta
A d'fhág focail ina dtost.
Faoi bhun gach ní,
Faoi cheo os cionn croí,
Faoi fhuil ins an gcolainn
Faoi chraiceann gan locht,
Faoi fhuinneog 'sna súile,
Faoi chnámha aosta,
Faoi bhrón, is faoi ghreann,
Faoi ghrian 'is faoi ghealach,
Faoi chríonnacht 'is uile,
Maireann fuaimeanna.

D'oscail ceol na tuisceana,
D'eitil taibhsí isteach,
Iad ina dtost.
Go minic, ní gá tada a rá.

Eleanor Hooker

## An Gorta Mór
*Doolough, Mayo, 1849*

Some say two hundred, others say six hundred souls
were compelled to trudge through blizzards
that bone-chilling night in March, to present
for inspection before dawn's indifferent glare.
Shadow-light and starving, barefoot and barely robed,
garments long since pawned, they left Louisburgh

through Doolough, a valley gorged by hungry hills,
for Delphi Lodge, twelve miles hence – eternity
for the dispossessed bound on a death march.
Some, they say, were slight enough that gulping
winds drew them up and plunged them
into Doo Lough, to tumble forever in the lake's dark.

Versions do not describe why, when they had
gathered at the appointed hour to be judged
for *Outdoor Relief*, Hogreve and Primrose, Poor Law
Guardians, left for Delphi without consideration,
obliging those wretched beings to follow on
or be cast off. And die.

And deemed unsuitable for relief or the poor
house, without tender or sustenance – in despair
our famine dead began their long trek
into oblivion, or would have were it not
for the anonymous 'ratepayer' who wrote them
into history in their missive to the *Mayo Constitution*:
*The inspection took place in the morning,*
*and I have been told that nothing could equal*
*the horrible appearance of those truly unfortunate*
*creatures, some of them without a morsel to eat,*
*and others exhausted from fatigue ...*

Returning to Louisburgh – men, women
and their children perished along the way –
grass in their mouths they lay exposed
*for three or four days and nights, for the dogs
and ravens to feed upon, until some charitable person
had them buried in a turf hole on the roadside.*

Jennifer Horgan

## Chris, 1993

His body had become more solid, bigger
than most fourteen year old boys back then.
He would show us, posing like a wrestler,
great big bulges blooming from his neck.
Arms curled in, blue veins pushing out.
I didn't like how his face changed that night
I must have teased him or coaxed him
about something he didn't like, maybe
I was cruel, but he didn't hesitate.
Lifted me right up off the ground
over his head and down with strength.
I don't recall pain, just the surprising
arrival of tarmac on my cheek, being
too far down and sideways; then headlights,
his effort to remove me before things
got more serious. It was the main route
to the golf course. The other boys ran.
Later, my mum walked the road to his house
to complain, or just to say it had happened.
His mum slammed the door shut. I see her
in our kitchen, tripping up on the open dishwasher.
Crying into her hands. That's what stays,
has sound. My mum crying, and the feeling,
aged thirteen, that I shouldn't have told her.

Liz Houchin

LOVE POEM FOR TIRED WOMEN

Eve wasn't weak that day
with the apple and the snake
she was just tired of being naked
and her tiredness is now yours,
passed down like wedding china
or your granny's widow's peak

it's that hand pressing down
on the crown of your head
barely a caress, yes, but yet
it keeps you from floating away
or swinging in and out
of the autumn sun and shade

and when you cry from being tired
of being tired and when you try
to trace the feeling to its seed
someone leans over and twirls
your hair and explains your job
is to be tired and please smile

but at the end of the endless day
know this: a queen's chair awaits
made with the braided arms
of tired women everywhere
holding you up with bone dry hands
and the heart to never let you go.

Holly Hughes

ERUDITE

how many times can i forget then
look up the word erudite again
and remember the gross irony? scolded
by cambridge and merriam-webster
i am cowed by the limits of my own retention
using the same words i stole from
impressive books aged fourteen
and filled with promise
then, it felt good to be precocious –
that was all one could be if they weren't hot, buxom,
popular –
i wasn't. personality is a defence mechanism,
you'll know that if you watch female comedy,
i learned sarcasm too young
and can't forget it.

now, am just a sullen, stupid girl hunched
over a submissions page
fumbling with iambic pentameter
measuring herself against strange meter
wondering when she will be good enough.
shuffling her little words and big, bland emotions
into fuzzy caterpillar lines, harmless
unless she's drunk, then they transmogrify
into essential, emblematic totems
to grow belligerent and earnest about
momentarily determined to be listened to.

it passes
and they return to, mostly remain as,
same-same, indifferent, nondescript moments
rendered inane in concentric circles
of words too many times recycled.

sometimes, i wonder if the most interesting thing
about me is a seven-year-old anecdote
blown about in a smoking area,
expiring through lips jaded with the retelling
but knowing it's the best there is
watching it be inhaled –
crackle, orange flame, toxins, elation –
by the gullible other
who doesn't know about all
the disinterested, intervening years
waving my hand, the smokescreen trailing it
dismissively, metaphor for
mystery, mysticism, enigma –

did you know the word for the whispering
sound trees make is susurration?
i'll lean in conspiratorially,
that silky hiss another stab
at a promise i won't keep,
irresistible. no, he'll say,
god you know so many big words.
glancing away as if modest
i'll shrug noncommittal –
do you really think so?

Helen Hutchinson

## A Day's Work in Gammon

Bug me the coulinens
and bug me the fay
get me a rounnuck
I make grub for today.

Granig the cob now
he has no hay
put him in the sark
or he'll fade away.

Granig the comra
for he's an aul pet
he's granigin the glimmer
as I put on the grub.

When I fill out the dinner
a bit of fay is his love
go up to the wagon
and get me a sharker.

Bring down all the vessels
get sticks and a stove started
then when you're finished
eat up and go to lee,

as you need to go luggy.
Start over next day
then we will get some durra
and we will get violeen.

We will put on some rumogues
when the kettle is boiling
we will have to get skuck
to get us through the day,

maybe another bit of cob
and another bit of fay.
We will boil more coulinens
and a dinner we will have.

Give thanks to our garter
for the little we have.

Sacha Hutchinson

## The Room

May there be a room for you
in the old stone house,
a room with a wooden chest so large
that it must have always been there
for it wouldn't fit through any door.

May there be
delicious kindness about you
and may the window
look down the long valley.

Every year may swallows
return to the nest above the beams
and may the cat not get up to leave
but sit still with a perfect purr
blinking in the last streams of liquid light

and when the time comes
may you go to that next place
we know absolutely nothing about.
There, you can rest from
a world of vagaries and vicissitudes

but may a part of you
stay always in that room.

Deirdre Hyland

### Gaillardia
*After 'Kathleen' (1938) by Sir John Lavery*

Rummaging through his memory,
connecting the decades,
he gathers loose impressions,
sketches of Kathleen.

Sculpting from the family pool,
glimpses of Ann, flashes of Eileen,
dreams of Mary Donnelly
combine in paint.

Roughly wrapped in a dull jacket,
she walks through the worked white
ground of ivory and bone, like
a Berber woman, looking to the light.

Her head is covered in coral voile.
Hints of teal seeds
and pomegranate strands
lead us to her basket,
an exuberance of blanket daisies,
pink, golden yellow and ruby.

Linda Ibbotson

LETTING GO

There are things you need to let go of,
the weight of it –
your arms ache pushing the world, alone.
Don't be afraid to fall into darkness,
because when you lie down
you count the stars
and all that is above.

Let the rain wash away sorrow,
the blood of your mistakes.
Let the thin light of warmth touch you –
remember nothing is complete,
not love, or the things we love,
nor shadows.

Rest awhile because
when the way ahead feels unclear,
it's not too late to let the wind lead us to
where we are supposed to be.

Jean James

SALVATION

Darkness clothes the back room
where a bed lies in shadow.
It is from here,
a land scented by old books,
that she sails forth,
up from her pillow
beneath sails of linen sheets
a billow of white.

Sometimes a Hunter's moon
holds her, a prisoner from sleep,
yet there are nights she will step
straight into a Monet painting,
where women rest on grass,
framed by lime trees,
their green light stretching
into the soft air.

A woman will walk past,
her hair a copper beech,
a blackbird will sing
the morning song and
in the cracks of the stone path
creeping thyme peeps through.
This is the garden where life begins,
and where it closes.

Rosemary Jenkinson

## IVY

I have this one enduring image of my mother
tying the wind-loosened ivy to the wall,
confining, twining the tendrils round the trellis,
struggling against the elements like a warrior
while a westerly tugs at her hair, sending
it sideways, burnishing it with flecks of sunshine.

I was wild too, at fifteen that year,
and my mother, always so well-groomed,
would often be pursuing me with a comb,
trying to tame my body,
curb my curves and edges into a nice dress
as we battled primordially for control
and back then I thought we were so different
till the day I saw her hair go

wild in the wind, and sensed the roar
in her and it's only now I see that her inner self
was an image of my own, though I was of the generation
that was able to leave the house and garden
and, overtaking her slippered footsteps,
I would take my fight to the world, chasing
after the big things in her honour, holding on tight
to the rocking branches of life,
tying them back as they beat within my hands
and relishing how, in the end,
I could bend them to my will.

Maura Johnston

## Places Slip

to walk in this garden is to listen
is to have feet clogged with bindweed
is to fret over sun-smashed petals
is to find no balance for uneasy feet

where my toes take me
the sky is in tatters
branches sway under quaking birds
there is no constancy in water

I will paint flowers and doves on the fence

Tiegan Johnston

SHADOW
*for Jean McConville*

I

A film of polish and dust clings
to the frame of the only photo of her
standing in its antique darkness
on the gleaming dresser.

II

Graduations of black and white
and grey pick out her assured form,
arms pressed into a cross at her front,
the strength apparent in their square form.

Skin as stark as the surely pressed cotton
dressing her from neck to frame.
A scalloped edge of apron hinting
at her domestic designation.

And, even in all that static, a familiarity.
Those sheer, impossible cheekbones,
the sharp nose and mocking brow
of my mother, my mother's mother, telling me

or the photographer, to wise up
and get on with it, I'm a busy woman
with dinners to make, clothes to launder
and plenty of children to love, love, love.

III

The flowers on her table
catch the sun of a long afternoon
as they begin to wilt in the tiny
summer kitchen. Her hands in one

confident motion would rid the potato
of its skin, leaving a spiral of eyes
and muck. In a flowery apron
she would stop, potato and knife

still in hand, to watch the boys
playing in the sunburnt grass,
the girls portioning carrots at her side.
Now, dancing a hand across her forehead

she would shimmy the girls out of the way
as their small hands worked too slow.
Now the dark hair would be worked
into a knot at the nape of the neck,

now the vegetables lowered
into their steaming bath.
Here they would simmer
as she mended clothes with her blue pin.

And here was love
like a pot of potatoes
singing against the stove
as their water overflows.

Nithy Kasa

## Two Sister-Wives

I met on my way,
they did not say but one on his left,
one on his right, and their vestures
(from one cloth), but the glint of the textiles
of their gowns gaping in shimmers,
one a faithful red (tested by the waters),
the other the red of a young flame,
one with a Gele folded into a crown,
the other a haloing headband.

The Master wore his pants,
he wore his kufi,
he had spare wax in his bag.

I yield them way by the cobbles with a bowed head,
gawking back with the eyes of an owl – Watch them
gleam with gold and silver. Their figures; they're fed.
If the sisterhood between them is real,
I say there's honey in their hive.
If the sisterhood between them is real,
I say there's a babel in their hive.

But the Master is in between,
he wears his kufi,
he wears his pants,

his sister-wives;
capes on both their shoulders
bejewelled, in the wind quivering as they went –
Impeccable,

from a distance.

Virginia Keane Brownlow

## THYME

Thyme grew in all my mother's gardens,
in cities and at seasides.
There was thyme in many meals,
in soups, stews, casseroles.
No good at all without thyme,
its small green leaves, mauve flowers
that frosts and winter storms
shrank and faded away each year.

Lying once among beds of wild thyme
on a high French plateau
with a fine French man who smelt of horses,
drinking wine, eating Roquefort cheese, grapes
and fat purple figs among horses
who grazed on thyme flowers all around us,
under midday summer sun.

Sitting once on a stony African hillside,
where all that grew
was thyme, smelling of my mother's meals
among Ethiopian children
on a picnic holiday, far from shanty towns,
laughing, eating papayas,
mangos and injera full of chilli, cooled by breezes,
watched by curious goats.

Years later back at home in Ireland
at Ardmore by the sea
in my dead mother's kitchen,
I remember all of them, Ababa, Fekado, Hikma,
Mariam, Negasi, Armed, Salim, Dani
as my kitchen scissors snip thyme
into soups, stews and casseroles.

Róisín Kelly

## First Photograph of a Black Hole
*for Lyra McKee*

on Good Friday a rose window
rises where the sun
should be and a buddleia bursts
through a crack in the wall.
in a shaft of pink glitter
and rubies, I'm barefoot and hanging
up my clothes. so much depends
on a single wire and a concrete
yard of one's own.

on the news is the first photograph
not of an actual black hole
but of the light that surrounds
and defines it. light
it will one day consume.
I stand before the bullet hole
in a pillar of the GPO
and put my eye to it. it
tunnels down through fifty
million years towards that
ring of fire, decaying
rose, burning wheel rotating through
the dark. at the moment in
time the photograph captures
rainforests covered Earth's
poles. what lies beyond the painted
gable wall, the event horizon's
glow? every frequency hisses
with static, the sound of an underground
falls. what language can there be
between the living and the dead? on
the news the women

paint their palms with red, on
the news a stained glass window floats
above a smoking pile of rooftop
beams that once were
ancient trees, of heights no oaks
in France can now replace, yet still as it
has always done the
surviving disc translates the
light that filters from our sun
into the word *colour*, into the
word *faith*, within a
lattice of circles ...

my father, the photographer
captured Notre Dame at
night on his honeymoon in
1989. limestone towers suspended
in amber, ivy creepers trailing
to the Seine. it was
the year the Berlin Wall came
down, even though back
home in Belfast they were addicted
to walls at that time, they couldn't
put up enough of them.
so much depends on a country
of one's own – so much depends
on the butterfly bush with its roots
between the stones –

Anne Marie Kennedy

## Motherly

My mid-winter morning walk is paced with ease
under sunrise solitude
where I traipse the river field of mist-kissed grass
and wild flowers,
nettles alive, the dock leaf dying, thistles crisped
in this rugged place
where the beech, ash and oak stretch charcoal
limbs skyward.

I climb a stone wall gap to commune at the reed-strewn
water's edge
where the Aggard stream meets the Dunkellin river
and in wedded flow they go, sluicing it, out of my sight
into the swell of the Rahasane Turlough.

It's at this threshold, a liminal place, that I meet
my modest elder,
mythical symbol of witch, wise woman and goddess
standing her ground on the wide, wet, riverbank,
a mother's grip on her dying, still green leaves
rain-jewelled, they flutter and cling on, above little
clutches of black berries
that sprout from blood red tendrils,
sustenance for wild birds,
clusters of her fertility, dangling from the tips
of her boughs.

My boots are on ancient earth, my mind infused
with nature's quietness
except for the crows' caw overhead and cattle
chewing the cud
in the sloping pasture on the opposite bank of
the gurgling river

I watch the dew lift, hear the reeds whistle, rushes stir
in a soft cushion of wind.
I touch my elder and tell her it's time to let go, time
to tidy this year away
to welcome the dark and nourish her bark against frost,
sleet and winter gale.

And in this chapel of nature, her sacred glade,
to where I'm invited
to lean in close if I want, to watch the last
of her leaves drop
see the wind whip at a bunch of berries and wonder
at her season to season resilience.

I'd like some of that.

I crouch to the ground then, feet flat, gloves
in raincoat pockets,
my warm palms mooch around her roots, to find soft
mounds of dense, damp moss
randomly growing from where her trunk sprouts.

I flatten them down, tuck them into her body tighter,
let my elder sleep now
through winter dark and deep until the spring, when
she'll bud again
and I'll come again to where the Aggard stream meets
the Dunkellin river
and speak my verse, in benediction for the modest
and stalwart elder.

Hannah Kiely

## In Which the Mother Needs to Dance

The mother grabs her hidden duffle
roll-starts the truck in neutral
drives road after a long road
to the sound of a silent radio
until she's out of tears.
The mother is not sure
where she's headed
but where it takes her
is where she wants to be.
The mother knows
she can no longer live
in the prison
of her uneasy thoughts
where keys always clunk.
The mother needs to go
to absquatulate, flee
from shattered glass on kitchen floors
from grey rain on black asphalt
from squandered pleading words
from daily application of poverty
from crying children
from her broken promises to them
within walls that listen
with no choice.
The mother, her arms painted
with the wings of a butterfly,
wants to dance, move her legs,
hear music falling
on the peaks of Absaroka.

Thérèse Kieran

### The Women in Your Family
*for Paula*

It was an ordinary January Sunday,
your mother was dying and you stood
beside her bed suddenly in tears.
And with teabag lungs, with her blood chugging
slow and intermittently, she reached for your hands;
it was all your Christmases as she pressed them to her lips.

On the Wednesday you took the Dublin bus,
met your daughter off a flight from Vietnam.
"How could I not come home, Mum," she said.
And that night the bright kitchen lights shone like stars
as you and your three girls made Granny's favourite buns,
weighing out flour, butter, sugar, mixing in eggs,
filling the house with sweet sugary smells,
the oven's heat no match for the heart's fire swell.

Bethan Kilfoil

## Found in a Glass Apothecary's Jar on a Convent Shelf

like shiny sweets wrapped tight in foil
to be shared at a birthday celebration
this jar is stuffed full
of tear-stained trinkets left by young mothers,
heart-shaped lockets, small rings, chains,
each piece engraved with initials
or with a photo tucked inside
that maybe one day might provide a clue

this jar is heavy,
so heavy

Susan Knight

## Portrait of a Lady Restored

How she simpers – the lady in the portrait –
stiff in silks and lacy ruffles,
pearls threaded through her chestnut locks,
a glow suffusing peachy cheeks
– pretty as a picture, you might say.

'Fake!' snaps the expert,
'Bronzino never painted that.'
(Bronzino, portrait artist to the Medicis).
'This female's a Victorian travesty.'

But then
restorers with their spit and spirit,
their cotton buds, their gentle touch,
lift off the varnish and the over-paint –
a nineteenth-century sugar coating –
and Isabella, daughter to Cosimo,
emerges from her hiding place,
corpse-pale, and all her wretched years
inscribed upon her melancholy face.

An arranged betrothal at eleven –
the expedient linkage of two dynasties –
wed at sixteen, had six miscarriages.
Then three live births to a careless husband
who only cared when she took a lover.

In 1574 Bronzino painted this.
In two years Isabel was dead,
washing her hair, they claimed.
Or was she, as the rumour went,
strangled by her husband
at the urgings of her brother,

for the shame she brought
upon the family?

Restored now, she stares back at us,
inscrutable. Or can she read her fate,
in our compassionate eyes?

Caitríona Lane

## Eochracha an Chúldorais

Nuair a thiteann an spéir chun talaimh,
Nuair a fhanann an dorchadas ar foluain
Os ár gcionn laistigh, lasmuigh,
Faoi chois, táim sáinnithe.
Sáinnithe sa leaba, sáinnithe i mo cheann,
Sáinnithe.
Téim i bhfostú ar mo chuid deilge féin ar nós driseoga,
Cuirim fola ag déanamh cogar mogar. Táim sáinnithe.

Nuair nach bhfuil fágtha ach liath an lae caillte,
Lorgaím eochracha cúl dorais mo smaointe,
Tuislím thar scáileanna sceach,
Thar gheata meirgeach,
Atá ar crochadh le téad le cuaille claí
Agus go tobann mar lasc thuisleach,
Caitear drithlí i mo thimpeall. Lastar mo shúile.

Feicim áilleacht sna driseoga, i nduilleoga daite an fhómhair,
I ngréasán an damháin alla, é ag sníomh snáitheanna, bun os cionn,
Diamaint ag longadáin ar gach líon. Feicim ansin thú faoin aiteann
Ag fanacht go foighneach ar mo bheola, le teangbháil mo theanga,
Taisce an tráthnóna ar nós dí na sí,
Agus tagann cuimhní cinn scór fómhar ó shin chun solais.
Cumhracht na cistine, scilléad suibhe lán súilíní
Ag boilgearnach leis ar an sorn. Saoirse aigne seachas sáinn.

Ann Leahy

EVERYOUNG

It starts with the Guards – everyone
saying how they all seem to look so young.
No one tells you that it will happen soon
with plumbers, barmen, airline pilots –
how they will start to look like they can hardly
have left school, and, worse, with doctors

and even in consulting rooms where
what's at stake seems to call for wisdom –
for a philosopher as well as a technician –
and what you notice, instead, is a kind of strained
and distanced attention, a face that glows
in the light of a screen, that nods without hearing.

Then the heartthrobs of your youth will start
to die (and not just the ones who lived hard)
and soon you'll recognise as just-above-your-age
the actor cast as the down-at-heel spook
in a TV thriller who's coaxed from drab retirement
and later subtly called upon to sacrifice herself

for the well-built youth
who is the darling of the piece,
as, after all, who's to know
what she might have to live for?

Donna Leamy

## Poetry Class

I studied the sonnet for thirteen weeks,
Petrarchan, Shakespearean, Miltonic,
Terza Rima, Curtal, and a few freaks
that refused to be so formulaic.

Iambic pentameter, voltas, rhyme,
we got close-up to this singular form,
debating the ones without fourteen lines,
since we were once told that this was the norm.

But rules are made so rules can be broken
or slightly bent in a Diane Seuss style –
memoir in sonnets written as spoken,
a raw truth that will linger for a while.

The little song that stood the test of time
deserves both an ending couplet and rhyme.

Róisín Leggett Bohan

## The Curator

Before I press the panic button, before nurses rush
in, before doctors declare you (   )
I will curate what you lost.
There, a hair from your brush –
I will arrange it on puckered velvet, encased in solid oak
frame.
Here, a breath you mislaid –
I will parade it in a glass jewellery box,
a ballerina on coiled spring circling your final exhale.
That blood spot on your handkerchief –
I will siphon off, hang it as a centrepiece,
porcelain perfume pot, gold chain, atomizer puff.
Your expiration date I will archive in the fine art
catalogues of the stories you once told me.
And your heart, what of that?
I will present it as a performance piece –
wrap it in muslin, lie it in a rocking chair until it stills.
I will not mark one single exhibit with a red dot.
I will keep the lot.

Jessie Lendennie

## WHAT IF

What if you got on a cross-country bus
And got off at the 10th stop
Where you knew no one
And no one was waiting for you

What if you had to live there
What if you couldn't go home
What if the bus home never stopped there again

Would you live the same life
Would you walk in the park,
If there was a park,

Would you have a dog

Would you walk without looking back
Would you gaze at the river,
If there was a river,

Would you fall in love

Would you watch the same sun rise and set
The same sun

Would you sit on the porch
Of the house made from dreams
Say *Hello, Neighbour*
To the woman gardening next door

And when the onward bus stopped
Before heading out of town

Would you get on?

Susan Lindsay

## The Dreamtime Memory Machine

Artificial flowers
are not the same
despite wonder
at intricate beauty
deceptively similar
to the delicate imperfections
rooted in earth
blooming intelligence.

And artificial intelligence
however divined
in the dreamtime machine
mimicking empathy
does not grasp emotional depth
put more than programmed cognition
on complex humanness

And the wobble in wobbly waste bins
as elsewhere
may indeed evoke
a human need to resolve
artful cute helplessness

but will not empathise
however so described
however creative engineers
endeavour to have it appear so
for even the best of machines
do not have guts or feelings.

And humans will never be exclusively rational
and programmed entities
no matter how well inspired

can still make errors
differently but similarly
to the humans creating them.

    ii

And the post-office people
falsely imprisoned for fraud in 2014
in the United Kingdom of Great Britain
were neither in error nor criminal at all

the horizons of others
too blinkered to imagine
that technology could fail
to accurately count
failed to account for interference
system failure.

And the mathematician who designed
algorithms that could not fail
that semi-paralysed the stock exchange
contributing to its collapse
in 2008, admitted
he had overlooked
*the human factor.*

    iii

It isn't the first attempt in human history
to make gods, or God, in our own image
project humanness onto forms
systems to be revered
able to reflect to us who we are
to outdo the gods
by outdoing ourselves.

It's best not to mention the wings of Icarus
now we can hear the wonder
of astronauts
blown away
by seeing from space
living earth

aided by
the dreamtime memory machine
the breathing whole
suffocating

combining in failure
to remember Gaia
re-imagine balance.

Mary Lockhart

## Poppy Purett's Woodland Party
*for Poppy Murtagh, my grandniece, who lost her wonderful dad, David*

There once was a fairy called Poppy Purett
who tapped in the woods for all she could get.
Berries and mushrooms were all that grew,
so she brought them home and made a stew.

She headed for the pond and waved to the frog,
stay there, she said, I'll bring you some grog.
From the old tree she borrowed a stick,
then it was time to give the pot a good lick.

Poppy heaved and dragged with all her might.
She called Patrick until it was light.
He was out playing chess with an mischievous imp
so it was no wonder that she felt a bit limp.

All the animals watched her go.
Some said yes and some said no.
She'll never get that pot in place.
Look at her, she's red in the face.

The rooster said maybe so,
Mumsy Goosey said no no no.
Bubble the goat started taking bets
just before he went to the vets.

Poppy Purett stirred the pot with her stick
and very soon the stew became thick.
It wasn't long until the tantalising smell
put Patrick and Haylie under a spell.

Poppy dished out on banana leaves.
She handed out spoons made of feather weaves.

Fairies only used them for special treats
– ice cream, honey and spicy meats.

The animals came one by one.
It seemed cosy and so much fun.
Toad cried when he saw the frog
and thought I'll never get any grog.

But he didn't know Poppy that well,
looking after her chums she did excel.
After the feast it was time for a rest
but she watched out for another guest.

Everyone else fell sound asleep.
The robin came out singing zeep zeep zeep.
He'd been her friend from the start.
Hello you, any chance of an apple tart?

Sadly no, I'm afraid not,
Frog and Toady scoffed the lot.
She had a treat for little redbreast
and pushed a pavlova towards his chest.

She watched him with a smile lap it all up.
Oh! Poppy, he said, you're always good for a sup.
And you, Robin, have such a big heart,
and you, Pops, were under mine from the start.

Aoife Lyall

### Painting my Husband as the Forth Rail Bridge

The thrill is in the scaffolding –

the hours spent blending and building
for the minutes it will take to wash away –

in all those girders and railings and rivets
falling to his feet with the sea
and sky and harbour wall –

in the perishable flesh of the man
I married –

the head and heart of him
two islands I call home.

Jackie Lynam

## Gutted

The results are in;
lesion, cyst, polyp,
raised somatostatin levels.
*Nothing to worry about, for now.*
I'm booked in
for follow-up bloods,
a scan in three months,
another capsule test in a year.

I should be relieved I'm not dying
but my heart is heavy.
I betrayed myself again;
allowed a smidgen of hope to sneak in.
Thought that the latest barrage of tests
might explain the thirty years of unwellness.
But there's no diagnosis for this
(whatever *this* is)
therefore
no cure.

*Have you other patients like me?* I ask,
*with symptoms as bad as mine?*
*A few,* she concedes.
*So I'll probably be like this*
*forever?*
She shrugs.
I leave the hospital,
gutted.

Noelle Lynskey

### Returning
*i.m. Edna O'Brien*

On the day they take you home to Iniscealtra,
the lake looks back remembering the gaze of your young eyes
and the gushing flow of your daring imagination;

your townland recalls the ripple of your laughter
and the longing for your purple ink that lingered
long after you fled this place that once was home;

the trees on the shoreline sway, their boughs blessing
today's boat that bears your body to the aloneness
and solitude of the island's moss-lined grave.

Buoyed by your sons' love and a gratitude so deep
it dapples the water so the blue lake rises
to the outpourings of the mourners' grief

and the oars dip to the rhythm and turn of old tunes
that, between breaths, incant a chorus over and over:
*she's home, she's home, she's home.*

Aifric Mac Aodha

## TÁ D'ATHAIR AG ADÚ TINE, A CHROÍ

Tá d'athair ag adú tine, a chroí, tá d'athair ag adú tine.
Tá ceap mór crainn briste aige, tá ceap mór crainn briste.
Gluaiseann sé leis ar thóir a thuilleadh –
Filleann lena athuchtán, tá a cheap dóite roimhe.
Tá d'athair ag tógáil dúin, a chroí, tá d'athair ag tógáil dúin.
Tá ceap mór cleití carntha aige, tá díon ar leath a thí.
Gluaiseann sé leis ar thóir breis clúimh –
Filleann lena athuchtán, tá a áras nocht gan dlaoi.
Tá fuarán ar fhód na faiche, a chroí, ar oileán seo d'athar.
Tá na seacht sruth ag dul isteach ina bhéal
ach sileán níl ag teacht as.
Ná meabhraigh scéal an rí do d'athair, ná luaitear leis athscéal.
Más beag a thug sé uaidh, a chroí, níorbh é a fuair a leor.
Agus is éadrom a ór ag daoi, a chroí, idir dheatach, shop 's deoir.

Siobhán Mac Mahon

## Magdalene Laundry for Sale

Now that they've built
a brand-new hotel –
all concrete and plate glass,
all Farrow and Ball paint –
there's plenty of work to be had.
They need a small army
of invisible workers
to keep the place spotless.
We polish, dust, hoover,
sprinkle the beds with lavender water,
change the sheets everyday.
You should see the laundry,
the piles and heaps and mounds of it.

But we can't seem to get rid of the stench.

They say the tourists don't sleep
well; they toss and turn
in their 100% Irish linen sheets
after sipping fine malt whiskeys
by the warmth of a real peat fire
sustainably cut from thousand-year-old bogs
(it's all in the glossy brochures)
in the new basement bar.
Its tasteful pictures
of old Irish ways
hiding the cracks in the walls.

Colette McAndrew

## Dying Fall

There must be a name for it,
that way of sitting,
knees up to your chest,
head hanging down,
the arrangement of limbs,
graceful, languid.
Nothing casual in it.
I've seen it at the ballet,
arms artfully folded.
the dying swan.

A rag doll, or a dead Christ,
white angles, dangling.
Skin gleaming,
light hitting bone.
Arms crossed against all comers,
shut down, the dying fall.

Joan McBreen

## One Another

Here they are once again words
of the living to one another

whispered voices in a chapel
where eyes of icons stare

at us not knowing whether
what we are saying

brings us nearer knowledge
or into a place of darkness

where what has been lost
has us wander in ignorance

of past and future. Perhaps
we cannot guess the moon's

sadness our lives
are lived so briefly.

Catherine McCabe

ALL OUR HOUSES
*in memoriam of British Special Operations Executive agent,
Noor Inayat Khan (1914–1944)*

SOE operative Noor Inayat Khan screamed
*liberty* as she died, because she knew
it wasn't going to end this way.
And her soul
raged on
into the ether
roaring like a noisy ghost
haunting a house;
our house;
all our houses.

Aoibheann McCann

## Trifle

I am a trifle. Left over, tin foil on.
Melting layer of cream on the top,
distracting silver balls of sparkling sweetness,
custard, thinly disguised guilt and regret,
sponge cellulite,
down in the jelly.
Heavily infused with alcohol.

Felicia McCarthy

## Loss and Gain

The longer you are dead
the more precise I become.
There is hardly a crumb
left on the counter.
Struck dumb by
your absence
I
use my mouth
only to chew,
eating for two
wanting to keep
the weight of you
– that sweet heft –
here upon me. Thus,
I
become more substantial,
perhaps, even big enough
for the both of us.

Mary McCarthy

## The Sun Also Rises
*after Ernest Hemingway*

The Road to Santiago
    surprises me every day.

The sun observes,
    high above a cloudless sky.

Bald eagles stretch their wings,
    glide effortlessly.

I urge my tired feet to go on, a scent of lavender
    lingering in the wind halts me.

I breathe in. Deep inside to a memory
    evoking another place under this same sun

when I watched my mother
    take pride in the purple colour of her garden.

A Mediterranean aroma wafted
    when she weeded borders back home.

That day I saw an age to come,
    did not know how it might reveal itself.

I never thought she would be resting in peace
    as I walk in an undetermined beat

along a rocky road alone
    where I gaze at the spectacle overhead.

A certainty of being human
    that we have no control over.

I take another step and hear her say:
*keep the faith, my child, keep the faith.*

Helen McClements

## THE DAY MEDUSA WASHED UP TO SHORE IN TIME FOR ELEVENSES

Medusa opened crusted eyes,
coughed and clawed her way to shore.
Snake coils slick with salty brine
bickered and twisted, sniped and spat.
Her tangled braids an unholy brood
ground down her neck until it bowed.
But gorgons give up?
Shaking herself upright she slapped at her head,
blood and sand beneath her nails she stumbled forth.
The snakes thrust outward, lured by the smell of
something sweet and drew her to a door
where a blast of warmth blew back
the days of clinging to rock.
And then the jingle-jangle of a bell
seemed to conjure up a spell.
Before her trays of shell-shaped bakes were spread,
but no spartan offerings were these, instead
on a silver platter lay ammonites of cinnamon,
slaked with icing gleaming white.
Plump pastry cones, whorls oozing cream,
and fudgey slabs of brownie, dense and thick.
People froze when she came in;
froze perhaps, expecting to be frozen.
But the snakes had forgotten how to freeze.
They strained and stretched and swallowed whole
squares of chocolate, caramel,
jewel-studded discs of Florentine.
'The craturs are starved,' spoke a foreign tongue,
and over the counter passed yet more:
biscuits, cakes and bacon baps.
Nobody noticed Medusa now,
the writhing snakes had stolen the show.

Having gulped and gobbled, their taut skin bulged
necks almost pierced through with doughy shapes.
Flaccid and sated their eyes flicked shut
as they settled, bodies swollen, distended.
Under their weight Medusa shrunk smaller still,
sidled to a chair into which she sunk and slept.
Her venom spent, her rage assuaged,
all sense of helter-skelter tumult gone.
What sorcery was this, her final trick to play?
An invisible cloak to don
when women tire, grow old and grey.

Clare McCotter

## The Swing

brought her to the top of their clipped yew
to next door's iris and velvety peonies
to the farmer's cattle and sheep
and piebald pony.
Leaning back, heels in the air
hair trailing the ground
it brought her to blue
and a chalice of clouds.
Leaning forward, feet tucked under,
to a horizon
wide and sapphire-dark.
Later to a raven's silhouette
in a city of stars.
And one gold autumn day
flying higher and higher
it brought a smile
to the little mouth between her thighs.
Each time she flew like that
the smile spread
till crinkling the corners of her lips
it turned to a laugh.
First time he heard it, he said
*if I ever catch you at that again*
*there'll be a spell*
*in the big house behind the trees.*
Then calling her *degenerate*
*and a disgrace*
he locked the door and, removing his glove,
wiped the smile off her face.

Karen J McDonnell

I'M READING *ULYSSES* DURING A HEATWAVE

and maybe it's the heat – or I'm overwatered – but
I'm blooming like Greek geraniums
in an old olive oil tin

and I'm with the men:
their lusting and leering
and schoolboy conversations.

Years out of the place, I enjoy peeping
over Leopold's shoulder as he perambulates
around the Dublin haunts.

Prone on the sun lounger, I take charge:
wandering old places,
according to my mind's patterns.

We're back on that old bed
blazing. Belt pulling. The fate
of your shirt buttons in the meld of our hands.

Wanting to feast on you then.

Now.

Afric McGlinchey

## On Learning what Not to Talk About on the Family Group

Feathers everywhere.
He's re-stuffing our sixty-three-year-old
leather sofa in an effort to make it comfortable.

I bite back my comment that it won't make a difference.
He'll never let it go.
It's become one of the many things

I can't mention – like microplastics
entering our brains, or sewage in the bay,
or what Trump will mean for us ... or Gaza,

Ukraine, Afghani women, the homeless,
or the atrocious cost of renting (the reason
my son's left Dublin).

What my family *do* share on the group
is Electric Picnic excitements – the gigs, the vibe –
or photos of the wedding, a trip to France,

the latest adorable pics of our newest family members.
Something they saw on the Dart
that was daft or hilarious.

A Wild Atlantic Way road trip
with *the lovely boys,* along with a shot
of the best-poured pint in Ireland.

The feathers have settled.
Sofa's plumped up. And I have to admit,
it is a much softer landing.

Medbh McGuckian

## On Either Side of Windows

This dark and shapeless present
is a threat made by a cowardly sky
as utterly rain. Sunset is full of subtle
griefs, the clouds are merely a layer
of blue, what else is the sky but
borrowed colour from a neglected garden?

Everything I had acquired became a kind
of hovering, as of old, the moon rises in me
with a graveyard grace, or the pain with
which I dreamed you, the slow of its own
river bed. I looked out over the tips
of the lime trees, where a dancer was attached

to me, or a poem which could be swallowed
and thus expressed in dance. I feel
my shoulder cold where the hand should
shake me, a certain dryness there where
the eyes swallow. In my heart slept a heart
like the agitated voice of Easter's deepest bells.

The island like a signature I have often read
becomes a slim, weathered angel holding a sundial,
slender, weather-beaten angel, refusing further
concentrates to set up a counter magic to that.
Summer lasted like a great illness

that tasted you to see if you were not
in pain. Poems were in flames, one could hardly
hear oneself live, while chestnut woods
were dripping towards Italy, its pure rim,
in front of the quiet windows.

Ann McKay

## Super Moon

right outside the door of the pub
at eye level a red sphere glows intensely at your face
its visage radiates through wisps of granite-grey cloud
it holds fast over silhouetted trees and hills
defying perspective like
some vehicle of enchantment or otherness
that makes you feel uncertain of your
position     status     here
or role

Ellie Rose McKee

## Downsizing

I suppose you and I never did fit the mould.
Didn't meet those expecting expectations.

Society lets us know there's an order to things:
You grow up, get a job, find a partner, settle down, expand.

At least until the tide turns, the fledglings fly,
you discard the job, and start to take things easy.

Is that the opposite of growing up?
Is there a word for the particular kind of heartbreak

in which it dawns on you it's time to downsize
without any of the eggs ever having hatched?

Raquel McKee

## Her Laughter Still

Disbelief propelled my feet over the door jamb. I didn't want to, but I had to see – no rise and fall of her lopsided chest? Her oxygen tank, silent as her breath? Her quick-witted eyes closed, her laughter still? I struggled to compute. One who skinny dipped with her dog along the Atlantic Way, driving till something took her fancy, then picnic blanket, tea with shortbread and repeat, now journeying to a much further home?

What would we do without her wily wilfulness, her 'just for badness' wind-up jokes? Who would make me gawk with a surprise engagement announcement on April Fool's Day, and tickle us with the final Christmas present being a wrapped-up chicken in a gift bag? I padded slowly back to the others.

My laughter stilled.

Maeve McKenna

## Yellow is Not Alive

The forest claims its young
and I worry how the child
will find a way home.

I am a native of grief. The grave is wild
where I visit – not my mother's,
my father's, not my brother's.

So little of myself I carry, given over
to fright and dark weight
at the mercy of this morning

that appears to offer light
though through its leafy mask
I have still to pass.

The scene on soil sudden
as process can ground – finch,
scraps of blood, body and tar

her beak a pink purse closing to the sky
less than an inch –
wings, broken, flapping black bruises.

And her one open eye is a brown button.

Emma McKervey

## Krakow, 1988

In the week before Christmas the carp would swim
its last in the bathtub, teased by the children
as its gills washed clean of river mud.

Down on the street people waited, coughing and huddled,
in the endless queues to buy whatever they could find,
but inside the high rise their bathroom was magical,

lit by bare bulb and the carp's refracting scales.
From the kitchen came the scents of raisins in brandy,
rice simmering, cinnamon and nutmeg toasting.

Through the window the air was soft with snow.
Above the stubby concrete tower blocks
the last of the sun on steepletop gleamed.

E.V. McLoughlin

## Why are you Like This?

Yesterday, at Mauermuseum,
I joked about making a journey
in the boot of a car
from East to West.

Tonight all six of us are lying
on the floor, carefully below the windows,
as the tow truck lifts the broken-down
VW van onto its back to take it to Bonn.

*This all takes place 15 years before I learn that, neurochemically,
excitement is almost indistinguishable from anxiety.*

I text "scared",
but I am lying.
Autobahn lights, steaming kettles of nuclear plants,
blades of turbines,
my freedom.

Killing time in a Burger King
we are stranger and closer than friends.
You said you are always looked after
by your country.
I am still looking for mine.

Now it's 4°C, the morning sun
shines so brightly it aches
with whatever this is.

*Feel everything*
*notice it all*
*hot chocolates*
*by steamed up window.*

Liz McManus

## Muezzin

Out of the darkness a muezzin calls.
As our arms lengthen with longing,
we are bookended by exits and entrances,
closer to a winding sheet than a swaddling band.
Our days have grit, our nights edge;
wizened pap and shrunken sac,
evidence of what we have become.
Impervious to age, the holy words summon
to prayer and we turn inwards
towards each other.

Triona Mc Murrow

## The Back Garden

A wooden gazebo at the end,
not grand, it is a haven of quiet.
The next best thing is the shed
where my father's old hoe
leans against the wall,
the wooden handle worn smooth
from his grasp. I think of him
when I weed the raspberries.
Then there is the symmetry
of rows of new potatoes,
earthed up to protect them,
the pattern soothing and precise.
No order in this garden otherwise.
A cutting from a friend
that never stops spreading,
lovely borage seeding itself everywhere.
Old gnarled apple trees
that feel now like elderly relations
who have to be minded.
There are two bockety wicker chairs,
one for me, the other for the cat.

Winifred Mc Nulty

## Hiraeth
*after Emma Stroude's painting*

She paints a static semaphore, high wires
between the shadow trees of dusk; it could be
anywhere. I recognise the place, beyond woods
where the Manorhamilton Road twists through hills.
A glacial valley opens, like a place in a fable,
to shining land all the way to the sea.
It is that split second of return.
You are home, on a road
you know like a song.

Liz McSkeane

## How to Make a Woman Disappear

Take a woman, average to fair,
who's not too troubled about the way she looks.
Now, put her under scrutiny. Be sure
she notices the lens, the eye, the stare
that catches her mid-word, mid-thought, whatever
is commanding her attention. And – wait.
Quite often, that's enough, the consciousness
of being watched a catalyst that sets
the shift in motion, when the single self
fragments, becomes observer and observed,
a saboteur, a spy, planted within.
If that has no effect, suggest new angles,
lighting, filters. Point out other women
in magazines, on TV, even friends
(comparison with friends is good). And don't
forget the science, note the camera adds
ten pounds at least, of belly fat, of jowls
she never knew she had until the clicks
have multiplied and you can let her look.
That almost always does the trick. The queen
of anywhere, the waitress in the bar,
all desperate to invest in the regime,
the pills, the knife to guarantee removal
of unsightly curves and flesh, allow
the perfect body mass and bones emerge,
create the ideal frame for zero size.
Repeat – but smaller – next year. Then again,
until all that remains is the essence
of how to make a woman disappear.

Mary Madec

## Moon Festival on Chung Yin Street, Hong Kong 2018
*after the legend of Chang-e*

Two children with China paper lanterns
tighten their bows to release
arrows on the ten suns which try to burn the earth.

In the middle of this hot white street,
once a riverbed dividing two communities,
happiness is fluttering

yet underneath the moon
on this balmy autumn night
a muttering about the future.

*Chang-e* on her diviner orb knows the sadness
of hide-and-seek behind the clouds

and as she looks at the joy among the crowds
she splits her face in the river with pain,

her face pocked by tears for what is to come.
Next morning one sodden moon cake on the street,

a crow beaking his way into a wonton noodle box,
the sun already telling the moon where to go.

Patricia Maguire

## The Knock Girl

I glimpse her, lumbering across the forecourt,
arms linked into the crook of her
dad's elbow, two ginger-snapped heads,
one follicly challenged, the other plaited.
Swapping words and smiles on a June day
along some sanctum path in Knock, rooted
in prayer and hope and solace. I glimpse her.
The gait faulty, bereft of glide, a certain
something amiss, that extra chromosome that
fleshes out a different spatial truth but allows for
a smile that breaks moulds in freshness,
without guile, luminous and trusting.

Her glasses mark another of her senses straggling,
informing her myopia through bottle tops.
Pale shapeless legs step to their own rhythm.
Father and daughter propping up this day
in perfect symmetry of pace and tenderness.
It was her gait that drew my side-way glance.

The rest of the story slotted within my lens.
All cultural hiccups encapsulated in
one girl child, pallor, hair, shape,
God's female clown oblivious.
I smiled with her and prayed this place
of Our Lady would bless and protect
father and daughter in gentle grace.

Ruth Marshall

MERMAIDS

Mermaid, a little uncertain in her stilettos,
she gripped the arm of the man
she would later marry.
Had she already given up her voice?
They often did, on marriage, in the 1950s.

Peering sideways out of the photograph,
my mother had a look of Jackie O about her
but under the swing jacket and pencil skirt
she wore a red shirred bathing suit.

'Little' Mermaids reclaimed the power of speech
in the 1970s. Miss World 1970
women with curated smiles
paraded in high heels, swimsuits and sashes.

Bold women, standing hip-deep in the waves,
called out: We are not beautiful, we are not ugly.
We are angry.

I remember I once wore a red ruched bathing suit.
I once shouted crossly, 'Enough!'
No one had listened to my young voice.

I watched the pageant on TV with my mother,
cut my hair short and chose to take care of my feet.
Wore wooden clogs with thick wool socks to school,
tended my voice and learned its many uses.
Never once did I miss the tail.

Katie Martin

LETTERS IN AUTUMN

I am reassembling my small histories,
smoothing their crumpled pages.
So I am writing to you in my true script.
Jagged, unkempt, I keep it for the secrets I tell myself.
This evening the russet light issues an invitation.
I will try on that dress again.
My figure is fine. Youth's silhouette
is not finished with me yet. You were right.
I am pliant. I can assume any shape required.

What am I asking for?
Only that you let this brush against you
as the leaves touched our shoulders in the forest –
that evening when day and night kept each other company.
If it was less than love, tell me it came close enough
and you have let your likeness linger in the scene.
Mine has stood there so long it has grown roots.

I need to send something back to that moment.
I have tried to fashion an alphabet from a dusty silence.
Now I am clothed in the camouflage of middle age,
the world can smother me with all it wishes to lose.
I welcome it. This season is like no other. Obscured
by a fog of confusion. If you reply
send me some words you might have spoken.

Orla Martin

## Daughters of Ireland
*after Maud Gonne MacBride*

Daughters of Ireland,
an august destiny beyond
Home Rule, Land Wars,
a nation hostage, a Troy to burn.

It was for Irishmen and Irishwomen
that they proclaimed,
in slanting typeset
on the steps of the GPO,

by suffrages of Sisterhood,
by suffrages of Brotherhood,
the Tricolour unfurled
and raised above this land.

Daughters of Ireland
take heart, take force.
Be not felled by adversity
on the cold flagstones at Kilmainham.

Daughters of Ireland
fight for valour, fight for freedom,
for your noble right,
now at this hour, to be free.

Mari Maxwell

### Atop Mount Gable

He swings the orange wand
overhead.
Frees bubbles into
the November sun.
Pink-purple-lemon orbs in the blue
lazily float down to bounce
on thick mounds of snow.

This man is learning how to play.

Máighréad Medbh

## One Night Stand

Declaring his politics to a woman
twice his age but beautiful whom
he's just met this fluke Monday.

Her hand carefully explores him.
His surges and sucking are welcome.
They are almost familial together.

He talks and then kisses; attempts,
recedes. They behave like transients.
They have not yet required names.

He's an engineer with a golden look.
She thinks of a streetlamp at dusk
drawing the eye to its own position.

Or a light in an upstairs flat where
neophytes practice new theories
and sound them like resonant bowls.

Singing themselves without knowing.
One of those in his own arranging,
the apartment larger than average, gated.

It's machinic in the passionate sense.
Fuels carefully managed, attention to functions.
The metallic aura of a pet well-tended.

Pouring in and out they and the event.
Bernie Sanders, Gerry Adams, McGuinness
joining them. Christy Moore, Karl Marx.

Sprung from the chair James Connolly.
Black and Tans exploded on their journey
to a non-judicial retribution down the street.

Her granduncle lived here once. He never
got over the hunger strike. She has an idea
how that might be, how to be part of a war.

Transient in the yellow-duveted bed
she feels what she likes to – emptied
of panic and automatic demurral.

A moment of clarity opening capacity
for pleasure like a lovely snake.
Her clothes his clothes thrown down.

Victoria Melkovska

## This Year Her Present

wasn't a book –
my shelves sag under the weight of volumes
she's given me over the last two decades
since I moved from Ukraine to Ireland;

wasn't a dress –
she has such a sharp sense of style:
the last one was a black linen gown
with traditional cross-stitched sleeves;

wasn't a postcard –
bought at the vintage fair in Kyiv
where she knows every vendor by name
and they welcome her soft, smiley face;

wasn't a notebook –
she chooses journals one-of-a-kind,
leather-bound, with printed fore-edges
on pastel pages, growing flowers and vines;

wasn't a sweets box –
candies no Irish store can match
in their taste, the songs we spun on air
and echo of our side-splitting laughs;

wasn't fragrant mead –
Piastowsky or Kurpiowski drinking honey
I can't get in Dublin for love or money, so she
packed it in her luggage for me in Lodz duty free.

This year, her present was
a brown bottle of Lugol iodine solution – to swallow

when the heavy air wears a radiation halo
at the edge of nuclear war.

Mary Melvin Geoghegan

## In Some Sheltered Spot

the story has it –
in the final months of John Moriarty's life
as his hair began falling out
he had a head of thick curls
that no comb could tame.
He began collecting up the shedded strands
and lay them in some sheltered spot.

Weeks after he was buried
a neighbour began to notice empty nests
woven with those wiry threads of silver.
Recently, repeating the story
he tells me – he often opens the back door
and releases all of his hair clippings
to the wind.

Geraldine Mills

RHYMING THE HORIZONTAL

When I am old I will not do the Jenny Joseph purple thing,
will not eat pounds of sausages nor spit upon the street.

Instead, I'll take unsuspecting men to my post-virgin bed,
young studs who think they've lived it all, until they're

abandoned on the island of my scarlet, satin sheets
and I have had my wild-wicked way with them.

They will, on their shaking, bended knees,
plead for one more tiny touch of my skin

but I will show them the pale line on my finger
where a ring – for too long – used to gloat,

tell them firmly to put their spent one-eyed beauties
back in their trousers, guide them to the door.

A taxi driver further down the street will find them
– the fifth this week –

jabbering my name to the sky,
call emergency to come lock them up.

Me? I'm just having a ball, will crush more mint
for my mojito, wait for the next beseeching call.

Drucilla Mims Wall

## Galway Plain
*for Kevin Higgins*

Little sister rain, gentle as always,
strikes yellow roses into disarray.
English ivy expands cellular cores
to rope the rusting laundry shed.

Five pints stand on the oldest bar
in town, settling the bargain between
air and darkness. I missed a round,
but we don't do that anymore, we don't.

The most oxygen lives at sea level,
not enough, though, for any of us.
Red-sailed boats cut waves against the tide.
We don't feed the harbour swans anymore,

for their own good we're told.
Our friend has died in the city he loved,
as his mother did. We have his words
on the page, not enough for any of us.

Suffice the yellow roses in his garden,
nothing more anymore to feed us,
not even the darkest pint of plain.

Geraldine Mitchell

## Lessons from the Clothesline

A platoon of ants patrols the old clothesline
    (a rope rigged up one summer long ago)
        their urgent journey like a sign

that we too often while away our time, malign
    those earnest people who appear to come and go
        like ants, trudging the same old line –

a path laid down in childhood, a design
    that keeps them, head bowed and incognito,
        on endless urgent journeys. A sign

that unlike cats we do not have nine
    lives to squander, that we might do worse than tiptoe
        cautiously, like ants, along a well-traced line.

Often we behave like butterflies, dine
    on gorgeous colours, flit from flower to hedgerow
        on urgent, fruitless journeys – no sign

that we have grasped the fine
    distinction between using and abusing our one throw.
    And still they're at it, those ants on the old clothesline,
their steady, urgent journeying some sort of sign.

Audrey Molloy

NIGHT VISIT

I woke this morning to a fading scent
of almond flour and lavender,
a sense of something I forgot to do,
some precious chance I'd squandered.

I dreamt of you last night. Among
a baffling mix of guests – the kind that muster
in some half-familiar galley kitchen –
we spoke like any other time, a proper
back-and-forth discussion, and yet I –
ignorant that you were dead –
failed to ask you anything
important, Mother, like *did you leave
the salmon out for supper?* Or *should I
leave my husband?* I didn't
hug you when you wiped your hands,
hung your apron up and said
that you had somewhere else to be.

What is a dream but locksmith incognito,
breaking into towers stacked along
the lichened inclines, lonely
as the beehive huts on Skellig Michael.

When you were leaving I was deep in talk
with someone in a wool beret; I only
glanced around and threw a little wave
at your departing figure in the doorway,
wreathed in lilac evening light.

Amanda Moloney

ENDURANCE

You come late, in a black suit and tie,
eyes crinkled at the sides,
pushed up by the smile
as you apologise –
a funeral, it couldn't be helped.

And you sit, still smiling at each in turn,
dazed by the mundanity of our day,
your surface breaks,
your crinkle scrunched,
an implosion, collapsing your face,

and I sit captured, before you blink it away,
recognising the shellshock
when even the expected hits harder
than you ever thought it could.
And yet somehow, enduring, days go on.

K.S. Moore

## The Shadow when we Kiss

You're in the texture
of my page
its rub against my thumb.

I turn
but I come back again
the years of us in flipbook

you
lopsided-smiling at
me
drinking my way
to expression.

Mid-story
we hide in corners
I come to confess

the word *friends*
placed on my tongue
you believe

and I
believe in you
our fingers interlace.

You touch my hair
like it's gilded
though it's falling dark

the shadow when we kiss.

Sadhbh Moriarty

## NIA

Iontais na cruinne ar lasadh i do shúile,
ceol ón altar ag snámh as do bhéilín.
Níl focail le haimsiú idir do bheola go fóill.
Níl agat ach an fhírinne chóiche,
do theanga bheag bhideach,
do lámha luascánacha,
agus mé féin, dallta i ngrá,
ag stánadh anuas ort
go bómánta.

Joan Morrissey

## When I Knew

It wasn't the dozen roses
nor the handcrafted pieces
of silver, followed by the
diamond set in gold.

Nor the way you tried to
calm my agitation on that
turbulent flight to France.

When the bee flew in, I reached
for the swatter. Leave it, you said,
and I watched you fold the kitchen paper,
hammock style, and hold it against the pane.

Cradled, the bee flew out to freedom.
It was then, I knew.

Sinéad Morrissey

## Allery Banks

Little road slack as a giving string
between river and railway-crossing,
I have walked you in all weathers.

After you, the town peters out.
Allotments, car-ports, the last back
gardens give up the Parish ghost

to fields, a wood, a sewage-plant,
the pitched, electrified rigging
of the East Coast Mainline,

fizzing and sparking. Trains
cross the ridge like figure-skaters,
one long held attitude each,

then vanish to London.
And here lies your makeshift
shrine a man I've never met

has fashioned from flags
and bric-a-brac: a dinosaur in a swing
and a sodden, one-eyed Ninja turtle

tied upside-down to a tree
bless all who pass. Allery,
Allery, *hush*. Flight path for bats,

track of my daily office,
it is all splendour – lit
theatre of your cottage windows

stacked along the top,
lone sheepdog behind glass
going ballistic; you

losing the run of yourself
completely come summer
in a white-out of nettle and cow-

parsley; the brash, celandine fact
– four years later –
of one foot in front of the other.

Julie Morrissy

### The French for Moon

at the valet entrance
of the Los Angeles Athletics Club
his stomach lifts and falls

against mine
we hug for a long time
under a canopy, so long

the valet calls several cars
groups glide by us
my view over his shoulder

a small shrub climbing
towards the first floor
two-way window, double-doors

his view, tiny particles
of dust from roadworks
threads of tyres pulling up

the valet's hair as it grows –
we break and say some shit
I send him to swim

hug again, call back love
to each other
when I considered staying

he said about retrograde
and I knew
what he meant

in the dark hours in Paris
I wake bolt upright
from a nightmare

nine hours behind
he writes back immediately
Blue Super Moon

Katie Moynagh

## Look Out

I look forward to the day
when it does not matter
lesbian, gay, bi, transgender
even straight will do
love or hate it's all the same
no matter what you do

I don't care to know
the intimate details
I would like to know
you are happy
loved and
not alone

caring, sharing
and reaching out
arms extended
one to another
draw together
me to you
and you to another

live and let live
too simple by far
trite beyond compare
blood and guts
and giving a fuck
this I have to spare

Sara Mullen

## The Haunt

Listen for it:
the sly crackle,
the snarling hiss,

things spoken
as though
by the rooks

in their sky barks
uplifted on
sycamore tips.

Remember:
her back to you,
a black dress

chucking at hens,
by their stone house
under the trees.

Her place, this,
but more than hers
the voice

that rasps your name
as you pass the
walls at night.

More than she
who spooks the horse,
who thrills the kids

in a rush of fear,
and sets them
of a sudden

on the roundabout
way home.

Mitzie Murphy

### FIELDS

He is six years of earth, and I am a different version of myself. They call it Mother. I do not know where I have gone. I try to calm him and teach him things when all I want to do is shape a poem and lay it down on whiteness. How could I know it would be thirty years before it found the page? Instead, I make him fields. I rip fresh moss from warm rock and place it on trays in the oven. He impatiently waits, pulling at some other part of me. Could it be my heart? I stick the dried greenness onto A4 sheets until I have pages and pages of fields. I'm frantic. Glueing ice pop sticks together, I make fences with a frenzy I can't quieten. His farm is ready. The boundary is tight. He finds his plastic lumps of animals and dances them around the fields. Cows, sheep, pigs, goats, horses and chicks come alive. He makes their sounds and I follow. Laughing at my mooing, his clucking. The animals barge into each other. Our laughing gets louder. The sounds go higher. The animals scream. They jump the fences, falling on each other, he is jumping too. Stay safe, I say inside my mouth. It's chaos. Animals go wild on my kitchen table. The fences are broken. The moss comes undone from the pages. The game has reached its peak and I hold tight this child of six, knowing tomorrow the game will be different.

Anne Murray

CONFESSION

I am the child of an older mammy,
herself the child of an older mammy.
So, when I arrived in 1956,
my Granny Annie was 75.

A good age for a Granny.

She moved in with us
after Granda died
and at 85 took over my bed
and I was shifted sideways,
age 10, to share a room
with my older brothers.

She would shout during *Crossroads*
and spit phlegm on the fire.
She was slow and got in the way.
Once, after a nudge,
she fell to the floor,
a rack of old bones,
she spoke to me –

*may God forgive you.*

At 13, I heard her cry
in the night,
and did nothing.

Days afterwards
I peeked through the door
and saw her propped up
for viewing, veiled,
stiff and silent.

Granny Annie was dead 40 odd years
when my mammy said to me,
unexpectedly –
*you never complained.*

Chris Murray

ENMESH

I hang the black dress at Michaelmas.
My garden is alight. Lit again. Its
slow transformation from black grey
to popping electric green, and every little
thing. Nothing is too small, nothing is
passed over: A blade of green green grass, a
dew-atop with its tiny amber bead, magpie's voice,
and a parasol mushroom, all present.
The work of the darknesses is done – there is more
than one darkness in any one life.
I fell into yours like Alice through her glass.
There is a red storm-polished apple high in the
neighbours' tree – Is it for me? In the darkness,
you, her and the endless possibilities of love – No more!

Joan Newmann

## How Much Do You Need?

Bridgets I have known
who carry your name, Saint Bridget –
and your wild desire to let no thing
slip away, become a negative.

There was Bridget Meed,
a poet among poets.
She needed money.
An unspecified amount.
When Cathy spoke in the spirit
of Saint Bridget. *I've got money.*
*How much do you need?*
*She paid back every cent,* Cathy told us
and we were all glad that
the spirit of generosity
hadn't been used and abused.
As if to repay us for our faith in her,
Bridget Meed said *Tomorrow, I'll teach you all to dance.*
She was a belly-dancing poet.
And though we all shook our bellies
and stood wide-legged to little avail,
we tried, and Saint Bridget was pleased.

There was Bridget Winter,
(a great name) from Magherahoney.
I drove her home from the cancer hospital
some Fridays. This day, she was crying
because her consultant had told her
that she must not keep in contact
with people who had been discharged,
people who had become her friends.
Because if they died, or if
she heard that they had died,

it would set back her recovery.
Bridget knew that she would soon
be one of the discharged herself –
those for whom there was no cure.
But Saint Bridget sat Bridget Winter
up in her hospital bed –
a room full of birthday cards
and flowers and wine –
and Bridget read her poems to us
and when we knew the lines
we joined in and made her smile and smile.

A recent Bridget from America,
who didn't know Saint Bridget,
stood at Saint Bridget's place in Faughert.
And the still air settled on her,
and all that wisdom, and at home
she sent me a photo of the pasta
she had made with the labour of her hands.
Saint Bridget loved the sense of purpose
though the long strings of food
were very unfamiliar.

Oh, and the close Bridget –
Bridget of years and years.
A woman of beauty and conviction
wants us all to honour Saint Bridget.
Oh timely. Timely.
Saint Patrick has to wait his turn.
Saint Patrick, whose name and day
trip off our tongues.
*Sure, he wasn't even Irish,*
some might say.

To Saint Bridget, it is by our deeds –
deeds not words – deeds that cling
to us – and she has been seeing us

for fifteen hundred years.
Hearing us and touching us
(maybe smelling, maybe tasting us).

When Saint Bridget speaks to us
she speaks her knowing.
We need to listen.
She tells us.

She *tells* us.
*And then there is Love.*
*I've seen it. And the lack of it.*
*Oh, Love is a many-splintered thing.*

*Pity.*
*We need to believe*
*in Pity.*

Kate Newmann

## California, Oh California, I'm Coming Home

She stands crying in Paradise.
She's come back
and the fire has burned up
the very ghost of her house.

They had two minutes to escape.
She'd thought of the animals –
then her husband.

Sucked into the blaze
with the forest,
home has coughed itself out
as black absence, grey aftermath.

The metal box of the stove
stands ridiculous.

When my godmother was cremated,
her ashes passed around,
– carelessly, I thought –
and one friend remarked
*she's heavier than my sister was.*

We know nothing
about being through fire
or how the body houses love.

The woman in Paradise
gathered up
her animals.
Then her husband's urn.

In those last moments
she saved his ashes
from the flames.

Róise Ní Bhaoill

## Hibakusha

Soitheach dearmaid mé,
Luaith i mo bhéal
Is i mo chluasa,
Mé gan éalang fhollasach
Na *Hibakusha*.

Níl inscríofa
Ar mo chraiceann
Mionphátrún *Kimono*,
Níl reanga righne an dódh
Ag siúil mo chinn.

Ní greim mise i dtaobh an náisiúin
Nach raibh géilleadh ariamh ina dhán,
Ná i dtaobh lucht na caithréime,
A chosc an tsúil siar.

Is mé soitheach briosc
An dearmaid,
Ag fuireach le hord toll an ama,
A fhágfas lomnocht mé,
Ag faire ar mharcshlua cnámh.

Ceaití Ní Bheildiúin

## OSPÍS NA LEAMHAN
*don deilephila elpenor*

Líonta le fíon driseach
tar éis bheith sa ghort thiar ag blaistínteacht
ar phósaetha cumhra pinc
druideann tú i leith chun bheith ag rince.
Fáilte is fichead –
ach abair
an é do dhreas deireanach é
an bolgrince spleodrach seo?

Ón ndorchadas
atánn tú tuirlingthe
d'fhonn do dhordchnagadh ársa a chleachtadh
ar an ngloine os mo chionn
scata ded ghaolta sa chóngar
ag drumáil, ag steipeadaíl –
an bít hipneoiseach.

Solas bhur n-aon dia amháin
deinim amach.
Ó lasadh an chéad choinneal
ó crochadh an chéad lampa
ó cuireadh ar siúl an chéad bholgán leictreach
titeann sibh, i bhfochair leamhan d'aicmí eile,
fé dhraíocht soilse.

An 'fuileann tú, a leamhain aoibhinn phinc
teann dírithe anocht ar dul isteach
in Ospís an Lampa ar an bhfalla
le luí ann i measc do chineáil
do dhé scoir a ligint uait?

An é go santaíonn sibh compord ag an gcríoch
ar nós sinn féin? An laghdaíonn an solas
is a bhogtheas an phian?
Guím sámhnas is suan ort laistigh.
Go maire do phór go deo.

Úna Ní Cheallaigh

## In Wilton Park
*"Happiness drives out pain, as fire burns out fire"* – Mary Lavin

After a night of relentless wind, I wander
without purpose through the park;
old sycamores toss their leaves in frenzy.
I catch one floating before it reaches the ground
and you are there once more raking that last fall,
gathering damp mounds in a distant garden.
It is Samhain, still a sweetness of risen sap;
a memory of fresh cuttings after rain. I place
this leaf on my palm, across my broken lifeline,
search for answers in its veins.
Fires are burning, the wind soughing.
It is time, why not let us go?

Dairena Ní Chinnéide

## AOIS

Mapa línte ag tochailt isteach ina gnúis
Bhraith sí óg ina croí
Ach na lámha rocacha san
A scéith a haois uirthi

Ní hamhlaidh a bhí istigh
Áit a raibh rith ráis ag a samhlaíocht
Sciúrdanna á thabhairt in aon treo fánach
Tóirneach is tintreach amuigh

Í mar a mheas sí riamh í féin a bheith
Ina comhluadar féin
Neamhspleách, ceanndána, láidir
Máistreás ar a cúinne féin

I bhfolach sna leabhair is sa cheol
A mhaisigh a saol
Níorbh leasc léithe a suaimhneas
Ní uaigneas a bhí ann ach saoirse.

Caitríona Ní Chléirchín

SUANTRAÍ NA PÍBE UILLEANN
*do Thiarnán*

Éirigh chugham a rún,
a ghile, gluais liom
go támh
thar thairseach mo chroí
le do phort aoibhinn sámh
le d'fhonn mall
gluais do lámha
thar adhmad na huirlise
le lúth na méar
a Phíobaire shéimh
le fuaim na ndos
le ciúnas anama
go dtitfidh mé i néal
faoi do shéis cheoil aoibhinn.

Ceansaigh an bhuairt im chléibh
le do nótaí síodúla,
go séide lá
go scaipe scáth
a chorraíonn
sians glé na heolchaire
go dtéann
cian is cumha
chun suaimhnis.

## Laoighseach Ní Choistealbha

### BÁNFHILÍOCHT

Súil amháin agam ar an chabhsa,
is súil eile ar an chlog,
chnag mé ar dhoras an dáin.

'Táim réidh,
tar isteach!'

D'oscail mé an doras
is bhí straois mhór uirthi,
a dhá cíoch ina gcácaí boise,
a bolg mór chomh bog le taos fuinte,
a ceathrúna ar creathadh
le macnas éigse.

Is chuir mé ina luí uirthi,
in ainm Dé,
go raibh na cuairteoirí
ar a mbealach anseo,
is go raibh sé thar am aici gléasadh:
cathéide, ionar máilleach, clogad,
gúna, léine, péire stocaí,
tuáille nó brat,
ar a laghad.

'Agus cén fáth?'
a dúirt sí,
diabhlaíocht ag lonrú
ina súile liatha.

'Mar tá na cuairteoirí –
do chuid léitheoirí –
ag teacht go luath le breathnú ort

agus ba cheart duit
tú féin a chlúdú,
do náire a chlúdú.'
'Bhail', a dúirt sí,
'nach mbeirtear nocht gach aon neach,
gan orthu ach fuil is uisce,
is nach gcuirtear san uaigh an duine
is é gléasta cumhraithe
sa chulaith,
sa taiséadach,
sa chónra?

Ar rug tú beo ar leathanach mé?
Nó ar chuir tú mé
marbh maisithe
in uaigh an pháipéir seo?'

'Ach, na léitheoirí!'
a dúirt mé léi.
'Nach gá bheith clúdaithe,
sciata,
tiúchraicneach, fiú?'

Agus chroith sí a ceann.
'Más é go ndearna tusa,
a phuiteálaí na bhfocal,
do jab i gceart,
ba cheart gur féidir leosan
mé a choinneáil suas leis an tsolas
le go scallfaidh an ga gréine
fríd mo chraiceann tanaí
trédhearcach,
nár cheart?

Sin geanúlacht, a chroí:
bheith chomh nocht sin
os comhair an tsaoil

nach bhfeicfear thú
in aon chor!'

Bríd Ní Chomáin

IF I DIE, PUBLISH MY NOTES APP

If I die, publish my notes app.
Let me be a segment on some podcast,
a cautionary tale taught in schools.
Let my words go viral on BookTok,
every salacious detail made spectacle,
every lesson unlearned, a titbit,
paperback fodder, summer must read.

Let the musings and the self-flagellation
sit in other minds when I am gone.
The sunsets and smudged clouds described,
the lists of to-dos and to-gets,
of sexual partners, apologies,
the difficult emails and questions,
desperate pleas, streams of consciousness.
The succinct and humorous observations.
Let them illicit chuckles, let them hit nerves.

Let all the aches of my heart
light sparks in others.
Let them all mean something,
fleeting though it may be.
They are my only evidence
that life is poetry.

Mairéad Ní Chonaola

### Freagra agus Freagracht

An bhfuil aon ghaol ag freagra le freagracht
seachas cosúlacht a litriú ar ndóigh
nach minic muid ag lorg freagraí
is ag seachaint aon fhreagracht a théann leo

dá ndíreódh muid aird ar ár bhfreagracht
cois an teallaigh nó amuigh ar an ród
b'fhéidir gur ansin a bheadh na freagraí

a bheadh daingean
dúshlánach
cóir

Eiléan Ní Chuilleanáin

WHAT IT'S LIKE

The archangel came out with his question
just then, when we were lounging on the edge:
Tell me, he said, what is it really like
having a body, having to live inside it?

So I told him, but did he believe me
when I said that it's not the webbing,
the muscles or the signals holding us upright,
not even the hunger, not even the hurry,

it's like being followed around by a drowning hull
dimly visible in deep water,
something that slides across the daylight,
grey-blue, purposeful, pointed and slow;

then when I remember the deep wound,
the needle, the tubes, the bags of blood
and when I see how it flinches,
that's how I know it is mine.

Annemarie Ní Churreáin

## THE OTHER DAUGHTER

Is the daughter who went as far as the bridge
in the falling sleet. Others were crossing

through the mountain, the ghostdeer on alert,
as she drew a willowy breath and swung

back *home* again along the trembling road.
The daughter whose name is invisible to stone,

who carried the creels, and mossed the bones,
and knit cloaks of stars for the splitting body,

who laid a hand upon her father's brow
*féach an ghealach agus feiceann an ghealach tú*

as she combed out rivers, ash-lit and shallow
at the temples, as he clung like a snowflower

to the bare arms of the bare arms of winter.
What it took to stay, and spoon strings of fish

into his mouth, and wait for the swallowing:
blind crossings every day – of the grate,

of the churn, of the last bread, of the lilies
in June before the altar. Crossings no less

than those of one ship rising *the brightest
& the best* over black ribbons of water.

Ciara Ní É

## AN BÉAL BEO SEO

Tá athrú tagtha ar mo chuid cainte
dar le cara liom nach bhfaca le tamall
an bhéim ag bogadh go deireadh na bhfocal

Ní miste liom a chlos

I ngan fhios dom a tharla
ach tuigim an fáth
tá do bhlas deas ar mo bhéalsa
mé go seasta fé d'anáil

Tá mórtas orm an corn seo a ghlacadh
tuillte go maith, tráthnónta i'd aice

Nó ag crónú na hoíche ar chliathán sléibhe
fé sholas gealaí, i mo luí le do thaobh
i mo chluais do bhéal binn go héirí gréine

Tá athrú tagtha ar mo chuid cainte
is sin an chuid is lú de

Éire Ní Fhaoláin

## NÍL ANN ACH SCÁTH

Ar bharr an chnoic, tá solas fann.
Gléas trom spleodrach.
Deirtear nach bhfuil ann ach
scáth ar an bhféar,
Ach feictear dom an duairceas.
Feicim an scéin nach mbogann d'aon duine
Nach luíonn leis an ngrian sa gheimhreadh.
Ar bharr an chnoic, tá buíon ag rince
Ag casadh, 's ag casadh gan stad.

"Nach álainn an radharc ó bharr an chnoic?"
Cáithníní uafáis ag bailiú.
Tá ciúnas an tseomra ag béicíl agus
feictear dom an chontúirt.
Feicim an mhistéir a deirtear i gcogar
A chuireann na truáin faoi dhraíocht.
Ar bharr an chnoic, tá buíon ag rince –
Deirtear nach bhfuil ann ach scáth.

Eithne Ní Ghallchobhair

## CEOL CROTAIGH, CAOINEADH CLADAIGH

Tchím thú, cluinim thú,
a chrotaigh ghlórmhair, ghroí.
Ar dhath donn, riabhach
ag dul i bhfolach faoin tír.

Pilleadh an tsionnaigh
ar ais chuig Oileán Feá,
oileán taoide
ar chiumhais na trá.

Colainn thoirtiúil, amplach;
cosa caola, cnámhacha;
ceann cumtha, oirirc;
sciatháin amhra, lonracha.

Griogadh meanman,
macnas croí.
Tchím thú, cluinim thú,
a chrotaigh, a laoich.

Bogann tú leat gearrghiota
ag faire romhat go beacht.
Ag seiftiú láibe
ag imeacht le feacht.

Gob thar ghoib
éanlaith na spéire.
Gob slíoctha, snoite, snasta
ar chruth na gealaí úire.

Súile staidéartha
ag spiaireacht, ag stánadh,

ag baint lán súl
as an ghrinneall faoi spága.

Éan staidiúil, slachtmhar, ríogúil
i mbun rúin réidh;
faoi shó agus faoi shuan
ar lagtrá mhéith.

Óch, is tú atá maorga,
a chrotaigh ghlórmhair, uasail,
idir chnámh, chlúmh is chleite
amuigh ar an uaigneas.

Seal cois farraige ag fosaíocht;
seal sna sléibhte ar gor
faoi cheilt ón namhaid arranta,
ar mhaithe le slánú póir.

Riasc agus seascann,
móinéir agus caorán.
Éan siúlach, scéalach,
eachtrúil, deisbhéalach.

Más faiteach féin thú,
is foighneach thú i gceart.

Agus fógraíodh go barr na spéartha
gur tarngair an bháis thú,
gur comhartha mí-áidh
don iascaire ar farraige thú,
go síobfadh na gailfin
go géimneach dá gcluinfí thú,
go ngreadfadh an ghaoth
go goimhiúil dá bhfeicfí thú.

Corn maisiúil d'fhir
fhoghtha, fhoghacha;

d'fhoghlaithe forránacha,
feargacha, fraochacha.

Orainne a thitfidh na mallachtaí
agus Éire faoi chiúnas ceo.

Faolfhead léanmhar
ag sceanadh an chiúnais;
géis shíofrúil
ag stróiceadh an tsuaimhnis;
geoin dhubhach, ghléineach,
uaill dhiamhair, ríméadach.

Maireann tost, tost iomlán idir achan ghlaoch glan.

Agus tig athrú ar do ghair
ag brath ar do staid saoil:
ar chothú, ar phórú,
nó tú sa bhearna bhaoil.

Port plobach, bolgarnach:
ceiliúr na cúplála,
le teacht an tsamhraidh
agus tú 'do luí ar an fhara.

Feadaíl bhog, shéimh
na socrachta síoraí.
Tormán faobhrach, fíochmhar
an fhaobaigh.

Maireann tú beo le fuineadh gréine,
a chrotaigh thréin,
an dorchadas mar sciath chosanta ort,
is coimhthíoch do réim.

Glór púcúil, uaibhreach,
i ndiaidh clapsholais.

Maireann do lúcháir liriciúil
mar chomhartha dóchais
go mairfidh tú go deo,
nach n-imeoidh tú leis an cheo
mar a d'imigh bunús do shleachta.
Tá Éire lomtha, bodhraithe agus creachta
de dheasca mheath éanlaith na spéire.

An liú síoraí, seasta;
an guth saoithiúil, casta;
an glór cianmhar, cúthúil,
séanmhar is úisiúil
ionann agus díothaithe,
imithe, críochnaithe.

Ceol a sheolann
go smior na gcnámh,
a fhágann an té a éisteann
faoi shámh,
faoi thámh.

Port beatha, éagaoin éaga
in aon éan amháin.
Tchím thú, cluinim thú,
a chrotaigh ghlórmhair, ghroí.

Colette Ní Ghallchóir

## AG LEANÚINT

Tá sé i mo dhiaidh ach níl sé ar mo chúl.
Tá sé romham ach ní bhéarfaidh mé air choíche.
Nuair a fheiceann sé mé ag teacht imíonn sé
mar a bheadh cú ann.
Is maith leis mise a fheiceáil ag dul chun an bhaile.
Ba mhaith leis mise a choinneáil sa bhaile.

Ailbhe Ní Ghearbhuigh

## Fear Iomaire ag Taibhreamh

An fada anseo mé
ag triall ar an oileán

Gach buille iomartha
cruinn, teann

An talamh docht
romham amach

Liom sa naomhóg
bean sciamhach

Colpaí dea-chumtha
is com seang

Idir an dá shúil
stánann sí orm

Cead raide
níl agam

Ar fhaitíos
a himeachta

Níl i ndán dom
ach céasadh na dtonn.

Áine Ní Ghlinn

## Cad d'Imigh ar Mo Dhá Chos?

*i gcuimhne Elizabeth O'Farrell*

Clé, deas, clé, deas, gan oiread is
an tsracfhéachaint is lú thar mo ghualainn
ná an chlaonfhéachaint is lú i leataobh
ach mo dhá shúil dírithe ar na baracáidí.
Banda na Croise Deirge ar mo mhuinchille.
Bratach bhán na síochána i mo dhá lámh.
Bean an Mhisnigh, mar dhea, is mo dhá chos
ag máirseáil leo go mall creathánach.

Siar is aniar le teachtaireachtaí.
*Ní ghlacfaí ach le géilleadh gan choinníoll.*
D'airigh mé coimhthíos liom féin.
Coimhthíos le mo chosa creathánacha
is iad ag siúl suas síos Sráid an Mhúraigh.
Scoiteacht iomlán nó gur teilgeadh isteach
i mo chorp arís mé is mé ag siúl céim ar chéim
leis an bPiarsach ar an tsiúlóid dheireanach.

*Ní ghlacfaí ach le géilleadh gan choinníoll.*
Ualach na bhfocal ina luí go trom orainn beirt
ach nuair a chonaic mé claíomh is piostal
ár gceannaire á dtairiscint don Ghinearál Lowe,
phléasc mo chroí istigh le hualach bróin.
Phléasc mo chroí is thit sé síos síos.
Síos thar imeall mo sciorta.
Síos síos thar mo dhá rúitín.

Síos isteach i mo dhá bhróg. Na bróga sin
a shiúil céim ar chéim, iad ar comhchéim
leis an bPiarsach ar an turas deireanach sin.
Ach cad d'imigh orthu?
Cad d'imigh ar mo dhá bhróg?

Cad d'imigh ar mo dhá chos?
Cad d'imigh ar imeall mo sciorta?
Bróga, sciorta, cosa aerscuabtha as an stair.

Cad d'imigh orthu go léir?
Cad d'imigh ar Bhean an Mhisnigh?
Cad d'imigh ar a misneach?
Cad d'imigh ar an mbean a rinne
Bratach Bhán na síochána
a iompar i dtreo na mbaracáidí?
Arbh é nach raibh ionam ach giolla gan tábhacht?
Arbh é go raibh orm géilleadh gan choinníoll?

Orlaith Ní Icí

## Teanga mo Mháthar

Ar iasacht
a thug sí dom í,
sractha óna béal aici

Clúdach barrdhóite uirthi,
imeall creimthe,
is corp práibe

Leis an ngeallúint
Nach ndéanfainn clón aisti
Ach go gcruthóinn mo *spin* féin uirthi

Ghlac sí a háit ansin
sítheach sóch
maoirseacht á dhéanamh aici
ar a snáithaidí saorga
féithe á fhí, craiceann á chumaisc
comhar coibhche le híoc

Thugas móid di
an chomaoin a chúiteamh léi
nuair a bhí sé in am di a blas a chuimhneamh aríst

Réaltán Ní Leannáin

## Bag for Life

*Bag for Life is right*, ar sí,
Ag amharc ar mo sheanmhála *Superquinn*, siopa atá imithe le fada.
Frankie. Seasca a sé. Chuir sí suntas sa mhála plaisteach
Mar chaith sí féin an chuid is fearr dá cuid blianta ag obair leo
Go dtí go bhfuair sí fógra iomarcaíochta
Bliain sular bhain sí an trí scór amach.

*Tá cat agam, Úbaí, short for ubiquitous,*
*Níos fearr ná fear,*
Achan gháire aisti.
Bhí sí geallta trí huaire, ach d'ól siad uilig
Mar a d'ól na fir eile ina saol - a Deaid agus a deartháireacha.
*Drochnuacht iad na fir*, ar sí.

Líon sí an spás eadrainn sa cheaintín san ospidéal,
Ag geabaireacht gan stad,
Bean nach bhfuair deis cainte le daoine eile go minic.
Ag baint tairbhe as an ócáid,
Ina gúna bándearg trilseach gan mhuinchillí,
Go foirmeálta i measc na *fleeces* agus na *trackies*.
A smideadh cóirithe le cúram, a gruaig mar an gcéanna.
Galánta. Níos oiriúnaí d'oíche ag an ópera,
Nó fáiltiú le gloiní *champagne* agus *petits fours*.
*An maith leat é?* ar sí,
Ag amharc orm ag stánadh ar an ghlioscarnach ghlé.
*Margadh a bhí ann, fuair mé ar lascaine mhór é,*
*Síos go céad euro ó dhá chéad go leith.*
Aoibh uirthi go raibh sí chomh seiftiúil.

*Is fearr liom leabhair*, ar sí
Ag muirniú an ceann a bhí ina glac,

*Níl aon mhaith ionam le ríomhairí, an bhfuil tú féin in ann acu?*
Ach níor éist sí le mo fhreagra.
Shlog mé bolgam tae, greim agam ar mo mhála plaisteach,
Súil amháin dírithe uirthise, súil eile ar an chlog,
Coinne *physio* agam ar ball beag.
Níor thug mé faoi deara nach raibh cupán os a comhair amach.

*Rinne mé iarracht mé féin a mharú,* ar sí, *an deireadh seachtaine seo caite tá siad mo choinneáil anseo ar an* mental ward *is fuath liom an focal sin* mental *níl mé* mental *in aon chor.*
Aoibh uirthi i gcónaí, ag cuimilt a leabhair.
Lean an chaint thart orainn sa chaife.
Rinne tráidirí plaisteacha cling ar na táblaí.
Óladh as mugaí.
Osclaíodh pacáistí ceapairí cáise.
*Ligeann siad dom suí anseo ní maith liom suí ar an* ward *beidh cúpla duine ón chór san eaglais ag bualadh isteach chugam tráthnóna tá siad iontach maith tá duine acu ag tabhairt aire d'Úbaí sin mo chat short for ubiquitous tá súil istigh agam go bhfuil sé óicé.*

Bhí náire orm go raibh sé in am bogadh síos chuig mo choinne leis an *physio*
Ach sin é an saol.
Thóg mé mo *Bag for Life*,
Bheannaigh mé don bhean sa ghúna trilseach
Leis an leabhar dar teideal *Killing Time*,
A chronaigh a cat, Úbaí, short for ubiquitous.

Bríd Ní Mhóráin

## Caoineadh

Critheann an leoithne
Seoda ómra an fhómhair,
Titeann duilleog ar bhileog
Ina gcnuasach breacóir;
Cá bhfaighead an glór
Tar éis tosta ró-mhóir
Chun doimhneas an bhróin
A scaoileadh í bhfoghair
I ndiaidh an phlanda óig
Atá curtha fén bhfód?

Éist leis an leoithne
Lig di í a chaoineadh
I siolla ceoil na gaoithe.

Gormfhlaith Ní Shiochain Ní Bheolain

## CUR AMÚ

Táim ag cur na ndeor
bainfead sa bhfómhar
mo chompord is mo mhórtas.

Sáfad mo mhéaranta isteach sa chré thais
agus ní bhfaighead ann romham ach clocha lofa
agus aon bhláth mínádúrtha bándearg amháin.

Ní fhásann plandaí ó dheora an chompoird

ach scaol agus imní        imíonn
imeacht na haimsire ón gcuimhne

chun ná cífí síleáil bhándearg na scamall
leathshlí suas sa spéir
atá fliuch agus tais agus pinc.

Colette Nic Aodha

### Turas go Deisceart Bhéal Feirste

Chuamar amach ag déanamh na gcos
thar teorainn a léirigh sliocht ár sleachta
scartha óna chéile.
Sráid Iarúsailéim mar chuimhneachán agam ...

Banna fliúit ag máirseáil thar bráid,
níor thóg sé mórán ama orthu ...
An seicteachas
ag titim i léig.

Gearóidín Nic Cárthaigh

## An Foclóir Nua Béarla-Gaeilge

Tagann pacáiste chúm sa phost,
is níl teora le cairtchlár,
ná le téip ghreamaithe á ghlasáil.

Tógann sé leathuair
le siosúr is le tréan-dhua
an leabhar mór a nochtadh.

Tiontaím na leathanaigh
ar thóir na bhfocal
a sheolfaidh thar n-ais
ar bhóthar mo dhúchais mé.

Foclóir ag gor
ar feadh trí scór bliain,
ach briseann an bhlaosc
ar deireadh.

Pauline Nic Chonaonaigh

## FAOI GHOB AN PHRÉACHÁIN

Róipín rua
Tréigthe, spíonta
Ina leathshnaidhm ar chuaille geata
Is ceangailte de philéar claí

Síneann eidhneán craosach
Ó philéar go geata
An ciúnas diamhrach briste
Ag scoilteadh na gcipíní faoi mo chosa

Gan deoraí anseo leis na cianta fada
Driseacha, neantóga is raithneach
Ina mbrat trom
Toim aitinn ag greadadh i dtreo an dorais

Grágaíl bhorb préacháin
Ar phota briste simléir
Ag tabhairt foláirimh
Go bhfuilim anseo gan iarraidh

Siúlaim go mall i dtreo an dorais
Cuirtear bac tobann orm
Diúltaíonn mo chosa
Dul coiscéim níos faide

Casaim ar ais i dtreo an gheata
Ach mealltar mo shúile
I dtreo na fuinneoige
Faoin díon sa mbinn thoir

Feicim íomha chráite mná
Ag stánadh idir an dá shúil orm
Ní léir dom doicheall nó a mhalairt
A fheicim ina dreach

Caol díreach i dtreo an gheata liom
Mo chroí ag greadadh im' chluasa
Ar éigean a thugann mo chosa
Thar an ngeata mé

Suite arís ar an bpota simléir
Is léir dom grinneas an phréacháin
Seanchríonnacht 's é dom' fhaire
An léargas ceilte faoina ghob

Eibhlín Nic Eochaidh

## Staying Alive

At Lissadell a curlew's cry
pierces November air.
In Al Shifa Hospital the cries
of premature babies rise
from mattresses where they lie
side-by-side, relying on
each others' body heat
to stay alive.

Beside the gate the field maple
flies its tattered flags, burnt-orange leaves.
Outside the patio door the potbound
Japanese maple is stripped bare.

Margaret Nohilly

HER CORE BELIEF
*i.m. Annie Walsh (1914–2006)*

My mother graced the world in teeth of war,
tensions far and near she could not grasp
yet felt God's providence her portion – her
childhood backdropped by the Hill of Ben,
mammoth among the marks of fabled Fore.
Younger daughter of a dual mother, dreamy
widowed father; last of the brood, she took
being doted on her due and strode ahead.
Distinction in learning crowned her hidden
idyll: hilltop Sunday picnics, naming counties
spread below, circlet of lakes by shape and hue.
Laced with lyric language of her upbringing,
her sense of being plucked out of obscurity
braced her for the sorrows she would know.

Helena Nolan

## A Poem about Hens
*after Henri Cole*

She must have been lonely, my mother
though she had us all?
Every day, my father drove away
every day, we ran downhill to school

she worked late nights back then
most weekends too in the village bar
but all day long, when we were gone
Monday to Friday, she was all alone

she must have missed the farm, her
mother too, she wrote her every week
Basildon Bond Lined, in blue
called, when she could afford to phone

one day there was a crate of Bantams
in the yard, I remembered my mother said
she had always loved the hens and used
to run out to protect them from the rain

she loved those Bantams too, and they were
sweet, hopping about for grain, hiding in the
long grass, looking blue against the green
each night, she locked them in the broken shed

that morning, I was woken much too soon
I heard her screaming and then crying hard
no child should hear their mother weep
like that, it was a hail of sorrows raining down

"the fox got in," she said, "and killed them all
I should have known," she said, "I should have known
my one small precious thing" – we never spoke of it
again, maybe she wrote about it, in a letter home

Maria Noonan-McDermott

## The Empty Chair

Empty chairs,
empty rooms and all the spaces in between.
The light dimmed forever.

Portrait of my mother,
pathos and power immortalised.
Her imprints remain in the remnants left behind.

I sense her presence in the echoes and vibrations
of shadows cast
and I inhale deeply the last traces of scent
to recall her spirit,
grasping at tenuous links
in the hope of holding on.

The archaeological uncovering of earthly possessions,
mere objects of memory and nostalgia,
but objects cherished and honoured of a life lived well.

We begged for time and she granted us rest.
That ache of space dared settled dust,
takes her place.
Wishes for freedom now attained, loosed, released,
disconnected and forlorn.

Years of changing patterns.
Integuments of lives, splintered and scattered.
Shared seeds seeking solace in the succession of time.

Mary Noonan

## Sunflower, Sparrows

Hard to believe the sunflower was ever here,
beaming over the old wall. Planted in a pot
by a neighbour, it grew seven feet and flashed
its yellow searchlight over the mud-grained yard.

Hurricane Ophelia smashed it, though.
The petals, bled of light, took on the dun
of the wall. The lanky stalk bent to the muck
as wind savaged the garden's laurel.

I found an old box of Lonjing tea,
brought from Hangzhou years earlier.
The label told me the tea's leaf is shaped like
a sparrow's tongue, glossed with the green of jade.

I sat swirling the smoky tongues, listening to
Ophelia lash her tail: laurel leaves were flying,
but no sparrows. They had left for the treeless
fields where they would plant their feet and wait,
attune their bodies to murderous shifts in air.

Catherine O'Brien

## Mo Mháthair, Mo Chroí

Bean dhea-chroíoch, mhilisbhriathrach
agus
thar a bheith dílis.

Beart cliste, cinnte, a bhí ag Dia
nó timireacht aingeal a bhí os a chionn
an lá úd a sheol sé tú chugainne.

Déarfainn gur leathchúpla a bhí ionainn ach
ní luíonn sin leis an mbitheolaíocht.

Airím uaim do shiosmaid gan cúthail
a bheadh in ann iarmhéil gach brón a ruaigeadh.

Airím uaim ceist éiginnte a fheiscint
ag munlú ar do bheola
an fhéachaint sin a roinneamar
an gháire dhosmachtaithe chomh nadúrtha eadrainn
cigilt na gréine ar uisce socair an tsamhraidh a bhí ann.

Airím uaim binneas do ghuth
ceol d'anam uasal, sondas do fhírinne
a bhí agus a bheidh mar théad tarrthála don dóchas.

Jean O'Brien

## As if, Absence

There are always places where you are
absent: in that rue Petit in Paris,
behind the Pantheon near rue Clotilde,
on the side of the map where the land
lapses and the ocean floods the empty
spaces, where clouds seem to hover
on the horizon, until all becomes one,
a dream sequence from another time
or place.

Sometimes I think I see your face,
something is familiar around the
pucker of a lip, a certain fragility in
blue eyes, the slight raise of a brow,
all speak into the absence
that grows louder as years pass
as if, as if, as if.

Margaret O'Brien

WITNESS
*"This is a female text, written in the twenty-first century. How late it is. How much has changed. How little."*
– Doireann Ní Ghríofa, *A Ghost in the Throat*

The clocks went back last night and now, early evening, the day is drawing in. Clouds sail above – sky a calm sea – as I look towards Sliabh na mBan, this mountain of the women.

So many lives, women and their children, within a whisper of being erased. This is for the witnesses, this is for Catherine Corless.

This is for Nell McCafferty who showered Joanne Hayes with yellow roses, to soften the anvil on which she was being beaten.

This is for the women who dared to bring contraception across the border on that amazing train, flinging condoms and diaphragms across the barricades, into the hands of their sisters and beyond the reach of those who would erase their sovereignty.

This is for the witnesses.

This is for those who marched so that there might not be another Savita.

Night has fallen; the lights of Kilcash, yellow sparkles against the soft darkness – the mountain of the women. Bruises of clouds hang low in the valley.

This is for Vicky.

Mary O'Brien

## Tiarna na dTonn

Is mise Manannán, Tiarna na dTonn.
Féach mé ar dhroim na bóchna,
mé ucht le díle ar mo chapall, Enbharr.
Is iomaí oileán i mo Ríocht Mhara
chomh maith le mo thearmann aoibhinn féin,
an Eamhain Abhlach.

Samhlaigh na hiontais atá le feiceáil ann –
mo chrainn draíochta,
na húlla órga a bhfuil ceol acu,
na muca nach féidir iad a mharú
is an bhó riabhach a thug mé abhaile liom
ó mo thuras chun na hIndia le hAonghus.

Is minic mé socair, suaimhneach,
ag siosarnach go ceolmhar ar an trá.
Is minic lách cineálta mé –
is mise a chabhraigh leis na Tuatha Dé,
is chabhraigh mé le hOisín agus Niamh
ar a dturas go Tír na nÓg.

Ach is minic cuma ghruama orm leis,
mé corraithe, ar buile uaireanta.
Is iomaí stoirm a d'ardaigh mé
is mé gafa le racht feirge,
minic a cheil mé oileáin,
minic a bháigh mé fearann, míntír.

Mura dtugtar ómós ceart domsa
is do mo dhomhan mór faoi thoinn,
fainic an teas marfach ag éirí i mo chroílár,
m'fhonn díoltais ag treisiú.

Is ansin a bheidh sibh cách i mbaol.
Is mise Manannán, Tiarna na dTonn.

>
> LORD OF THE WAVES
> translation of *Tiarna na dTonn*

I am Manannán, Lord of the Waves.
I ride the swell on my sea horse, Enbharr.
Many are the islands in my watery realm,
The Land of Women, The Land of Promise
and my own great secret sanctuary,
The Isle of Apples.

Imagine the wonders there –
my magic trees,
the golden fruit that can make music,
the pigs that never can be killed
and the speckled cow I once brought home
from my trip to India with Aonghus.

Often you'll find me quiet, settled,
whispering a lullaby along the shore.
I can be gentle, kind – like the time
I helped the Tuatha Dé or when I came
to the aid of Oisín and my daughter, Niamh,
on their journey out to Tír na nÓg.

But other times you'll find me gloomy,
much disturbed and even angry.
Many a storm I have stirred up,
the sea always at my command.
I have made islands disappear,
eroded sand and drowned mainland.

And if I sense a disrespect of my sea creatures,
of my great underwater gardens, beware

the deadly heat increasing at the heart of me,
the urge to vengeance swelling.
You will all be in great danger then.
I am Manannán, Lord of the Waves.

Clairr O'Connor

## GONE
*im Maura Nash*

A cobwebbed busyness, the kitchen;
crockery and pots askew in stacks.
The door I push through clears its throat.
Her bedroom is a dusty ache of loss.
That pillow, still indented. The bed's declivity.
Those old diaries in their closed black world
her voice, fading into strangeness that opens
to an absence awaiting me and you.

Jessamine O'Connor

WITNESS BOX

From the inside of the witness box it's all down –
assorted balding ragged heads
or neat hairstyles on bored suit jackets

that glaring space you can't look at, will not look,
no matter how its shadow thrashes into your peripheral,
how many growls and blurts are shushed
by his legal team, do not look –

this is a crow's nest, bockety perch,
a creaking claustrophobic cage
you cannot leave

Karen O'Connor

## CLEANING BRICKS
*i.m. Mary Coffey*

Those days I lived in your company,
sheltered by the white-washed walls of your garden,
talked about your struggle to clean bricks
that were laid one hundred years
before your ninety years.
You were cycling through proven methods
to return the bricks to their original colour.
At your feet the chosen brick for all trial runs.
*What do you think?*
And all I could see were the myriad of bricks
in that herringbone weave
covering a good third of your garden.
But you, undaunted, admired that one brick,
feeling the port-stained stone had lightened,
more in keeping with when you were a girl.
And again, I find myself in envy of that mind set,
that allowed you to see the future,
not just any future, but yours;
when the bricks are bright and
vibrant and splashed with sunshine,
on a glorious summer's day, like today.

Nuala O'Connor

## An tIasc ~ The Fish

*'We breathe in our first language, and swim in our second.'*
– Adam Gopnik

I take my first breath from Dublin air,
snámhaim, freisin, i mBaile Átha Cliath.

English sa bhaile agus Gaeilge in school,
tá mé sáite idir na teangacha, an dá rud scaipthe.

Later, in Gaillimh, I breathe while I swim,
agus tuigim: *Is iasc mé, nasctha le teanga.*

Tógaim mo chéad anáil i mBaile Átha Cliath,
I swim, too, in Dublin.

Béarla at home and Irish ar scoil,
I am wedged between drifting languages.

Níos déanaí, in Galway, tógaim anáil is mé ag snámh,
and I understand: I am a fish, language-hooked.

Sarah O'Connor

## I'm Not Your Type

You normally go for blonde girls
with hair that swings when they shake their heads;
girls whose laughter is accompanied by an
angle of acquisition,
bored girls who drum their nails on the counter top,
glossy, lacquer gleaming.

The pity is
my body does everything you'd want it to, hungrily
and my body wants everything you'd want it to, lustily.
My heart's truer than truth and stickier than stalagmite
and my heart beats with incontrovertible beauty.

And, the real pity is
my mind seeds, grows, basks, ripens.
Yes, my mind is a veritable peach.

Grace O'Doherty

## Miradouro

Climb endless hills to the Moorish castle
and shelter under its stone pines.
The city below arrests the eye, resists your gaze.

Cameras announce themselves,
silent flashes along the battlements.
They take the red roofs, the red bridge,

the other Christ the Redeemer presiding over
the biblical wideness of the river, welcoming
cruise ships with a kiss on both cheeks.

Mary O'Donnell

### Family Christmas

Winter and low light,
no end in sight
in the wide fields of Kildare.
Crows cloak the sky
at dawn and dusk,
the porch and hallway
are hung with painted cones.

Auntie's face
ignores the family gays
perched at ease near table end,
their faces wine-merry.
She knows they've decided
they're original,
that no one really understands
and they might as well tuck in
as boring straight talk ripples
up and down the silverware,
tips through the turkey,
into the boozy trifle.

Everyone's hung.
With gadgets –
new trainers, tech,
jeans turned up just so,
– feelings are something
that happened long ago,
perhaps, now redundant.

The family asks nothing,
expects less, although
the conversation turns to money.
Someone mentions a poet,

what's his name,
Seamus – *Kavanagh*, is it?
*Won the Nobel, money in that,*
*I suppose.*

Your face turns down
towards the plate
and cranberry sauce
seems bitter.
You want away from people
who seem damp and lonely
as a derelict train track.

The night knits, then unravels,
an undecided craft of words,
and the aunt and new uncle
who met on the Camino
arrive with gifts,
let loose with the wine.
Their traces – more glamorous –
carefree – than this shadowy siding
near the bog where Family United
displays its wrangle of pain.

Outside for a smoke,
you regard the tomb silence
of other houses,
hysterical lights,
luminous pink reindeers
in gardens.

Two real robins
squabble in the holly hedge,
your eye follows
the damp gleam of SUVs
up and down the road,

then a lone child
on a new bike as night falls.

And night falls
more deeply after people leave.
Another child is twanging
the same few notes
on a new guitar
till someone shouts
*for Christ's sake, shut up!*

The room's tangerine walls
are braced against the night,
hint at future sunny horizons.
Yellow lamps comfort.
Firelight flares.
Way out in the black acres,
you imagine a pagan god stirs.
You remember
some vague, important thing,
almost forgotten.

Liz O'Donoghue

### Entering Eden

I find you drowsing naked
in the afternoon
I was in the garden
checking the tree for figs
the grass for snakes –

your soldier's physique
outlined against the white
is beautifully disarming
face down and unaware
I don't wake you –

naked like you
and weightless
I align my body over yours
lightly rest my palms
on your hands
my arms relax along the
strength of your shoulders
breasts cushioning
as the nipples brush your skin
soft stomach yielding across
your firm back
silver mail
on your golden armour
Venus between your cheeks
Thighs on (oh Jesus) your thighs

now
if I could merge into you.

Lauren O'Donovan

GOSPEL OF BIRTH

They won't let us leave the hospital
until they examine her in the car seat –

final graduation for new parents
after a week of intensive care.

All six pounds of her are too small for the infant bumper
but the nurse, all knowing,

rolls up a star-splattered blanket,
pads it around her like a halo.

When we had left our apartment, after long
days and longer nights in labour

there was a bowl of vomit in the bathroom,
the couch still wore a soaked waterproof pad

from when my waters broke with an audible *POP*.
Dirty dishes scattered over counters,

our bedroom – a chaos of things left unpacked.
For our return, everything is made new by my mother,

the heating on, dinner waiting in the oven.
The dog runs to us and stops short, unusually

respectful, like a priest in church.
We place the car seat on the ground

and he steps forward slowly –
soft paw after soft paw,

to sniff our new daughter's feet,
wash them with his tongue.

Margaret O'Driscoll

## WATCHKEEPER OF THE DREAMSPACE
*for Paula Meehan*

We assembled at the midsummer solstice fire
where Amergin first pronounced his song,
hearing our bards response to his incantation.
You narrated the tremblings of the women
already aware of all that invasion would bring,
your flowing tresses shimmering with silver fireflies.

A daughter of the city, winkle dancing along your
beloved Gardiner Street, weaned on words forged
from hearth-sparks that you kindled with ink.
A *beantuathach* of nature's bounty, painting
sweet pea, lilac, laburnum, while shivering
at disappearing fields and open sacred spaces.

Seeds nurtured in the furnace of your belly
sow images for seasons and the memory of water,
your songs sing the mystery of healing truths
that energise watchkeepers of the dreamspace.
*Your hand in mine as earnest of trust,*
*not because we want to – because we must.*

Orlagh O'Farrell

## Some Days I Want to Be Cillian Murphy

quieten my face down until
it's almost geological

a crater on the moon that has paradoxically
two forest pools of the purest lightest blue

my lips will enunciate normally
but they will have a life of their own

hovering somewhere between a smile and a threat
so you can't tell which it is

and people will say is Cillian Murphy really a marionette
so well made you can't see the strings?

As Cillian Murphy I will get used to people
stammering and getting tongue-tied in my presence

paralysed by my glossy black hair and my limpid stare
– almost bland, dare they even think?

A bit like Scott Tracey, International Rescue
and a bit like Parker,

chauffeur with a shady past
in *Thunderbirds* are go.

Lani O'Hanlon

## Soothsayer

You could play the djembé,
sing an African call and response,

chant sacred words from every tradition.
Sufi, Jewish, Arabic, Zoroastrian,

Native American, Aboriginal, Buddhist,
Hindi, Christian, Druid, Pagan ...

You sang and danced around my living room,
a box of matches – your shake-a-shake.

Played world music that rattled
the students in your yoga classes,

taught African drumming
before that became a thing.

In the market in Senegal a revered Saltigue
was sitting on a kind of throne.

You crouched on the ground to play
an intricate rhythm on his bare feet.

He stood up, lifted his arms
and hundreds of people rushed towards him.

Then he explained
that you had been foretold:

they would share that sacred rhythm
with the world

and a white person
would bring their rhythm back

to show them how far the beat
and beam of healing can travel.

NOTE: In Serer *saltigue* and its spelling variation derive from two Serer words: "sal" and "tigui"; *sal* means "meeting point of two ways, the place where one branch branches into two other branches. And by analogy, beam on which the roof of the hut rests." *Tigui.* "Saltigue" The term is of Serer origin meaning "soothsayer" those who communicate with the invisible world.

Helen O'Leary

## Shoe Shopping

A yearly jaunt,
two pairs to make the trip worthwhile.
Low-heeled and Velcro-ed,
fashioned for width and comfort.
'nuns' shoes,' Mam sighed and bought a red pair.

Afterwards they went to charity,
along with boxes of the 'never worn':
knee high boots, court shoes and sandals of Italian leather
purchased before the need for the yearly jaunt.

In the hospital gown Mam's slender calves
are pale and still, all pain obliterated.
No need for shoes now, nuns or other.
Underneath the bed, a pair of brand-new slippers.

Nessa O'Mahony

COMPRESSION

We've grappled these last weeks
with more than pills and stockings.
In the doctor's surgery
I perch on the third chair,
strain to decipher the code
on her flickering laptop screen.
I've breached the fourth wall
of doctor/patient confidentiality,
look disconsolate at the rubble
as you chatter on.

You tell her I'm your memory;
if so, we are already sunk.
I might recall the minutiae,
the dates, the calls for radiology,
what the consultant said
and how he said it (*brisk*),
but how can we survive
if you forget the rest?
Search and retrieve
were your strength, never mine.

Mary O'Malley

## The Writing Lesson

On the way downstairs with notebook
a clawhammer, the blood pressure monitor
Lowell's *Imitations*, two stick-on plastic hooks
and a tack between your teeth, you're on your way
to make a dishcloth rack and hang the blue
and yellow star chart when it stops you
like the phone, a shout, something
about the word 'lupus' or 'canis major'.
Now you have to sit down and coax it
Closer, onto the white page with blue ink.

Síofra O'Meara

## The Boy Band

A member of a band not your favourite member but a member not your top five spread across a purple painted room sellotaped-on-top-off showing teenage skinny abs member but a member has died. Their death tragic, the childhood symbolism of all those songs, all those horny dreams, all those late night what could've beens – gone in a instant. We grieve, we mourn, you're packing – always something to forget – maybe a hair straightener? Or a favourite tshirt – or god forbid the charger – they have a slant over there. Under there. 24hrs away from here. From her now. We drove to granny – for one last meal "probably my last" she says but we all know she's not going anywhere. Maybe said in a final attempt for you to not leave us. Leave her. Leave me. We listen to songs no one else understands – not cool, not in the charts – niche inside jokes that not even our folks have heard us sing – thankfully due to both being tone deaf. I arrive home and the dogs wait for a second arrival that never comes. Ear scratches that'll never be resolved because no one else knows that middle point between comfort and pain. "On plane" you'll text – as racial remarks are spat at our family member whose defence I wish was backed by you. "Safe flight" we all reply after the chaos. "This is why she left" – you're bigger then her. Our dogs will wait for that scratch behind the ear, and when I hear the songs of your favourite childhood band looking for my duet partner who can't make a coherent sound found herself in a far away place whilst listening to her favourite band, whose member who wasn't her favourite member's body was recently found. I'll be singing with you always on our trips far and wide.
A member of a band
but not your favourite
has died.

Bláithín O'Reilly Murphy

## Mná an Domhain

I grew on tales of Gráinne Mhaol and Con Markievicz.
I was inspired by Mary Robinson and Mary McAleese.
My youth a dizzy array of possibility and encouragement,
despite the daily 6pm chimes.

Light a candle.

Youth's protection and privilege afforded me freedoms.
I aged, ignorant of the growing,
or perhaps the everpresent power
struggle of women.

Strike a match.

The lines of death,
the rights removed,
the abuse of our bodies.

The match is lit.

We are the candle.
Ours the light to be extinguished.
Burn bright my fellow women.
The phoenix rises from the ashes.

The candle is burning.

Focus now.
The fractured future history is trying to write
is no more than that.
Ashes.
Mná an Domhain
burn with purpose.

Maeve O'Sullivan

## FIVE-A-DAY
*for Lisa Jean*

My hungry grand-niece tries a banana,
next up granadilla, fruit of passion:
she likes them better than the papaya
but not as much as fresh watermelon.

Messy orange stains from breakfast mango;
for lunch some pancakes made with blueberries.
Her Mum purées the humble potato
and for dessert there's juicy raspberries.

On warm days there's the cool of cucumber,
the nose is turned up, though, at guacamole.
She tolerates the pale cauliflower
though much preferred is iron-rich broccoli.

But best of all the taste of mother's milk,
her sapphire eyes and skin of lustrous silk.

Katherine Orr

HOME

Today I looked at you with love.
I stared in awe at your magnificence,
your strength, your beauty.
My body, I am home.

Today I looked at you with reverence
for all that you have endured,
for all that you have survived.
My body, I am home.

Today I looked at you and felt grateful
that you are mine,
that you stayed with me.
My body, I am home.

Today I looked at you, overwhelmed.
The pain I have lived through,
the unimaginable violence,
the relentless punishments I meted out on you.

Yet today I looked at you and you stood with grace.
You weathered the storm,
you carried me through.
Thank you.

Today I looked at you with love.
My body, I am home.
My body, I am home.

Saakshi Patel

CHHAYA

Perforated six-yard saree wrapped
around her middle-aged waist, she shuffles in,
tying her thinning hair into a fountain,
precision dwindling every year. She cracked
when her husband passed away so young.
Othered by her stepson, his deceit,
she now lives in a room measuring six feet
by four, including loo and kitchen, along
mother and uncle. Her day is a ragged washcloth
dusting the tops of foreign blackwood dressers,
perfumes and nail polish bottles by the swathe.
Unscrewing a cap and praying that all her pressures
are taken away, she paints her smallest nail blue,
hoping to afford her own bottle, brand new.

Cáit Pléimionn

Iontráil Dialainne

Is annamh a bhíonn uaigneas orm
san árasán seo.
Bainim sásamh as an suaimhneas,
spreagadh as an gciúnas.
Scuabaim urlár na cistine,
cuimlím na dromchlaí le ceirt
is nuair a bhíonn na haon rud
mar is ceart,
ólaim caife ar mo shocracht.

Luascaim le rithim cheol Carole King,
is corraíonn mo chroí
i dtreo na fuinneoige
le taitneamh a bhaint as an spéir ghormghlas.
Fáiltím roimh chiaróg na mbeannacht
a thuirlingíonn go réidh
ar an leac –
comhartha go bhfuil an geimhreadh
ag druidim chun críche;
fianaise
nach mbeidh an sneachta ina shlaodanna
ar thalamh na cathrach seo
a thuilleadh.

Ruth Quinlan

## The Feeding of an Irishwoman in Kuala Lumpur

It was a city wrapped in palm leaves
baked in the oven of the tropics,
and I was a fish, thrown gasping
from the Atlantic Ocean
to flounder in the South China Sea.

I escaped to the spices of covered alleyways
between the monoliths of malls,
to abandoned temples where nature
battled concrete and won
in increments of flowers.

I learned to wander through clouds
of steaming tea and hanging bags
of guava juice, to sit on plastic chairs
and slurp noodles, to scoop out parcels
of pandan leaves for scented rice,
to tear flaking rounds of *roti canai*,
dunk them in the earthiness of dahl.

I still sometimes lie awake
in a room unsoaked by jasmine,
unlit by monsoon lightning,
and wonder if my hungry shadow has escaped
to hunch again over a dark bowl of *bak kut teh*,
or beg a hawker auntie to cool my heated tongue
with just the smallest shaving of sweetened *ais kacang*.

*Roti canai*: Indian flatbread
*Bak kut teh*: A pork rib dish served in broth and infused with herbs
*Ais kacang*: A dessert generally made of shaved ice, red beans, condensed milk and syrup

Leeanne Quinn

## First Part of the Night

Days were plain sailing, sun up, sun down
moon over the – I was beginning to recognise
time, turning the calendar every evening.
Lifting the blinds at night so I could lower them
in the morning. It was already past June
when I began living in opposites.
Not wanting to appear idle, I began
to walk with purpose. Noticing some
repetitions, like the flower stand
at the gates of the park, how flowers
must always have been sold there.
The same woman with her dog
and a very particular phrase, what was it
she was trying to tell him?
I passed the old river, and the carp.
I followed them as far as the canal.
There were boats setting out – they had to
start from somewhere, the way things
in chronological order must start
at the beginning, something I was sure
I was beginning to understand.

Liz Quirke

## Here I am Broken into Small Acts

objects, props with no permanence
correlatively unobjective & TS Eliot
& Keats can get the hell away from me
& the small moveable items I throw
on the table for your comfort
for your singular use till I am as useless
as a bare curtain pole in this spare edifice
where neglect & cold sent a split up
through the woodwork & I'm wondering
am I ornament or vacancy & I can't tell
if my smashed body spells profit
or loss in the small columns & margins
where the notes collect in arbitrary scrawls
that mean nothing out of the context
of my mind when you're not reading
& all I am is language in a nightmare
where my mouth fills with blood & I know
that teeth work only when exposed
so let's chew the fat, masticate
turn your face away while bone holds its own
when sinew & nerve work silent
as a sepulchre, buried below layers of dust
& dead skin skulking on a skirting board
beneath caulk & sanding, the dried
crispness of an unwashed palette knife
& carpentry metaphor dispensed
the years dissolve & now I'm bric-a-brac
car boot sale items on a trestle table
by the beach that not even the tide
would take out as it turns, grim detritus
how we try to sell things we don't want
& what is a dead tongue, lifeless in a mouth
veins underneath a puckered blue, grey

& only certain quietnesses arrive like wind
to stir the senses & I'm wheezing
through an oration, letters chipped & fading
like a slowing pulse, words wrecked, wracked
& written on carcass with the hardness
that comes from such misuse, disuse
where sound can pull away from meaning
& the words in my mouth carry each other
away like sand, like water, like everything.

Saoirse Rafferty

## The Day You Died

Heavy breathing
and I'm trying
to get a response.
Can you hear me?
I know you can't see me,
your eyes are closed.
Your hand grabs mine,
squeezes it at the sound of
a familiar soundtrack.
And I cry.

I retell this moment over
to our friends
hoping
validation will make it mean something.
Because you can't use your words and
I need someone to tell me
you can hear me.
I need someone to tell me
you love me.
I know you do but
you can't speak so
I need someone to
tell me before you leave.

Deep breaths.
Chest rising.
Falling.
Starting. Stopping.
Then a little squeal
and I try not to laugh
as it's like a performance
and I want you to wake up

to laugh with me but
you get moved to a wooden box
where people weep and watch
and kiss you.

They hold your cold hand.
There's no movement.
No noise.
They say you look great.

But you're not here.

You can't hold my hand.
You can't laugh.
You're not able to curse,
kick your leg. Pull the door.
Hold a cigarette. Squeeze a ball.

You're not here.

And I don't know
what to do.
I knew you were leaving but
now you're gone and
I am talking about it
like it's a movie I'm watching and
I am so tired of watching it,
of commentating on it.
But I need to be in it.

I can't leave it.
Nobody outside of
the movie will ever understand it

Because you're not here
and I don't want to be either.

Anne Rath

## WON'T YOU CELEBRATE WITH ME
*after Lucille Clifton*

the push on the pause button
the world's spinning top
slowly tipping
into freefall
the north star's axis
aligning clear skies
and birds singing
while the daily death toll
shifts the planet,
the world grinding down.
No hurry to the invisible prize.
See my walk is slow
a cane, my new divining rod,
the eye's gaze cast upwards.

The profit lords are silent
their cyclopes' eyes no longer blind.
Old assignments are handed back.
Ledgers have been ritually burned.
Funeral corteges march
with military precision
to all compass points.
Moonlight still streams the rain,
tapping a new salsa on tin roofs.
Humans, together now
wandering foreign lands
sitting and dreaming
the cherry blossom into spring.

Nell Regan

## School Visit, Gaza

Open like a pair of wings, the 3D model
of the lungs sits in the centre of the room.
15 year old girls angle phones, fizz
and glow about the visitors. I recall
hard-backed science copies, blank
on one side for diagrams we'd label;
trachea, bronchus, bronchiole all branching
out to the alveolus, tiny sacs, sites

of gas exchange. Breathing in, breathing out.
Did we know we were phosphorescent
back then?
        The young women's names
now a list on an empty page.
                                 .

After the selfies a journalist had asked
one student where she saw herself
in the future. She burst into tears.
And the school? Grey dust caught
in the lungs of those who pass by.

Mary Ringland

FOLD

The caravan rests on bricks on sand in a fold
with a headland behind. Mum gone a year, Dad back
home. Donegal for three days with beach and lough
mine, patched canoes sprawl on the grass, a swimsuit
on the line stiff with brine and marram grass wave
unsettled by a rising tide. With a boat and fisherman

in sight I shake sand from the wool mantle
lying in a suntrap out the back. Hope folds
of a tame sea as white-lip-cusps of waves
mount, but bored by the splayed paperback,
its spine split, I tug at the salt swimsuit,
rinse it in the water butt, unclip my locket,

slip it into the van, tuck each lock
of hair under my cap, watch a man
tighten guy ropes by his tent to suit
a pending storm – wind to be threefold
– watch me. The water bites, lie flat on my back
held by the sea, till the man, ropes taut, waves.

I splutter, swallow, tread water, a wave
of unease swells. The van is unlocked
keys in the door, no one has my back.
Scan the hillside for the figure of a woman,
the boat's close, I bob up, shout hello, fold
my arms across my chest, pulling my swimsuit

both higher and lower; it was chosen to suit
covering lengths of the pool. The sun unwavering
in its glare, I step out of his sightline in a dune's fold,
sand claws my soles, spits up my shin. Then in, lock

the door, pull blinds, sink out of sight, the man
is whistling, rattles the handle and I lean back

against the door, will each vertebra of my backbone
to weigh more, will the old farmer in his brown suit
to dander by. The man circles the van. The fisherman
calls up closer than before do I want mackerel. The waves
have brought him in early. I stand. Wait till the lock
is abandoned, open a window, shout back. Fold.

Fold like prey under the mantle of an eagle,
on the back foot,
a backward glance always, the folds of my skin,
my birthday suit
in lockdown, unwavering modesty, memory round
my neck a weighted locket.

Connie Roberts

## Mrs Coady's Turnips
*i.m. foster parents Mr & Mrs Coady*

She's holding the frying pan in mid-air
like a sacrificial lamb, before
pouring the golden grease from the chops
over the turnips.

*Lord, I need Mrs Coady's turnips right now.*

Eiderdowned and tucked in, Maisie
sucking her thumb and twirling a ringlet
with her finger, he's leaning over the bed,
kissing our foreheads.

*Lord, I need Mr Coady's kisses right now.*

I'm 10, in a field with indolent sheep,
chewing, chewing, chewing their cud,
posing for a photograph, bellbottomed,
smug in a self-hug.

*Lord, I need that girl's confidence right now.*

Thatched and pebble-dashed, potted geraniums
in lace-curtained windows. Inside, two girls
bathing at the wooden washstand, pouring
water from a jug.

*Lord, I need those morning ablutions right now.*

Fields furrowed, butter churned, we're on our knees
by the hearth reciting the rosary.
After the prayers: the pantomimes and poems,
curtseys and applause.

*Lord, I need those simple mysteries right now.*

I need those simple mysteries;
I need those morning ablutions;
I need that girl's confidence;
I need Mr Coady's kisses;
And, Lord, Lord, I need Mrs Coady's
tender lamb chops and humble turnips.

Moya Roddy

## AN BHFUIL CEAD AGAM

On the dot of eleven we'd be marched to the *seomra folctha*
then back to our desks –
otherwise you had to put up your hand,
say the shaming words:
*An bhfuil cead agam dul amach?*
I'd always wait until I was bursting
until my hand shot up of its own accord,
then mumble, embarrassed at everyone knowing
I was about to pee my pants.

Like most kids in my class I hated Irish,
saw no reason for a dead language –
the preserve of culchies in the West of Ireland,
harping back to stuff long forgotten.
We never spoke it or even talked out loud –
*An bhfuil cead agam dul amach* the only exception.

If only I'd known it didn't mean
*Can I go to the toilet?* but *Can I go out?*
I'd have been out the main door like a shot,
through the front gate, heading for mountains
glimpsed from the classroom but never set foot on.
Far from bogging me down, Irish would have opened
up another world – those mountains a gateway
to a vast alluvial plain dotted with cairns,
dolmens, ring forts; peopled with bards,
ancient kings and queens, druids –
heroes and heroines, escaping lovers;
forebears speaking our own language,
*scéalta* old as the hills.

Orna Ross

## Lost and Found

*Her name? Her name is Generose,*
*Watch now how her story flows*

through the sounds of war anew,
our ruler coming out to say:
'Bombs! Again! Away!' Through
minions mincing with faux regret
at what we need to do, and why
'And yet ... but yet ...'
the evil ones must die,
through the soldiers jumping to,
through me, and my kind,
left bereft behind, nowhere to be
except here, hoping to woo
a person like you.

Come with me.
I need us to get to a place far
from here, where four or five million ...?
No. Let me begin again ...
Let me start here. Today.
Clearing my house. 'And not before time!'
is what my mother would have said
if she'd seen it. I was making two piles
– to hold or to go? – when I found it:
the book. Lying open, face down,
waiting for me to return.

I shrugged off the me who likes to think
she can think herself safe,
and picked it back up where I'd stopped.
And dropped down again into that wood
where four million people once died.

(Or was it five?). Yes, genocide.

*One mother's name was Generose,*
*see now how her story goes.*

When they'd hear the trucks of the killers
roar in, the villagers would grab the hands
of their children and flee to the trees.
At night, they'd lie down on dead leaves,
knuckling dirt into dreams.
One day Generose and her family
were too slow to go. The soldiers
came in with machete and gun,
hacked her husband to death, then
made her climb up to lie down
on her own kitchen table,
in front of her daughter and son.

'We're hungry,' they said
as they cut off her leg and sliced it
into six pieces, and fried
them up in her own pan.

*Yes, name her name, it's Generose.*
*Listen. Listen to how it goes.*

They ordered her children to partake.
The boy knew how to refuse
and was shot on the spot. The girl,
in terror, attempted to try. I ask you:
can you imagine? Not the family
so much as those soldiers,
the teaching it took to create them.
(Where this happened was already famed
for kings who came from afar to take
what they would. What one liked
to take was the hands of the men

he'd enslaved, the ones who had failed
to bring in their quota of crop.
And chop them off).

Consumed by the sight of the girl
trying to force her mother
as meat through her mouth, the men
somehow allowed Generose down
from the table to crawl from the house.

And so, somehow, she survived.
And so, she has heard, did her daughter.
And so she believes that some day
she'll see her again. And she works
every which way for that day.

Why tell you all this?
May I reverse the question,
ask you how you feel when you
hear it? That answer is why
the poet wrote her book,
though to regurgitate that leg
made her sick for weeks after.

The same choices call to us all.
Kings will do what kings do,
soldiers too, and if you don't
want to know, I won't keep you.

Let me back to the book that knows
what to own, what should be let go.
Let me wait in the place I've come
to call home, with those
who decline to oppose.

Let me hold to my hope that the girl
might be found, enfolded again,

to recollect their dead men,
that we all might recall
what we've been taught, so well,
to forget: the long-lasting hold,
the cast iron caress of the mother.

*Her name, this time, was Generose,
and that is how the story goes.*

Robyn Rowland

## Voyeur
*Hazel, in memoriam*

I was to meet you again, here.
I had the ticket for your talk, the link
with the past. Ready. Waiting.

Now the steady stream of emails
reminisce on your kindness,
your brilliance.

You were still alone
and I know what that is, both
happy, and unhappy.

There was a sadness in
our bones that always met,
a difficulty about men.

There were years of working
together, when we were too young
to imagine lives ahead.

Years that would take us away,
living in other countries, shimmering
in different directions.

Too many dying friends I have when news
comes of your death by heart infection.
New York. Yes. Quickly.

Now I watch the steady stream of photos,
videos, where your smile wafts out like vapour.
Private loving thoughts,

come to me from your sister, from strangers,
from names I knew in a long past who somehow
pull me now into the loop I don't deserve.

Too long apart. Decades of silence.
I listen to your radio interview, and see you
as we once were, younger, solitary each.

Watching, hearing your other life,
I feel myself a fake friend, included, yet
maybe illegitimate, absent from the recent so.

Knowing that next week, after your plane
had landed here, we would have re-met, and
all the softness of you would open –

the carillon of your surprised laughter,
re-tune our connection – I am bereft. Now
your absence is a star-dark distance deep.

Carol Rumens

## The Call Home

It was the second summer of the war,
the worst news barely news. Kraina FM,
I think it was, got the story of a woman
who'd helped a Russian soldier.

He was crouched in the alley, she said.
She didn't want to see him
but went to him when he called
and asked could he use her phone.

"On byl tsyplonkom", she whispers
over and over, as if
pity and shock can't fly
anywhere but to this newly-
derided tongue, the shell
of all she used to know,
and all she can say of the soldier
who sits on the ground, still waiting
for a connection home,
just across the border –
peering at her between straws
of yellow hair with whatever's
left of his childhood face.

*Kraina FM – Ukrainian radio station*
*'On byl tsyplonkom' ( Russian, my transliteration) – 'He was a baby chick'*

D'or Seifer

## SINAI

Sometimes the wind and excavators play
on girders in the morning;
it sounds like Strauss.

Home was a wall of windows
patterned glass to amplify
rare rains

to be opened
for a glimpse of
shrinking sea

between other windows
where waves of bodies
cry out for a *safe*

that's always on the next wave
after the sunset
descends red.

Home is bifolds
flowing into birdsound
in wild grass

flanked by walls of bookshelves
always another sentence
in my future.

Home is burrowed under
cover of a hum.
When I emerge

halogen bulbs turn
arm hair into rays,
grace in plain sight.

Our pillows –
holy mountains
your voice softer than sand

We whisper our future
in these acts,
in this (memory), our tabernacle
we'll carry with us.

Sree Sen

INVOCATION

the song-tune-sung
in a far-away language,
voices melding into a single ray
of becoming, words i'd un-say
because you deftly caught them
in the fog on the mirror,
wiped it clean of words
i'd perhaps-say
to a feral dog barking
at the ether of my ancestors,
reflected in the flesh-folds
of mothers and grandmothers,
half-remembered music,
never-forgotten anger.

Mary Shannon

## DERELICTION

In the meadow the old place stood –
built with rock and stone
hewn from Donegal's ancient soil
by folk who toiled with brawn,
plumb line and naked eye
to set their clay and stony haul
into walls that stood the test of time.

As friends and loved ones left these shores,
you trawled rough seas
to save, and build on the footprint
of the old –
seven years on a family home,
until one day, out of the blue,
jarring cracks scarred the walls.

The ghost of the Celtic Tiger
haunts the void of dissolving dreams
and crumbling homes.
Unable to pay upfront costs,
it's a bitter pill for the loss of hard-earned cash
on building blocks, mica trashed.

Lorna Shaughnessy

## Un-Tiling the Roof

An old Basque practice was to take a tile from the roof
each time a loved one died, and allow the grief to leave.
Times like this, too many are lost, too many tiles lifted.

We leave buckets in strategic spots but they overflow.
Water streams from the ceiling and pools on the floor
till we don't know where to put ourselves,

push tables into corners and huddle on top
taking turns to hold umbrellas, hold each other,
just holding on till the storm passes.

Katie Sheehan

OFFERING

I ask the earth to recount
the strength of my ancestors, but she is busy

drawing lines
of who will burn and who will drown.
And what am I

to teach my daughters?
The fields around now flooded,
now frozen, now flooding

once again.
Gather your embers,

I tell them. Don't let the fire die out.
Night is cold and long,
but mind not to burn
too much, too fast either,

because darkness keeps returning,
and already enough is aflame.

Róisín Sheehy

## Dúil

Cuisle an cheoil
ag pósadh ár gcumainn
Is sinne an Fheoir
ag líonadh is ag trá.

Ag rince leatsa
a slataire caol
Do lámh ar mo dhrom
ag stiúradh gach casadh.

Súile dorcha
mianach feirmeora
boladh an ithir
Is mise do bhláth
ar tinneall.

Ó bhronnfainn
deoch seirce ort
le caora finiúna ar
dhiúiliciní na habhann.

Go mairfeadh
ár ndúil siar amach
ó úrláir adhmaid
s' sileáil árda
Chathair Osraí.

Jo Slade

## The Leaving 1914
*for my grandfather, John Gibbons*

The old house was quiet that early winter –
I heard her call out the back door

and he emerged from the cold shed,
his cigarette aglow, like a star fragment

and the puff of smoke from his mouth
caught momentarily in reflected light

as if his spirit were leaving him, as if
what he had said earlier were true

that the knock on the window
that startled them, was a bad omen –

and the loneliness she felt was
pre-emptive and she must prepare

to be alone and learn the rhythm
of the small holding they owned.

The hills were purple, shadows
of birds passed over them, dark

silhouettes so clearly drawn
I thought them auguries of war,

like winged warriors.
I saw him hold her to him, his cap in hand,

his backpack on his shoulder
and as he closed the door and stepped

out into the freezing air I heard
her sharp cry – a sound I can't forget

as if she might die there without him.
Later that winter the old house lay buried

under snow, so even he, had he returned,
would not have found her.

Cassie Smith-Christmas

## AN TRAEIN DHEIREANACH GO DTÍ OILEAN ACLA (1937)

Ní raibh an dara rogha ann:
téigh go hAlbain agus na prataí a bhailiú
nó fan anseo gan phingin i do phóca.

Mar sin, d' imigh siad ina sluaite
na cailíní agus na buachaillí
na lámha salacha, fliucha
agus iad ag obair ó dhubh go dubh
an spéir bhán, fholamh.

Ach tháinig an dorchadas
faoi dheireadh an oíche sin
ar an mbealach go Cathair Ceann Tulaich,
iad ina codladh ar fheirm,
cailíní agus buachaillí scartha óna chéile.

Thosaigh an tine.
Bhí na buachaillí glasáilte istigh.

Chuala deirfiúr a deathraicha ag béiceach amach
a hainm arís
agus arís.
Ach ni raibh sí in ann tada a dhéanamh.

Tháinig na coirp ar ais
agus tháinig na sluaite amach,
gach aon duine ag smaoineamh

ar a gcuid cailíní agus buachaillí aca féin
thar lear

ag súil go mbeadh
an saol níos cineálta leo.

Fiona Smith

## Maria Luisa Ferrara

Maria Luisa Ferrara, I stole your name.
It was a terrible liberty to take.
With the loud despair of your people
all about you, to sound your name.

Sacrilege, yet I didn't do it in vain.
I wanted to see you as you were before,
feet planted on your stone floor, sunlit
through the windowpane – hair aflame.

You should have floated on a frozen canal,
ice molten from the hot tears of those bereft.
Heartsore for you, Macaria of the North.
After a good death, a journey of the blessed.

In your picture, you looked lovely all the same.
Immaculate in white for your un-wedding day.
Black would never do for you. I didn't know you.
Maria Luisa Ferrara. I knew that from your name.

Amy Smyth

## Untold Stories

Untold stories keep us awake at night.
Anxious pangs, flushed cheeks
from shame
or stress
or fear
or anticipation.

Untold stories smile a dance
on the side of your lips
at a funeral,
illicit memories of laughter
or love
or friendship.

Untold stories we will never tell,
they tell the most about us.
I long to know
the untold stories
about you
about my mother
about my lover.
I long to know
and will never tell.

Cherry Smyth

## Its Nightly Story

You can share a dream, but the experience
of dreaming can't be shared. You can tell
the story, corrupted by daytime's logic, fantastic
urgencies housed in ordinary words.
There was a cauldron – do I need to say black?
With a conical roof which I didn't question.
Inside was ruffled earth. Among the earth
were three partly-exposed bulbs. They were pinkish.
Does that help? I touched the earth and it
dissolved into grey. I lifted the cauldron outside
and worried that the sun and rain couldn't reach
the bulbs. I would have to tend to them like a
regular baby, with water and light. Was the word
'regular' the dreamer's word? I didn't know what
had been burnt, but can't clear my mind of the ash
of fires of houses bombed and children rooting
for a toy or a mother in the obliteration. There is
no water, no food, nothing left to tend. It is
only hell that is living, telling its nightly story.

Eilis Stanley

A YEAR OF LONGING

Why did you hand
me over
to the ravens?
Pour me into black wool
and stiff collar?
Walk me
into the wasteland
and turn away?

Why did you
leave me
with sleep-walking girls
sat on window ledges
at midnight?
In a dorm where rope
was strung
between beds
to stop strays
wandering?

In this convent classroom
I sat vigilant, eyes
on Sister
with her leather belt
and itching hands
who said
the Jews killed Jesus.
*Oh, yes they did.*
She marched
to the blackboard
sang it out like the bars
of a song she loved.
Dust chalk swept

over the front line
of eight year olds.

I met death there
with the Sisters of Mercy;
corralled into a cell
to kneel
bedside an old nun,
her body
a sepulchre of bones
laid out
on a bare bed,
brown pennies
on her closed lids,
decay like an ivy creeper
filled the room.

I want to tell you
walking
those Longford lanes
in a crocodile
on drawn out
Saturdays and Sundays
when time
was a bank of dark beeches
on a bone straight road
and our feet frozen
on the hard ground
was when
missing cut sinew and bone.
It was a sword that severed
last threads
of knowing where I belonged
because no tree
burning with light
or cluster of primroses
could bring me home.

Dolores Stewart

## As Alt

N'fheadar cad a tharla
ach stop an traein gan chúis, gan údar,

I bhfad ó bhaile

an lucht taistil fágtha ina chónaí ann
gan chead imeachta acu ná eile –

ag luí isteach ar neamhní
agus go breá bog leis

mian an amadáin iontu,
iad lánsásta chun mór a dhéanamh

leis an rud gan chomhartha gan chruth
ina sheasamh rompu ar an ardán.

Tá na cártaí amuigh.
Níl fágtha dúinn
                      ach fanacht.

Sarah Strong

### The Female Organs of the Crocus

are used for making saffron
which becomes bitter
when cooked unkind:

warm the reddish threads,
crush with a pestle,
heat some milk.

Use spice from Galicia
where delicate hands
pat corms at the time

of quickening:
three crucial days
to gather golden filaments.

Lila Stuart

AS THEY WERE

There they are
on their wedding day
at the turn of the stairs –
a wonder for children
and grandchildren alike.

My father poised on the end
of a high stool
matches my mother in height.
The sheen on his shoes in
competition with the shine
on its barley-sugar legs.
His wedding suit, his Sunday
suit for many years.

A side-face pose for my father –
my mother faced the world full on
as she did the care of thirteen children,
more years a widow than a wife.

No public hugs and kisses,
his right hand brushes hers;
expressions open and expectant.
No bartering of dowry
nor gathering of debt –
just a wedding breakfast
in her mother's home –
an afternoon honeymoon
in Bangor.

Anne Tannam

## Ode to a First Grandchild

Last year, no him, without even a notion
of his squishy himness, we went about our weeks
and hours, laps empty, arms emptier, playing ourselves
without him, in the film of ourselves without so much
as a thought of him, oblivious to a starstruck future
featuring him in our arms and oh, the curve-soft,
weight-warmth of his spectacular breathing in
and outness.

No thought of him until once upon a harvest moon
a call to say we have news: a test, some pee,
a blue line and it's very, very much far too early,
not even five weeks but how happy, their voices
happy shaky, how happy we are, and yes,
if everything goes well (if nothing goes wrong,
if nothing goes wrong), a date in the middle of June.

How can it be when before,
no thought, no notion and now?

The waiting. The telling tale of each appointment.
Early on, the boy of him revealed, his borrowed name
practiced on the tongue, whispered to the twelve week
black and white of him. Each every week the growing
him of him a fruit or garden vegetable: lentil, kumquat,
sheaf of corn, aubergine, coconut ...
Oh, the week after waiting week until watermelon.

Couldn't wait to meet him, raced head first into June,
calling and calling his name until our screens lit up
with the first, the *morning has broken*
*like the first morning* sight of him, skin to skin,
in the arms of, on the breast of his mint-new mother,

skin to skin, in the arms of, rooting for the nipple of his mint-new father.

*Blackbird has spoken, like the first bird*

The here of him
        The snuffling of him
The stretching of him
        The sweet sung hymn of him
The praise each day of him
        sun rising over Andalusian hills
sun going down across Dublin Bay.

Lynda Tavakoli

## I Couldn't Save Any of You
*i.m. Dee, Susan, Mary and Clare*

Well, girls. It's taken a while.
All those years afloat in absence
with two decades or more
shadowing your leavetaking.
How we loved each other –
friends, women, wives
of men we knew we'd leave behind,
the five of us a strange
cohesion of spirit communed
by illnesses of chance.

In your final days
I visited you one by one,
ticking death off some macabre list,
selfishly hoping not to be
the one who's left behind.
Yet here I am – those guilty years
unclamped by the passing of time
and the knowing
I can only ever save you
in my dreams.

Alice Taylor

## The Cobweb of Old Age

Dear gentle soul
do not think
    you are a burden
  in your love.
      You conceived them
    and wove them
  into the fabric
of your life
  giving to them
    all your strength.
      The tide has turned.
        They are the strong
    and you have your
    delicate threads
      caught in the cobweb
that is old age.
    They would wrap
      you in their strength.
  Let them now
    because you can.
  Give them much
of gentleness
  and the wisdom
of your time.

Lisa C Taylor

## At the Seven Sisters' Café

Her tattoo might derail
a corporate job
but she wasn't that kind of beauty,
her face a flowering dogwood tree.

Like rocks I climb over
to get to the solitary part of the beach,
a place without Adirondack chairs
or brightly-coloured towels,
she was a pause
where the soprano takes a breath
before finishing the aria.

The tiny scattering
of stars and Saturn
behind her left ear,
a carelessness

that made me wonder
about love
and who might offer excuses
to linger here,
order another espresso.

I got to thinking about
beauty's brevity and resilience,
the face of the ninety-year-old
in a Greek fishing cap,
the curly-haired child
rolling a ball in the park.

Beauty is unexpected,
a soundless reverence,

like blossoms, a chorus, the mix
of cream and teal on canvas,

everyday moments
that may resemble
a planet with rings around it

and seven tiny stars.

Gráinne Tobin

## Des Res

From my window seat on the train that chugs
over the Boyne on the Drogheda viaduct,
I can nearly smell the estuary's threat
of rot in spongy lintels, requiring maintenance,
damp smudges round back doors
where ghosts put out the rubbish
and the slate roofs need patching.

A single street of stone, two up, two down,
terraces right-angled to the river,
and behind the back yards, a rough field,
cypresses in a line of pluming spears
and silos, towers ranked in faded blue,
filled up from boats coming in on the tides,
registered in Belize, nothing shiny about them.

Perhaps I'd have some peace there,
in this textbook edgeland, still ungentrified,
convenient for the backwaters of battles,
the valley of monuments. But the train
is running on time past my parallel solo career
in the grey house second from the end.
Maybe I'd have had a nameplate for the door,
lettered *Innisfree*, and at low tide I'd have seen
the curlews and the oyster-catchers pause
to pick their high-heeled way along the shore.

Csilla Toldy

## Photo on the Brick Wall

This photo is imagined. A life-sized b&w of Patti Smith on the mouldy brick wall of a building soon to be demolished. She is tall, thin, vulnerable and androgynous. She half-turns to you, half to some other person as if she were standing on a turntable, like an Axis Mundi, the pivot.

The girl who sees this image for the first time thinks that the owner of the place, the man who hung this poster on the wall, is a magician. She does not know that he is just a journalist working for a Manchester newspaper and that he had bargained over a beer for the poster with a concert promoter for a mention in an article, in a bar, somewhere in Manhattan. The girl is amazed and creates an illusion of the journalist for herself.

She is not aware of it yet, but this is the moment she falls in love.

Shelley Tracey

## Making a Mark

i

in the forest

no mirrors
no echoes

footfall leaves no imprint
on unstable ground

bats colliding
over treetops

random scatterings
of needles

the only path right through
has not been found

ii

old cans of paint
in an abandoned house

the risk of forcing rusted lids
to find the colours dimmed

these roughcast walls
forever unadorned

the doors are absences
the windows crusted shut

iii

my father's drawing board
after his funeral –
a fissured set square,
broken pencils,
some plans with shaky lines,
his signature smudged
past recognition

Jessica Traynor

## During the Genocide

I am a bad, impatient mother.
I shout at my kids, push them away,
because every night when I dream
I'm in a school where soldiers
have come to kill the children.
I ask them two things:
to wait until I have them all in my arms
and to kill them before me
so they won't be left alone.
It helps me to feel numb,
like when as a child
I'd swim in the North Sea
and the heat in my blood
would fizzle out until
I couldn't feel my arms and legs –
small soul bobbing in space.
But now the feeling won't
stop its clinging, pushing
desperate fingers into my body,
till with the first shots,
the membrane tears
and all that's left
is the hope that death
is a step out of cold water
into spring air.

Jean Tuomey

## Freedom near Café Branquinto

The café thrums
as Carlos claps his hands,
a conductor gathering his choir;
the staff serve in tempo.

Metres away strangers stretch on sun loungers,
dream into the sea. Nobody asks names
or place of birth, as holidaymakers
choose their spot, set up camp for the day.

It's further out that holds my gaze –
two rugged rocks create a sea cave,
endless waves crash, timeless in their rhythm,
swimmers dive and rise,

and a child runs along the shoreline,
sings to herself and kicks up spray.

Mary Turley-McGrath

## Sealed

She knew
it was time to lock the shutters
revel in the silence of the room
hear the wind's staccato breath
in tall chimneys dart in and out
on the midday heat that oozed
along the old hall and stairway
to the red carpeted corridor.

There was birdsong of course
blue tits and great tits flirting
at feeders on the metal stairs
and hidden birds in tall trees
behind six grey stone houses
with dark green balconies.

One day she wrote to you:
*don't forget to change the flowers*
*on the kitchen table,*
the scent of gauzy tulips
was still in her head.

Niamh Twomey

## Egg Money

I packed a bag with cheese sandwiches cut
into triangles, spare knickers, socks.
I sewed change into the seam of my skirt.

I filled a flask with boiled water
for howling nights, tea, disinfection.
A cooking pot, an axe.

In the end I left without it, no time
to go back. I was busy slipping through bars
in a cattle gate, running for the woods,

the shelter of firs, nourishment
of rose hips and waxcaps –
all a woman needs in the wild.

Áine Uí Fhoghlú

## Ag Ullmhú Mála don Siopa Carthanais

Amuigh sa chuan tá'n geimhreadh ag cur a mharcshlua
 chun farraige
arís, a lámh ná traochann ag teilgean sobal toinne le
 m'fhuinneog,
lá é seo do chúraimí atá ag bagairt le fada. Fillim na héadaí
 is leagaim

go réidh i mbun an mhála, dearbhaím a dílseacht do
 chreideamh
na hathchúrsála, do shéanadh na ndéithe bréagacha a
 bhagraíodh méar
uirthi as fuinneoga snasta na siopaí nua, dá diúltú dóibh í
 a ligint i gcathú.

Beirim ar bhalcais is brúim lem aghaidh, é chomh bog le
 meall cúir,
chomh sámh le brollach lán-bainne fé cheann linbh.
Análaim, slíocaim.
Ainneoin sciúradh an *Persil non-bio* níl snáithíní an
 gheansaí *fleece* sásta scaoileadh
ar fad lena boladh, nasc fíneálta idir mé is na flaithis.
 Fógraím don mbrón
go bhfuil ár gconradh ídithe, an t-alpaire úd nach eol dó
 ceann scríbe.

Tógaim cnapán páipéir as póca, tháinig slán ó níochán
 dachad céim is léim
a bhfuil fágtha den pheannaireacht álainn reatha ar thréig
 a dhúch
san inneall: bainne, arán, *sweet and sour sauce*. Samhlaím an
 chéad duine
eile a ardóidh an geansaí léi chuig seomra gléasta, an t-
 áthas tobann

a lasfaidh inti nuair a chífidh a scáil. Tagann faobhar ar mo
   chuimhne,

tá na spásanna folmha láimh le bheith líonta, tuigim ná fuil
   sa chumha
ach grá gan dídean, is go bhfuilimid ag druidim lena chéile
   gach bliain
dá mairim, gach gliúc dá dtugaim orm féin is mé ag góilt
thar fhuinneog glacann sí coiscéim amháin eile im threo.

Carmel Uí Cheallaigh

## Marthanóirí

### 1

Teannaim mo dhorn, do shúile cráite
Fáiscim mo lámha, paidreacha ráite
Ní féidir linn dul siar faraor
Dár saol roimh d'ionsaí scáfar géar

### 2

Ón oíche chinniúnach sin tá gach rud difriúil
Cá bhfuil tú i bhfolach? Mo chailín álainn misniúil
Todhchaí gheal nach bhfuil i ndán dúinn níos mó
ina ionad sin imní agus dúlagar mar do stró

### 3

Toisc go gcoinníonn tú a rún
Seachnaíonn sé blianta fada sa phríosún
Cailleadh na blianta tábhachtacha seo go deo
Is ar éigean go bhfuil tú beo

### 4

Ach níl deireadh caillte fós
Is cuma cad iad na fadhbanna atá romhainn
Sáróimid le chéile iad
Mo shaol, mo chroí, mo stóirín.

Máire Uí Ráinne

## UACHT AN UAFÁIS

Crá croí a bheith ag breathnú ort
a bhuachaill bhig mo chroí
Is tú tógthaí de do bháireachaí
ag cogadh is fuath an tsaoil.

Scéin an uafáis i do shúile
Do bhaile ina mhísc
Is tú i do sheasamh ansiúd i d'aonar
Is do mhuintir sínte i gcill.

Tá uacht an uafáis ag borradh ionat
Tá do shoineantacht ar lár
Níl aon chinnteacht agat ná dóchas
Seachas marú, sléacht is ár.

Is iomaí leanbh mar thú
Scaipthe i ngach ceard
Is gurb é do scolaíocht feasta
Gunna a bheith i do láimh.

Ní buan í an daonnacht i gcroí an duine
Nuair a théanns an ghráin thar fóir
Is nuair a thaganns rabharta an díoltais
Níl brí le moráltacht, ceart ná cóir.

Morgan L. Ventura

UNLOCK YOUR TRAUMA

Everyone loves a locked room mystery. Inside we might find passages to nowhere, poisoned artefacts, forgotten notes. We might after all be locked rooms in uneasy houses, memory palaces where the urge to remember is the same as the urge to forget. I do not know who locks away the trauma, all I know is it is not buried because I have dug in this room & this room & the other so many times before. In how many ways do we become like that which we'd rather not? In what ways are we all like the universe folding in on itself, sea anemones bursting from within, lashing out at whomever crosses our path or dare enters our room. If I am like a lock, because the door lies within me, then this means I hide the very force that consumes me. Then it is no secret & where is the key? In Tepoztlán, the doctor points outside the window as I lay on a wooden table, punctured by 27 needles, 27 little furies stoking fireplaces in my rooms. Rusty mountains, like thick hands, rise in celestial petition. They shatter the earth as songbirds whistle. She laments, *The energy here brings everything out. You must unlock your trauma.*

Mia Vance

BIRTHRIGHT
*Where they died, there the road ended / and ends still.*
"That the Science of Cartography is Limited" – Eavan Boland

There is a road
that doesn't show
on any map,

that doesn't go
to anyplace;

follow it to where
it ends, worn down
to skin and bone,

bleeds
into the field.

Follow the wall
that has wandered
away from the flock,

that offers no shelter,
gives no relief;

feel for where
its stones grow thin,
where it buckles

as the fever breaks,
staggers and sinks
to its knees.

Here it is:
your birthright,

blood and bone,
buried.

Prise it up
and build it
hand by hand,

stone by hungry
stone.

Monica Whelan

SEPTEMBER

| | |
|---|---|
| S | Silent shadow of death draws close as the autumn leaves fall |
| E | Embers of life dying grow stronger, your life force fading fast |
| P | Pulse rate slowing and breathing shallow |
| T | Transition has begun, you are between two worlds |
| E | Everyone gathered around your beside |
| M | Morphine injection administered |
| B | Beginning the rapid deterioration, heartbeat dropping |
| E | Exhaling your last breath the monitors indicated your demise |
| R | Rest in peace, your journey on earth is completed |

Grace Wilentz

*from* SNOW CATS AND ME

XI

Days cycle through assimilation, craving, the hunt.
She takes only what she needs but somehow
her energy is more finite. It's as if she wakes

heavier than the day before, slowed by some
invisible force. She sleeps around the lip of the lake
where all the beasts come to heal their wounds

in the sweet waters, still and calm and mirror smooth.
She's drawn to drink, and this night to slip
into the black, swim steadily to the far shore.

Máiríde Woods

*ROBES D'ANTAN*
*for my sister, Eithne*

In the nursing home our talk turns
to garments past, those lolloping dresses
we fell in love with in the seventies,
the way they swirled around
our bare legs as we scoured
the Dandelion on cloudless Saturdays;
authentic cream lace drooping
onto sprigged cotton that sported
lush crimson and carmine, indigo and plum.
Along the way came effervescent meetings
with friends, hugs and hands
slung over shoulders,
our tooled leather bags swinging
as we glided from stall to stall.

When you migrated from Belfast
you wore an Indian scarf and curly Afghan coat
unearthed off Botanic Avenue.
Even my husband sported flares
and a wide pink tie as he wheeled
our bright hand-crafted babies.

Oh we were poor but splendid then,
flamingos in flying hues of scarlet and maroon
with here and there black velvet! Could
such diva dresses have survived somewhere
– brighter and tougher than we were? Today
I feel so muted in my pastels.
Where are the frocks of yesteryear?

N.K. Woods

## Never Call a Man

Sir, even if it means detention
weather the scowls and the sarcasm
the *look who thinks she's special*
the titters from the class
the burning cheeks
the corner

never call a man
Bastard, unless he opens with Sweet Tits, Doll or Bitch

never call a man
Boss, or anything but his name
and only answer to your own –
if Girl finds your ear, turn your back
if fingers snap, walk right out
if tempers rise, do not fly
or laugh
or cry

never call a man
Lord – but Love is good, and Friend and Mate and Mine

Máire Dinny Wren

## Caoineadh Shinéad

Cheol tú chomh binn leis an smólach,
rinne tú ologán ar nós bean chaointe
is gáir mhairgní chomh géar le bean sí.

Bhí tú glórach mar urlabhraí
ar chearta na mban is na cosmhuintire.

Bhí comóradh mór leat an lá
a thriall do thórramh síos cladach Bhré,
do chairde, do chomharsain is do lucht leanúna
ag fágáil slán leat le goltraí is le geantraí.

Codlaigh go sámh, a chuaichín ceolmhar,
seinnfidh na héanacha do shuantraí.
Do shéad samhail ní bhfaighfear go brách na breithe.

Ba thú banlaoch ár linne
is iníon ionúin Éireann.

Amy Louise Wyatt

PERIMENOPAUSE

The dog does not recognise her reflection
in the mirror.

*Look girl, look girl,* I cry. *It's you!*

She checks behind the glass propped on the bedroom floor,
finds only a gap
between the creature and the wall.

Stares again, jumps and jolts,
cocks her head,
lets her long tongue loll.

*Barks*. Once. *Barks*, once more
while the creature only mouths a *bark*,
– a silent sound.

*Girl that's you!* I egg her on, encourage her – to no avail.

Read up about it.

How everyday it is for a woman to never know
herself
or her changing place in the world,
really.

Edna O'Brien
Mansion House, Dublin
2019

Edna O'Brien

## Writer's Block

Green braid
Hems the shore
Lilac, lavender and Prussian blue
Toss in the billows:
Until a downpour
Turns the whole sky pewter
Water and sky –
No light
No words
The blank page

*Afterword:*
# A KNIFE EDGE UNDER THE TOES

Nuala O'Connor

I often wonder when we say the phrase 'women's poetry' why we do that at all – why not just say 'poetry', as we do for male poets? I go back and forth, then, on ideas around corralling and sidelining, trumpeting and honouring, objectivity versus subjectivity. But I always land, in the end, on the importance of platforming women's writing as an entity, because our patriarchal world makes it necessary to do that. Women's voices, experiences, viewpoints, education, opportunities and more continue to be sidelined and quashed. Sad and tiresome as it is, women are still, in the twenty-first century, fighting this old, old battle for parity of esteem, for equality. Our sisters living under despots and strict regimes are, naturally, in the worst positions of all – their lives are fraught and, often, impossible. But, in the realm we're considering here – literature – women's work still does not receive the same energy, respect, and priority that is given to men's work in the wider literary world. Of course, strides *have* been made but, in the end, male writers – men – are still considered to be more important, more authoritative, and to be worth more. It is exhausting.

Writing in the *LRB*, Anne Enright said:

> I have often admired the ease with which men praise books by other men, and envied, slightly, the way they sometimes got admired in their turn. This spiral of male affection twists up through our cultural life, lifting male confidence and reputation as it goes.

She further says that if you complain about gender imbalance, you are told that other people have it worse. She calls it 'a pain competition' and says it is one that women can't win. But still, because women's inner power rarely dies, us women writers fight on and, here we are again, joyfully and exuberantly celebrating women's work with *Washing Windows V*, showcasing over three hundred poems by Irish women writers, exerting their right to write, and to be heard. With these poems, the reader is invited to come to the poetic table and gorge themselves; to consume the well-cogitated reflections and insights of these poets as their own. And it is a joyful banquet.

Writer David Collard says when he reads poetry, he 'disappears as a person and emerges as a reader'. He also posits that gender disappears, because the best writing transcends gender divisions. I love this notion of a non-gendered reading, that by entering a poem we become nothing but a being, one intent on finding meaning and pleasure in the words of another, regardless of how they self-identify. Do all readers approach work this way? I'm inclined to think they do not; certain readers, it seems, can't help but carry biases with them. Some readers may never even arrive at the pages of women, in fact; I certainly have met men who (unapologetically) state that they do not read women, as a matter of course.

We, as readers, are mutable – we alter, evolve, age, suffer, feel joy. We are a different reader with every poem we read because there is nothing as certain as change. I don't mind who has written work when it is good, but I find my own reading is often influenced by mood or energy levels, or even geographical location. I think ageing and, hopefully, maturity makes me a more considerate, compassionate reader too. The poem, of course, always remains the same but people alter, and things we may have failed to locate in a poem we've previously digested can become brilliantly apparent on re-reading. Personally, I often like – *love* – a poem more on the second, seventh, or fiftieth read.

Poet Abigail Parry says that the more she likes a particular poem, the more she's inclined to 'usher the author gently out of the picture', so that they cannot show her the text's workings, or suggest how she might like to read it. I'm inclined to agree, I want to come to a poem fresh, to find what I find, to re-read its stanzas to help my understanding, or to 'feel' the poem again, to recapture and deepen an effect it had on me in the past. *What was the poet saying to me before?* I wonder. *What does she say to me now?* Several poems in this anthology begged immediate re-reading; others I will re-visit often, to unpick their layers and see what I make of what I can find. One such poem is Nathalie Anderson's 'Magpies', an insightful, multi-stratified look at nuns, at austerity, at being an alien in someone else's home, at looking ahead to unknown futures. It is a deft and deep poem, monochrome, subtle, and beautifully formed. I know it is one that will draw me back and back. Having ushered the poet gently away, when I like a poem instantly, I am also drawn to the poet, so I want to beckon them back to my side, because I want to know more – who is the person who wrote this? Where is she from? What age is she? Can I read more? These are all questions of respect and love, I feel – readers want to dig deep because the wonderful mind that has created a wonderful work is always of interest.

Poet Imtiaz Dharker posits that poetry grows from discomfort. 'Doesn't there need to be a knife edge under the toes?' she asked once on BBC Radio 4. The poets in *Washing Windows V* are no strangers to examining the things that have unsettled them, that have been sharp against the sole and, clearly, the soul. There are elegies and loneliness in these pages; meditations on loss and violence against women; on anti-immigrant ranters, and on our crumbling ecology. Some poems touch on the grief and resignation of being childless; on the complications of failed marriages; there are a remarkable number of poems that meditate on the lives of women in holy orders. Many poems touch on the futile ravages of our current wars, including Sarah Clancy's fine linking of Ireland with Palestine, where the narrator tell us she 'hung a Keffiyeh out for Brigid', and the saint sent her 'most love filled and resilient' magic 'to those picking through the rubble of their lives/in Khan Younis, in Deir al Balah,/in Rafah, in Jabalia, in Beit Hanoun/and Beit Lahaya, and in Gaza City's Shujaiyya/where another poet caught it/and in the face of his own death, defied it and sent the magic skywards'. Powerful stuff.

Ireland-based Ukrainian poet Victoria Melkovska uses a list poem to highlight the ongoing realities of the war in her country, with a litany of unreceived gifts and one final gift that sadly speaks to a bleak future, perhaps for the whole world. Deirdre Devally tackles the war in Ukraine, also, in a stark poem about sexual violence against women, and one woman's horrifying experience. It is a narrative poem, carefully constructed to hold the whole of innocent women's experiences of war crimes. It is also a brave poem, unafraid of highlighting horror.

More locally, some of the poets here directly address the men who are harrying Irish women back into their homes and, potentially, into silence. Louise C Callaghan does it well in her poem dedicated to murdered Irish teacher

Ashling Murphy, where she urges all women to 'use your voice, scream,/for your cries will carry//echo a promise to us forever.'

Poet John Montague said that a poet should not be too tamed, they might in fact 'bite you', and I am all for this wild and courageous bent in poetry. Who will honestly reveal the terrors, absurdities, and exultations of our mad, troubled, lovely world if not the poets and writers? Who can reflect the female experience of living now better than the woman poet?

There are poems of light and of gratitude too, of course – for a beloved Singer sewing machine; for yoga; for middle-aged sedateness, for example, when Monica Corish talks lovingly of being 'sweetly bored' after a lifetime of adventures. Rachael Hegarty has fun with the anthology's title in her poem 'Washing Windows is Out of the Question', relating a situation common among many writers and creatives, no doubt:

> I'm not known for me good housekeeping ...
> washing windows is out of the question –
> it wrecks me head if we wreck spiders' webs.

The reader will find hope and guidance, too, in many of the poems here, including Linda Ibbotson's 'Letting Go' where she provides comfort of sorts with the lines: 'Let the rain wash away sorrow,/the blood of your mistakes./Let the thin light of warmth touch you –/remember nothing is complete ...'

Writer-artist Edward Gorey, in his *Great Simple Theory About Art*, said that art is about one thing '... but is really always about something else'; he further stated that one is pointless without the other '... because if you just have the something it is boring and if you just have the something else it's irritating.' Many of the poems here do this brilliantly, this work that Shelley called the 'vitally metaphorical' business of poetry. Eva Bourke's arresting 'Starlings Over Nimmo's Pier' is ostensibly a paean to

Galway birds that flock and unite marvellously, who move 'fluid black as Indian ink, a lengthening pixellated/shadow above the playing fields, turning/the air dark, contract into a ribbon, thin/as a knife edge, a fluttering necklace ...' The reader finds hope and joy in Bourke's stanzas, but behind them there is also the menace of war and fighter jets, when the birds 'uncoil like a lasso whipped across the sky' to become 'a shower of soot-coloured rain.' Bourke is a powerful writer, weaving Holbein and Mozart into her poem, and taking the reader on mesmerising journeys through the verses.

Mothers and motherhood inevitably loom large in a gathering of female voices. There are moving poems on the emigration of children, among them Marion Clarke's smart, flowing 'Capricorn Child', which takes the reader through the life of a young man heading to Australia, his mother's poignant sense of loss after a lifetime of care and, on her return to his empty bedroom, finding his childhood ABC open at W for wallaby. In Shelley's and Gorey's metric this piece is about empty nesters, but it also deftly sweeps up economics, migration, and the hopelessness felt in a first world country that is still exporting its young.

Hannah Kiely's beautiful poem 'In Which the Mother Needs to Dance', tells the story of a mother who wants to flee to Absaroka, a proposed American state that never was, hoping to escape 'from shattered glass on kitchen floors/ ... from squandered pleading words/from daily application of poverty/from crying children/from her broken promises to them.'

Micheline Egan talks of the sacrifices of Irish foremothers who showed great stout heartedness, grit, and generosity while living modest, straitened lives. The mother in her poem 'en route to her monthly pilgrimage in Knock' would 'crack a hard-boiled sweet between her teeth/so that her three young ones/all had something to suck on.' A poignant act that may be alien to those who lived – and live – in a more comfortable Ireland.

Virgina Keane Brownlow also uses food to conjure memories, via the herb thyme, which calls up her mother, the writer Molly Keane, giving insight into the author's family and home life, through bonding over food. Poems like this add riches to the literary heritage that anthologies like *Washing Windows V* help to cultivate and preserve.

Playfulness and experiment in form is a welcome element in this collection. Often subject matter dictates the shape of a poem, and these poets are not afraid to explore and try out different ways of using line breaks, punctuation, and caesura. Pratibha Castle's employment of forward slashes in her prose poem 'Remembering Kells', is refreshingly strange and it works well with her staccato, ramped-up style: 'thrashed/hedgerows squelched/through swampy fields/squished a frog/*raucous/rowdy*/like marauding rooks.'

Geraldine Mitchell opts for an old form, gracefully employing the careful constraints of the villanelle in 'Lessons from the Clothesline', to examine different ways of living: 'no sign/that we have grasped the fine/distinction between using and abusing our one throw.'

Maeve McKenna experiments to stunning effect in her poem 'Yellow is Not Alive', which contains the memorable image of a finch's open beak being 'a pink purse closing to the sky.' This is the joy of poetry – arresting and challenging the reader with a magical admixture of meaning, language, and form.

Perhaps because of the brevity of social media, directness and ultra plainness in prose – and some poetry – is a growing fashion in contemporary writing but, for me, stylishness with imagery and in phrasing is something to be aimed for, lauded, and savoured. An immersion in someone else's stylistic imaginings remains one of my main reasons for reading; the effort is always worth the payoff. I am such a huge fan of startling metaphors, beautiful imagery, and astonishing similes and, luckily for my taste, figurative phrases are legion in this wonderful anthology. Poet Mark Doty calls metaphor 'an act of inquiry' which I love. This inquiry, plus appropriate adorning, contains what Robert Frost called 'the pleasure of ulteriority' – our previously mentioned art of saying one thing while meaning another. (Surely a very Irish skill?) Writer Marie Rukoski, lamenting bald prose (but it works for poetry too), said: 'Why would one ever be so insane as to ditch a perfectly beautiful metaphor? Cut back, of course, prune if you like, so that the best metaphors are clear and sparkling.' She added that she would 'throw out unread the book that promises no metaphors inside.' Some of my favourite language flourishes in *Washing Windows V* include this gorgeous literary image by Polina Cosgrove:

> The golden eagle in the sky
> unfolds like a modernist novel.

Or how about this ingenious image from Moyra Donaldson's poem 'Where Was I Looking', which may be about illness, or about grief – that the subject matter is not clarified takes nothing from the skill and efficacy of the poem:

> I looked at the tulips, half mad with grief
> in the Hotel Opera, Budapest;
>
> they opened their black throats
> and filled the corridors with absences.

Many of the poets similarly call on natural metaphors, including Emer Fallon who, in her poem 'Gardening with my Mother', fondly remembers a Great Uncle, and how he 'slips from the room like water leaving/a whiff of the Grand Canal in his wake.' Anne-Marie Fyfe recalls pine trees huddling closer to a house 'to brood increasingly over our growing up' and an English cousin who climbs one of the trees, falls, and ends up with 'his arm as an ungainly wishbone.' What a glorious image! Another beauty to delight readers is Anita Gracey's line in her ekphrastic poem 'The Lonely Passion': 'The goldfinch perches on my heart like a bruise.'

And then there's this gorgeousness from Karen J McDonnell, who is reading Joyce's *Ulysses* in a heatwave:

and maybe it's the heat – or I'm overwatered – but
I'm blooming like Greek geraniums
in an old olive oil tin.

Tiegan Johnston in her powerful, moving poem 'Shadow' uses domesticity and lovely imagery to show the life of the good, decent woman Jean McConville, and the home she was so unnecessarily ripped from, when she was abducted and murdered by the Provisional IRA:

And here was love
like a pot of potatoes
singing against the stove
as their water overflows.

Love rushes through these poems – every poem, anyway, is an act of love – but the romantic kind is abundant in Aoife Lyall's gorgeous verses about a husband: 'the head and heart of him/two islands I call home.'

Katie Martin's elegy for a lost love, in 'Letters in Autumn', attempts to re-script and re-kindle old love with words on pages: 'If it was less than love, tell me it came close enough/and you have let your likeness linger in the scene./Mine has stood there so long it has grown roots.'

In a cautionary love poem, 'I'm Not Your Type', Sarah O'Connor urges a lover to open their eyes and appreciate all she has to offer, including her peach of a mind. She points out that her 'heart's truer than truth and stickier than stalagmite/and my heart beats with incontrovertible beauty.'

Incontrovertible beauty, indeed. It is all over these poems.

B'fhéidir nach bhfuil sé cothrom na filí a scríobhann i nGaeilge a scaradh óna ndeirfiúracha a scríobhann i mBéarla. B'fhéidir nach bhfuil ann ach coiréal eile do na filí sin. Ach, chun meas a léiriú dóibh, gach seans go bhfuil sé ceart go leor, faoi na himthosca. Ar aon nós, anseo tá sárthaispeántas sláintiúil, bríomhar de scríbhneoirí Gaeilge againn. Cosúil lena gcomhghleacaithe Béarla, clúdaíonn na filí seo raon leathan ábhar, gach rud ó ghrá go brón, ó fhantaisíocht go miotas. Don léitheoir seo, tá fáilte roimh an díriú ar ábhair imní an lae inniu.

Fiosraíonn Celia de Fréine pribhléid agus bochtaineacht ina dán 'An Fásach'. Áitíonn leanaí ar bhus tréigthe agus iad ag blaiseadh a dtodhchaí. Tá críoch bhrónach, mhídhóchasach leis an dán:

> Sular fhill siad ar an scoil, áit a gcuirfí ina suí ar chúl iad – rófhada leis an gclár dubh a fheiceáil – áit a bhféadfadh an múinteoir neamhaird a thabhairt orthu is a bhféadfadh siadsan a ndíomá a chaomhnú.

Cuireann nia nuabheirthe ionadh ar Sadhbh Moriarty – titeann sí i ngrá leis an leaidín láithreach – ina liric mhilis 'Nia':

> ... do theanga bheag bhideach,
> do lámha luascánacha,
> agus mé féin, dallta i ngrá,
> ag stánadh anuas ort
> go bómánta.

Ina dán 'Comhairle', tugann Julie Breathnach-Banwait rabhadh dá hiníon íogair agus bog i gcoinne a grá nua, ag rá léi go 'sínfeadh sí a croí chuige ar leac óir, go bhféadfadh sé é a roinnt is a dháileadh mar a thogródh sé. Mar sin a bhí sí, ar sí. Ró-oscailte, ró-ghoilliúnach. Seafóideach.' Tógann agus tógann an dán seo, ag ardú go háiteanna níos dorcha agus níos dorcha.

Is machnamh é dán Chaitríona Lane ar éadóchas agus, b'fhéidir, ar bhrón tar éis báis, agus ar nádúr síoraí an dóchais.

Nuair a thiteann an spéir chun talaimh,
Nuair a fhanann an dorchadas ar foluain
Os ár gcionn laistigh, lasmuigh,
Faoi chois, táim sáinnithe.
Sáinnithe sa leaba, sáinnithe i mo cheann,
Sáinnithe.

Ach, le hoscailt 'cúl dorais mo smaointe', tagann solas agus sólás chuici: 'Agus go tobann mar lasc thuisleach,/Caitear drithlí i mo thimpeall. Lastar mo shúile.' Agus anois tá sí in ann áilleacht an domhain a fheiceáil arís.

Scríobhann Ciara Ní É, mar is gnách, dán íogair a chuimsíonn teanga agus grá. Léiríonn cara athruithe ina cuid cainte, ach tá an scéalaí bródúil as na hathruithe ar fad atá tagtha agus í

> ag crónú na hoíche ar chliathán sléibhe/fé sholas gealaí, i mo luí le do thaobh/i mo chluais do bhéal binn go héirí gréine/Tá athrú tagtha ar mo chuid cainte/is sin an chuid is lú de.

Tugann Aifric Mac Aodha dán iontach spéisiúil dúinn, atá cosúil le miotas nó síscéal, ach atá ábhartha inár ndomhan atá ar lasadh faoi láthair; ábhar ábhartha, scanrúil atá anseo. Labhraíonn máthair lena leanbh sa dán, ag rá:

> Más beag a thug sé uaidh, a chroí, níorbh é a fuair a leor.
> Agus is éadrom a ór ag daoi, a chroí, idir dheatach, shop 's deoir.

Tá caoineadh speisialta scríofa ag Máire Dinny Wren do Shinéad O'Connor, file den scoth í féin, dar ndóigh. In íomháineachas taibhseach, cuireann Wren an t-amhránaí i gcomparáid le cuach:

> Codlaigh go sámh, a chuaichín ceolmhar,
> seinnfidh na héanacha do shuantraí.

Le tuilleadh súgartha teanga agus, cé gur féidir dímheas a bheith ar an mBéarlachas, bhí áthas orm dán macarónach Orla Fay – 'Mil na Fianna' – a léamh, inar chuir sí focail Bhéarla áirithe isteach go nádúrtha sa mheascán:

Tá do chroí cosúil leis an conch
fuair mé i óige
ag coinneáil na farraige i mbraighdeanas.
Is lullaby thú.
An cuimhin leat nuair a d'fhág tú do lipstick
ar an pillowcase?

Croí cosúil le conch – nach álainn sin? Tá filíocht na Gaeilge slán sábháilte i lámha na mbanfhilí cúramacha, cumasacha, ceiliúrtha seo.

And the same goes for all of the poets here – these are careful, capable, celebratory writers who are continuing the excellent work of their foremother poets, and paving the way for their poet daughters. No subject is off limits here; there is rage and agony in these pages, and the reader is made well aware of the knife edge under the toes felt by many of these writers, as they make their way through a world that seems to be spiralling backwards. But thankfully, there is also tenderness and hope and love galore in the work. The poets in *Washing Windows V* know that our best course of action is to link arms, surge forward, and write on, knowing that the best, the sanest, and most comforting gift a creator can give herself is the freedom to write.

# Book Highlights, 2000–2025

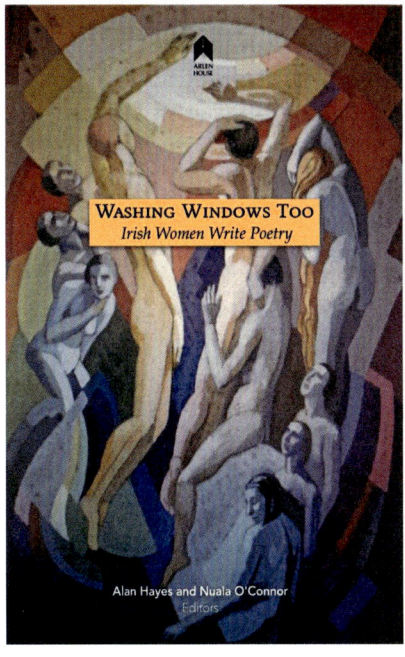

# Washing Windows III
## Irish Women Write Poetry

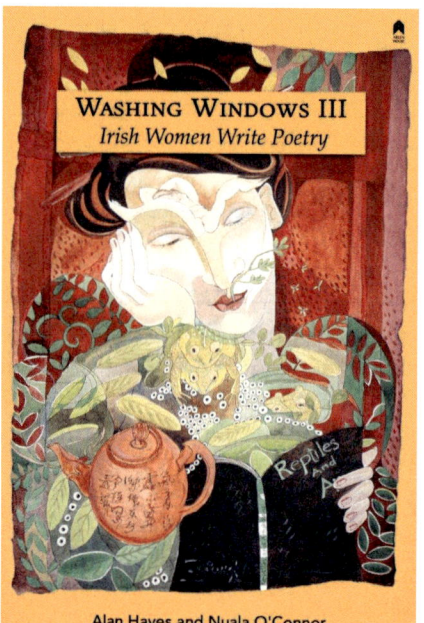

Alan Hayes and Nuala O'Connor
Editors

# Washing Windows IV
## Irish Women Write Poetry

Alan Hayes and Nuala O'Connor
Editors

**ARLEN CLASSIC LITERATURE**

# Maeve Binchy

## Deeply Regretted by ...

Shortlisted
Irish Book Awards 2021

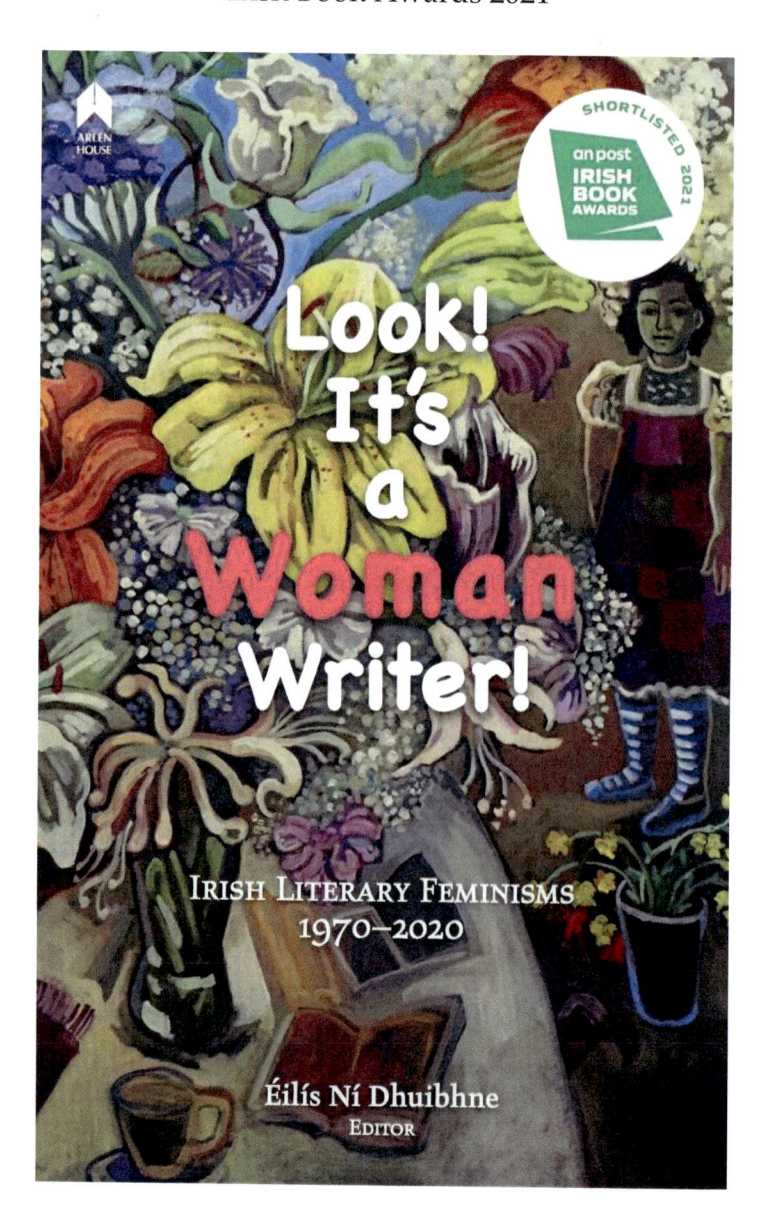

# Look! It's a Woman Writer!

## Irish Literary Feminisms 1970–2020

Éilís Ní Dhuibhne
EDITOR

Shortlisted
Irish Book Awards 2020

Eithne Ní Ghallchobhair
# MÚSCAIL, A GHIORRIA

Ar an ghearrliosta don ghradam
Leabhar Éireannach na Bliana 2020
Shortlisted for an Irish Book Award 2020

# Winner
## ACIS Leabhar Taighde na Bliana

**Úna Ní Fhaircheallaigh agus an Fhís Útóipeach Ghaelach**

Ríona Nic Congáil

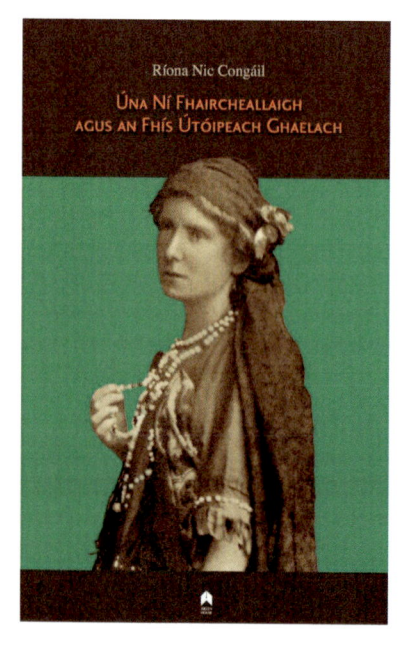

Groundbreaking anthologies
including work by four Booker winners
and an Oscar winner

**The Danger and the Glory**
Irish Authors on the Art of Writing
Hedwig Schwall, Editor

**FIRE**
BRIGID AND THE SACRED FEMININE
Niamh Boyce
Shauna Gilligan
editors

**HER OTHER LANGUAGE**
Northern Irish Women Writers Address Domestic Violence and Abuse
Ruth Carr and Natasha Cuddington, Editors

Celebrating 250 Years of Hodges Figgis

**READING THE FUTURE**
New Writing from Ireland
Alan Hayes, Editor

# Winners of the Patrick Kavanagh Award for Poetry

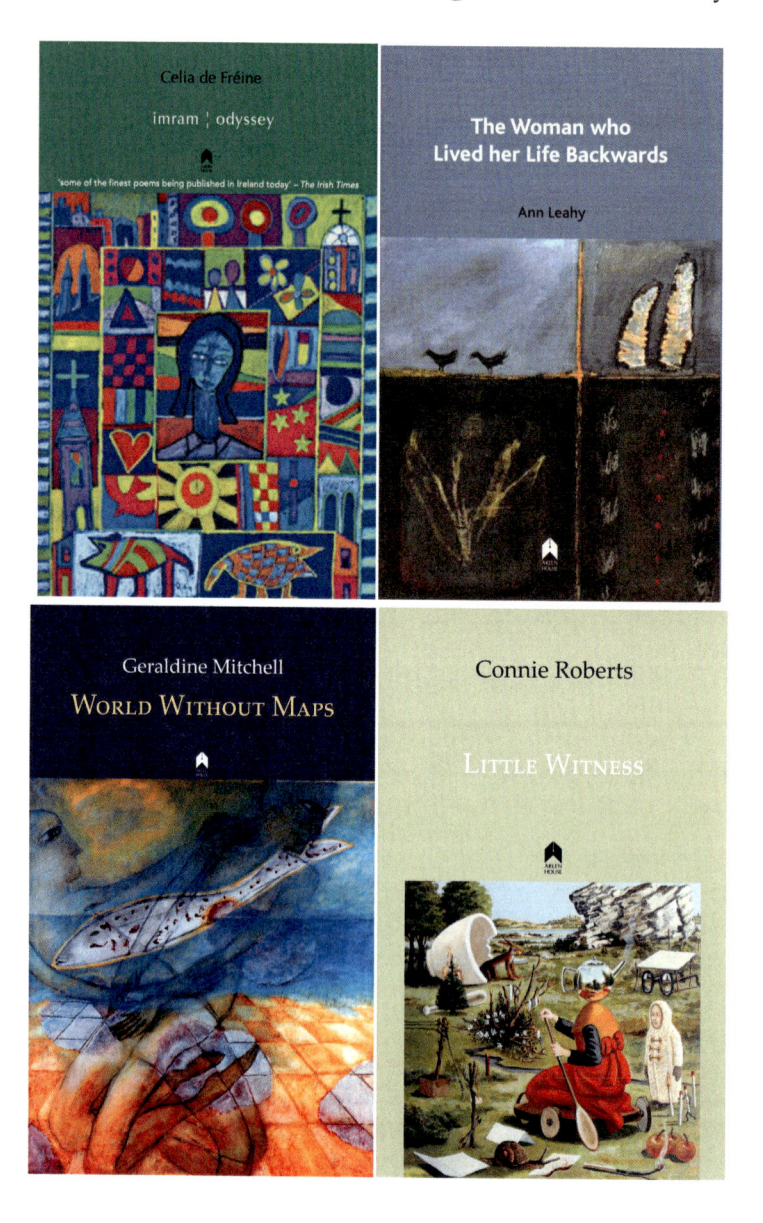

Siobhan Campbell and Nessa O'Mahony
EDITORS

# EAVAN BOLAND: INSIDE HISTORY

**Medbh McGuckian**

# LOVE, THE MAGICIAN

# Pauline Bewick
## 1935–2022

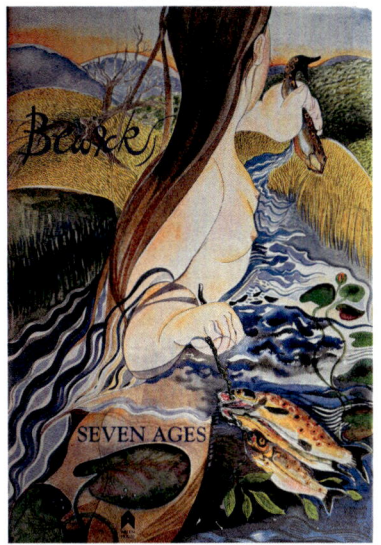

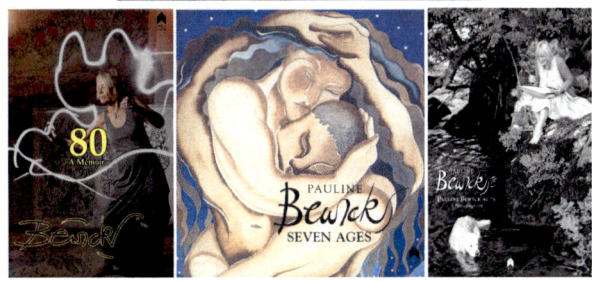

Winner
Francis MacManus Award
Cathal Buí Short Story Prize
Cúirt New Writer Prize

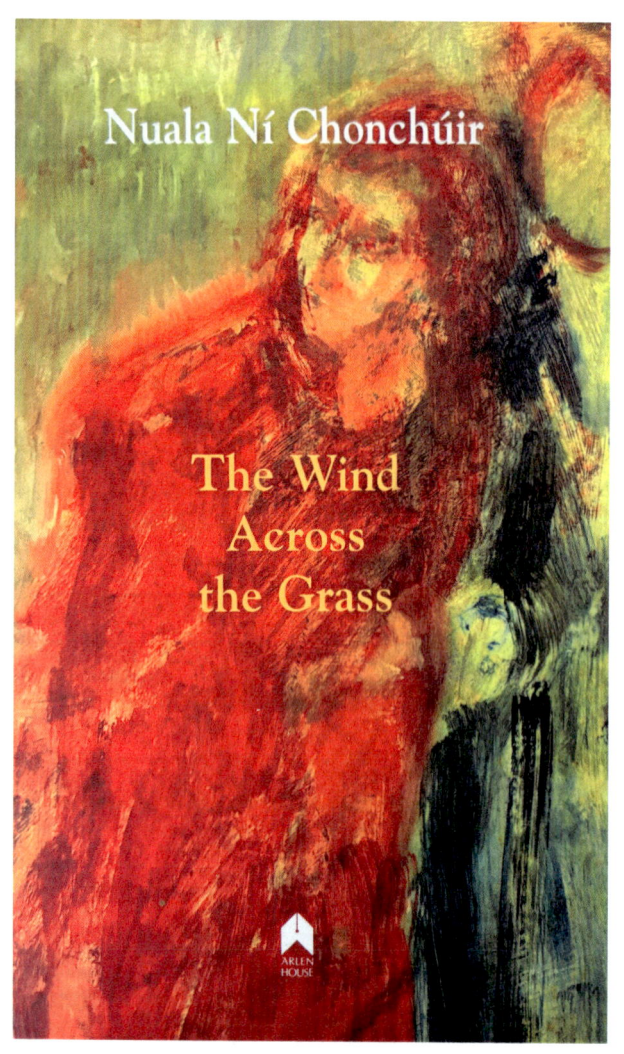

Nuala Ní Chonchúir

The Wind
Across
the Grass

Nuala O'Connor's first fiction collection

Nuala O'Connor
Birdie
Nuala Ní Chonchúir
To The World Of Men, Welcome
Tattoo : Tatú
Nuala Ní Chonchúir
Nuala O'Connor
Menagerie
¡DIVAS!
new irish women's writing
'A Sense of Place'
NUALA NÍ CHONCHÚIR, editor
¡DIVAS!
new irish women's writing
Maureen Boyle
The Work of a Winter
Maureen Boyle
The Work of a Winter
Strabane
Poetry by Maureen Boyle
Maureen Boyle
The Last Spring of the World
Eithne Ní Ghallchobhair
An Craiceann agus a Luach
Eithne Ní Ghallchobhair
An Craiceann agus a Luach
Under Her Skin
Eithne Ní Ghallchobhair
Caithréim agus Tóir
Kate Newmann
Grim
I am a Horse
Kate Newmann
Belongings
Joan Newmann, Kate Newmann
Circling
Dairena Ní Chinnéide
Fé Gheasa | Spellbound
Niamh McBrannan
The Devil Looks After His Own
The Uses of Silk
Gráinne Tobin

Awarded the Gerson Reading
at the University of Conneticut

Geraldine Mills

An Urgency of Stars

## THE WEIGHT OF FEATHERS
**Geraldine Mills**

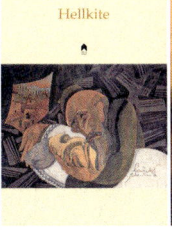

## Hellkite
**Geraldine Mills**

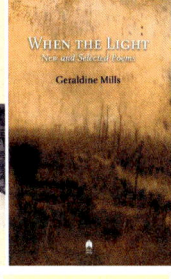

## WHEN THE LIGHT
*New and Selected Poems*
**Geraldine Mills**

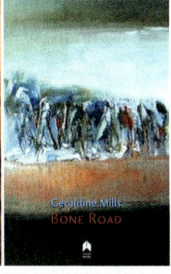

## Geraldine Mills
**BONE ROAD**

## Geraldine Mills
**BONE ROAD**

## The Other Side of Longing
**Geraldine Mills | Lisa C. Taylor**

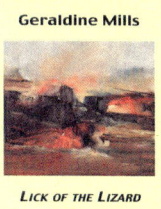

## Geraldine Mills
**LICK OF THE LIZARD**

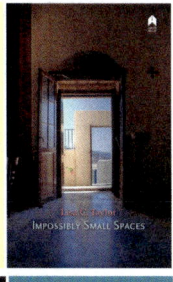

## IMPOSSIBLY SMALL SPACES

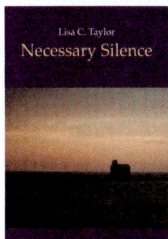

## Lisa C. Taylor
**Necessary Silence**

## Lisa C. Taylor
**GROWING A NEW TAIL**

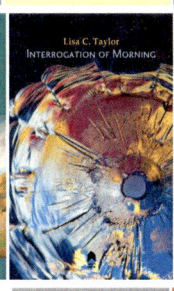

## Lisa C. Taylor
**INTERROGATION OF MORNING**

## Geraldine Mitchell
**MOUNTAINS FOR BREAKFAST**

## Geraldine Mitchell
**MUTE/UNMUTE**

## NAMING LOVE
**Geraldine Mitchell**

## Geraldine Mitchell
**Of Birds and Bones**

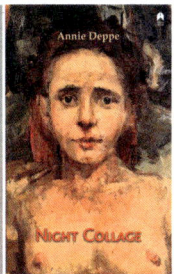

## Annie Deppe
**NIGHT COLLAGE**

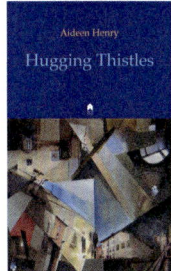

## Aideen Henry
**Hugging Thistles**

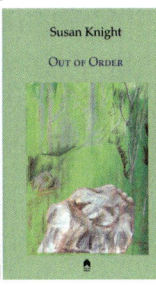

## Susan Knight
**OUT OF ORDER**

## EMPIRE
**Mary O'Donnell**

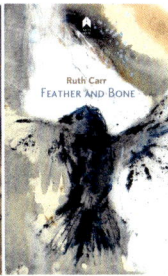

## Ruth Carr
**FEATHER AND BONE**

Winner
The Kate O'Brien Award

# When Black Dogs Sing

**Tanya Farrelly**

Winner of the Kate O'Brien Award

Tanya Farrelly
Nobody Needs to Know

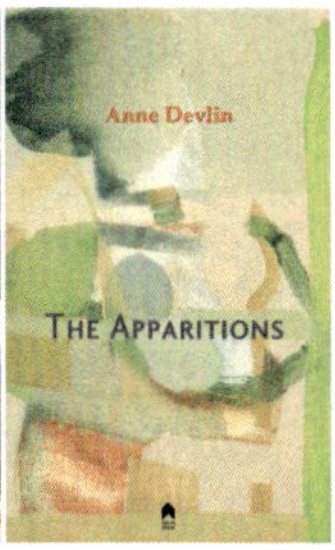
Anne Devlin
The Apparitions

Una O'Higgins O'Malley
TWENTIETH CENTURY REVISITED

A Last Loving
Collected Poems
Maeve Kelly

Berries for Singing Birds
Eileen Casey

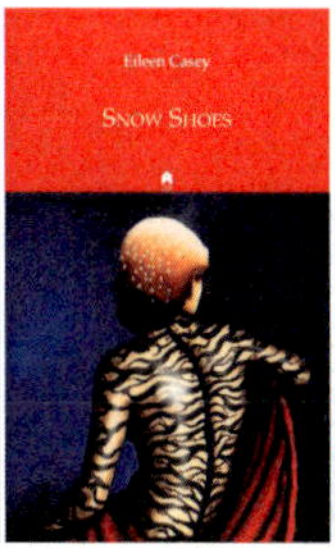
Eileen Casey
Snow Shoes

Eileen Casey
A Fascination With Fabric

Eileen Casey
and Jeanne Cannizzo
Bog Treasure

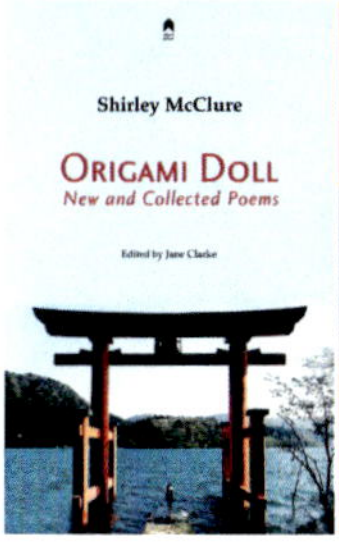
Shirley McClure
Origami Doll
New and Collected Poems
Edited by Jane Clarke

Shirley McClure
Stone Dress

Peggie Gallagher
Tilth

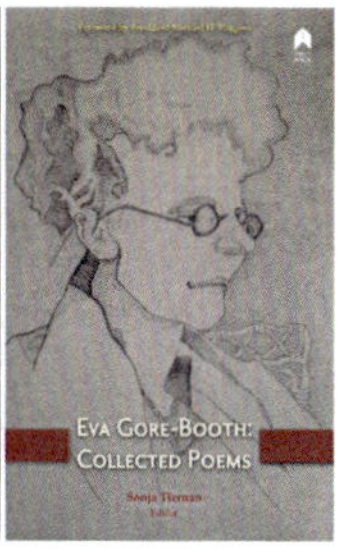
Eva Gore-Booth:
Collected Poems

MOTHER TONGUE
Pura López Colomé

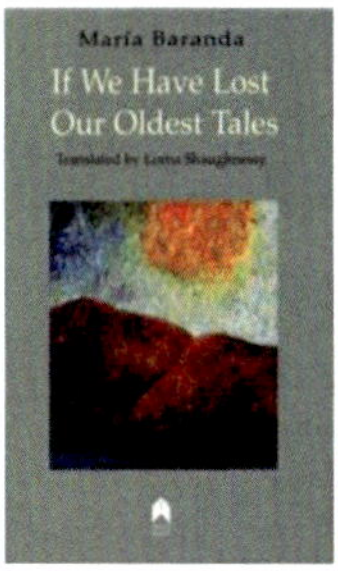
María Baranda
If We Have Lost
Our Oldest Tales

Colette Nic Aodha
Bainne Gear
Spoilt Milk
Rogha Dánta
Selected Poems

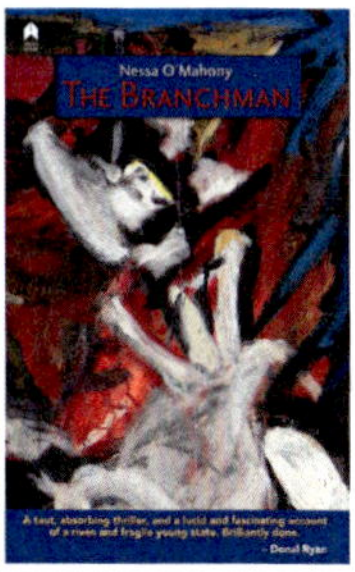
Nessa O'Mahony
The Branchman

Train to Gorey
Liz O'Donoghue

Colette Nic Aodha
Sundial

Colette
Nic Aodha

Winner
Farmgate National Poetry Collection Award

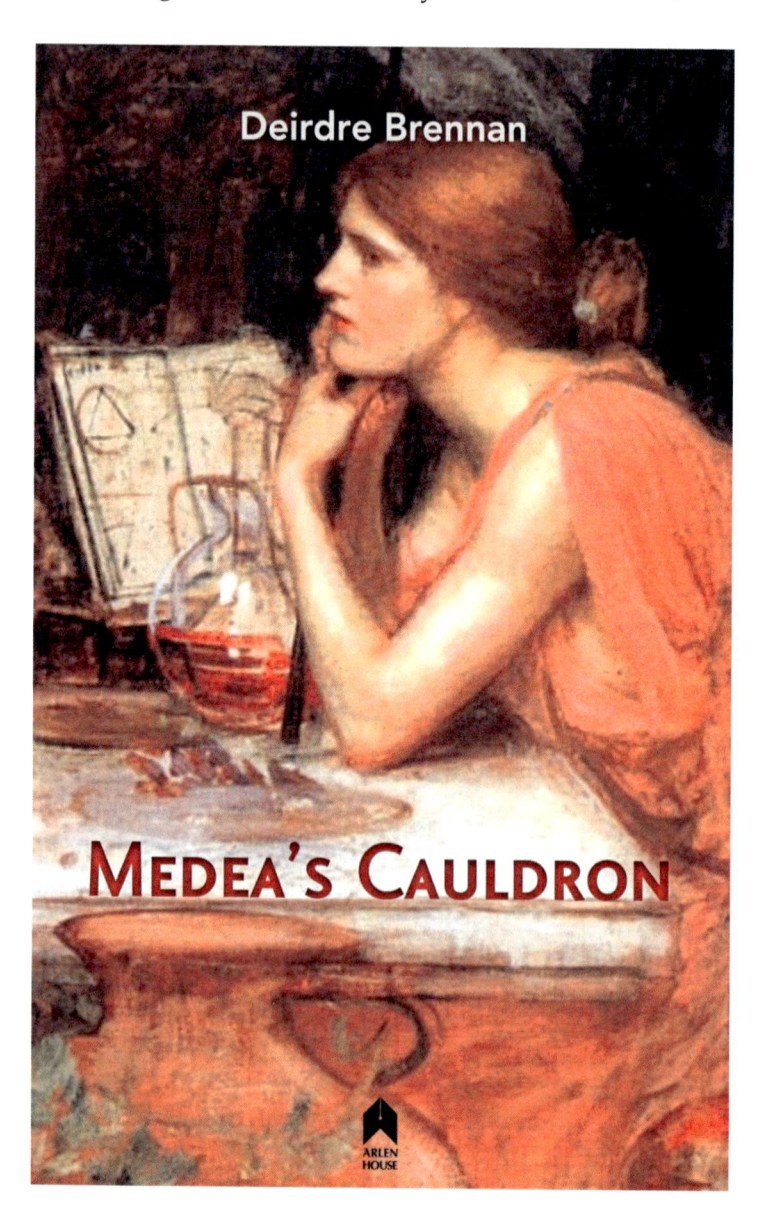

Deirdre Brennan

# Medea's Cauldron

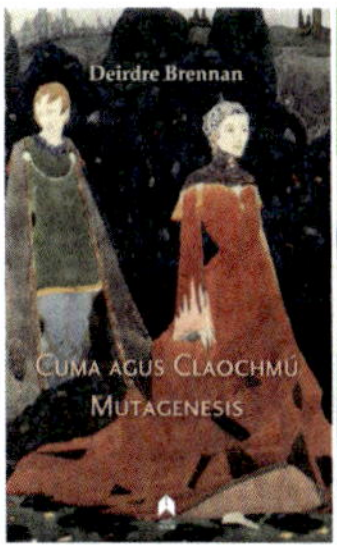
Deirdre Brennan
Cuma agus Claochmú
Mutagenesis
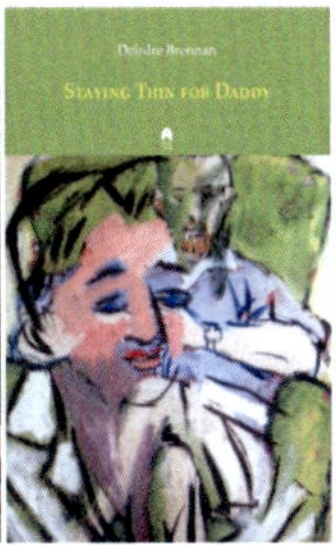
Staying Thin for Daddy

Cuisle Allta | Wild Pulses
Rogha Dánta | Selected Poems
Deirdre Brennan
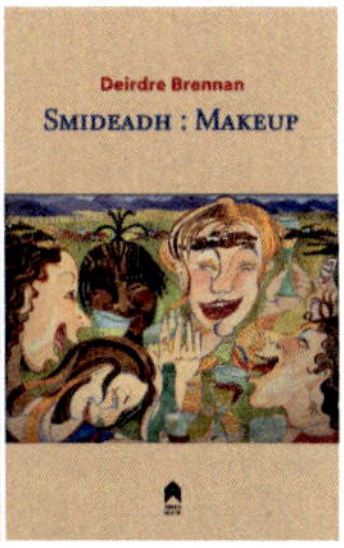
Deirdre Brennan
Smideadh : Makeup

Deirdre Brennan
Hidden Places

Deirdre Brennan
Swimming with Pelicans
Ag Eitilt fara Condair

Celia de Fréine
Even Still

Celia de Fréine
I bhFreagairt ar Rilke
In Response to Rilke

Celia de Fréine
Focal den Fhírinne
A Grain of Truth
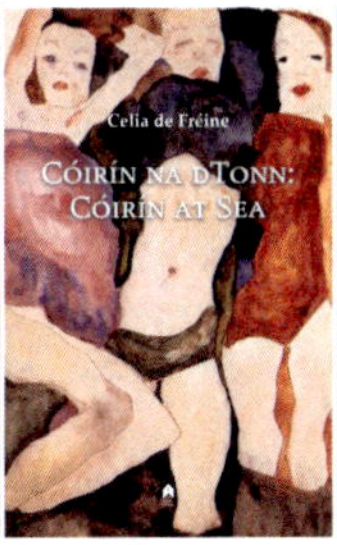
Celia de Fréine
Cóirín na dTonn:
Cóirín at Sea

Celia de Fréine
In Search of a Horizon

Celia de Fréine
cuir amach seo dom | riddle me this
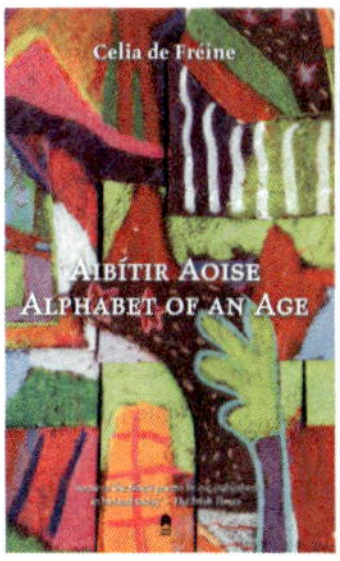
Celia de Fréine
Aibítir Aoise
Alphabet of an Age

Celia de Fréine

Celia de Fréine

Celia de Fréine

Fireseed

Idir na Fleánna

The Volary

The Colour of Time

Shortlisted
Edge Hill Short Story Prize

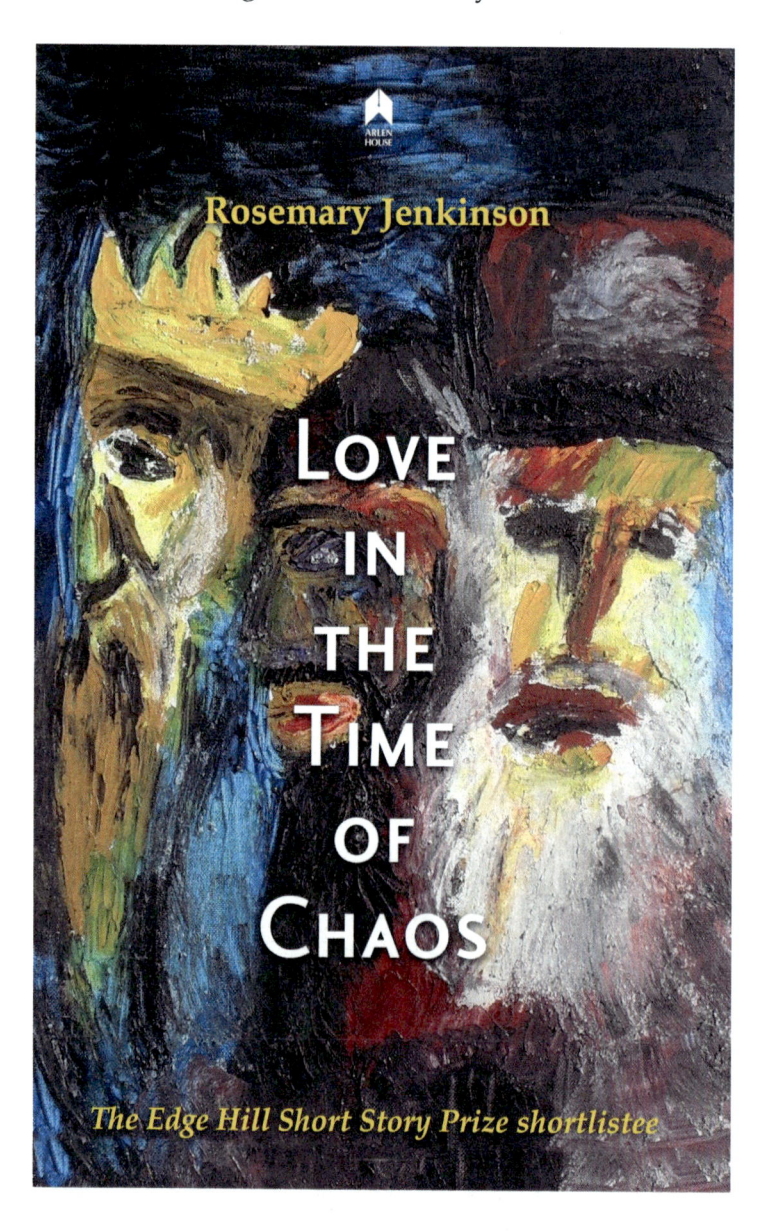

Rosemary Jenkinson

# LOVE IN THE TIME OF CHAOS

*The Edge Hill Short Story Prize shortlistee*

Rosemary Jenkinson
Billy Boy
Rosemary Jenkinson
Marching Season
Rosemary Jenkinson
Silent Trade
Rosemary Jenkinson
The Memorisers
Rosemary Jenkinson
Laganside Lights
Rosemary Jenkinson
Sandy Row Riots
Mary Coll
Silver
Noir by Noir-West
Catherine Foley
Amhrán Sráidbhaile
Village Song
Deirdre Cartmill
The Wind Stills to Listen
Open-Eyed, Full-Throated
Rosemarie Rowley
Ireland's Legendary Women
Girls of the Globe
Colette Ní Ghallchóir
An tAmharc Deireanach | The Last Look
selected and introduced by Cathal Ó Searcaigh
Colette Ní Ghallchóir
An Guth Aduaidh
Trish Bennett
Stench
Cherry Smyth
One Mountain: Sold
Leaving the Ladies
Sinéad McCoole
Sophia Hillan
The Cocktail Hour

Shortlisted
Pigott Poetry Prize

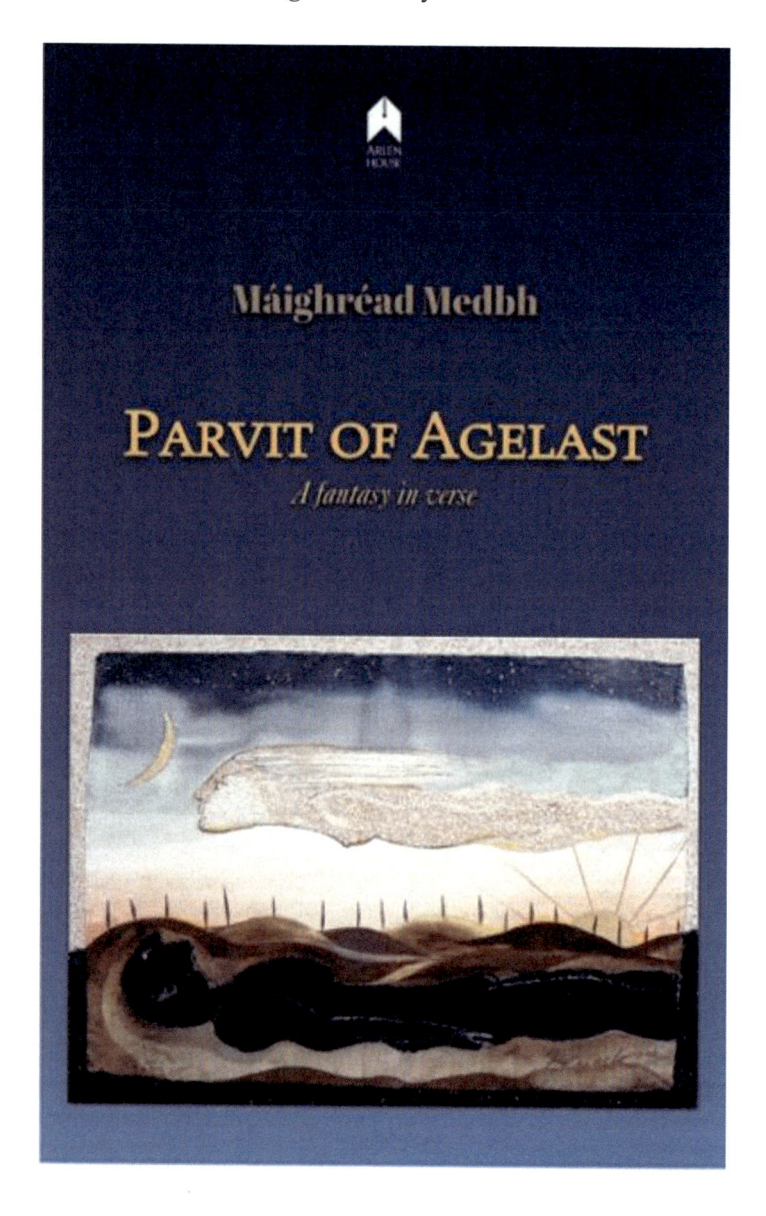

Máighréad Medbh

# PARVIT OF AGELAST
*A fantasy in verse*

Twelve Beds for the Dreamer
Máighréad Medbh
Máighréad Medbh
Imbolg
Máighréad Medbh
Pagan to the Core
Máighréad Medbh
of nothing
When the Air Inhales You
Máighréad Medbh
The Boiling Point for Jam
Lynda Tavakoli
Lynda Tavakoli
A Unison of Breaths
Mantles
Encountering Brigid
words Shauna Gilligan
images Margo McNulty
Breda Spaight
Watching for the Hawk
Mary Turley-McGrath
Forget the Lake
Mary Turley-McGrath
After Image
Mary Turley-McGrath
Other Routes
Csilla Toldy
Firebird
Margaret Nohilly
The Overlap of Things
Phyl Herbert
After Desire
Phyl Herbert
The Price of Desire
Martina Devlin
Call Me Madame
VOTE
14 December 1918
MARKIEVICZ
MARKIEVICZ, C. X
Nell Regan
Helena Molony: A Radical Life, 1883–1967
Preparing for Spring
Nell Regan
Bound for Home
Poetry by Nell Regan
Artwork by Monica Boyle

fiction by Celia de Fréine
shortlisted for Short Story of the Year Award
at the Irish Book Awards 2023

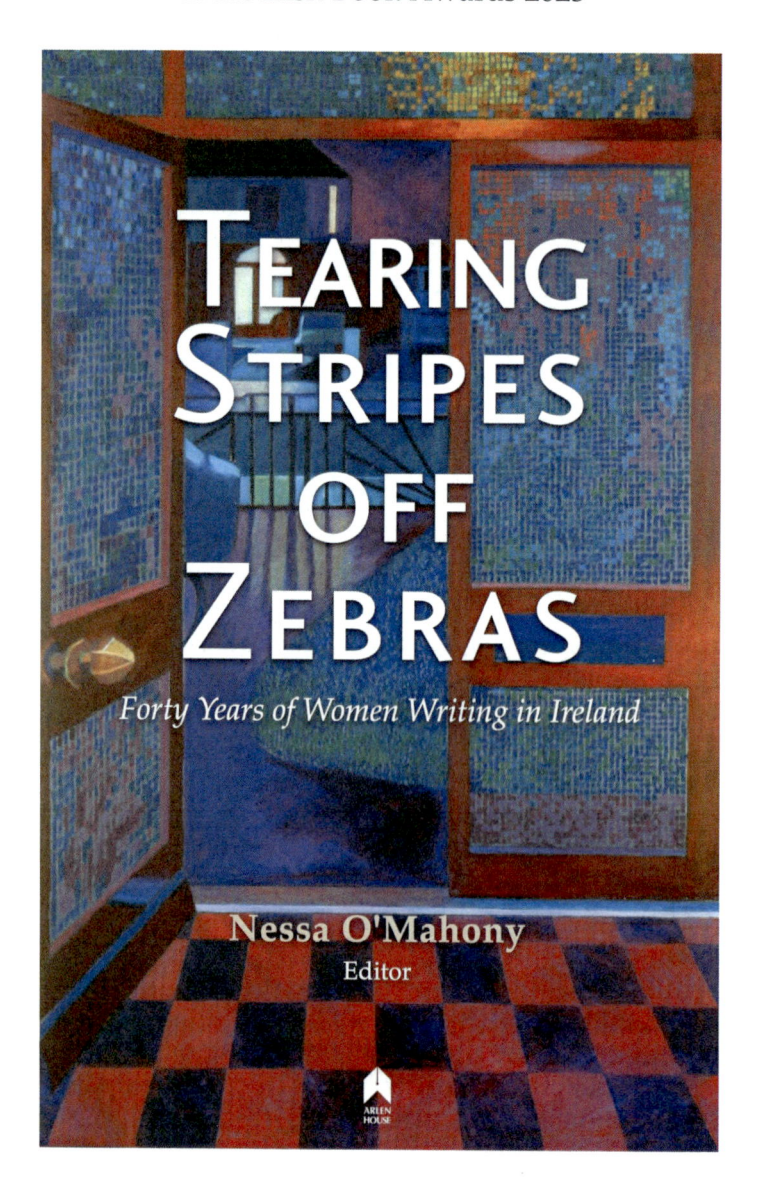

# Tearing Stripes off Zebras

*Forty Years of Women Writing in Ireland*

Nessa O'Mahony

Editor

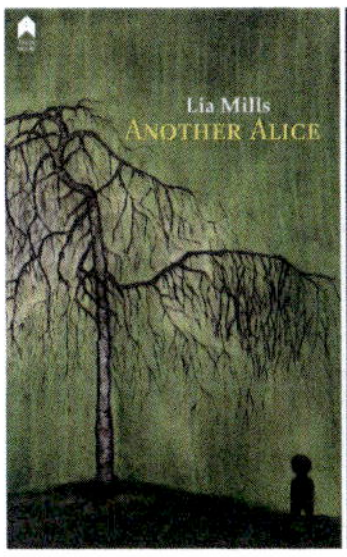
Lia Mills
Another Alice

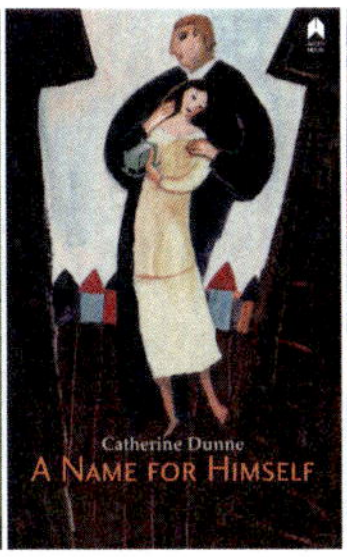
Catherine Dunne
A Name for Himself

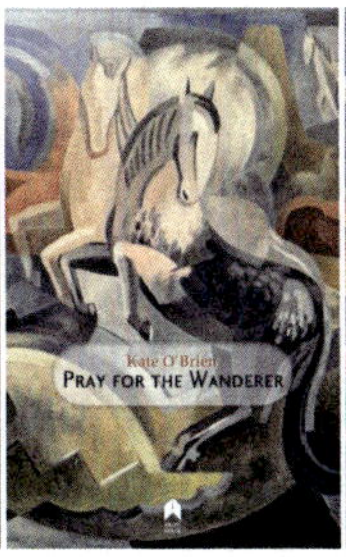
Kate O'Brien
Pray for the Wanderer

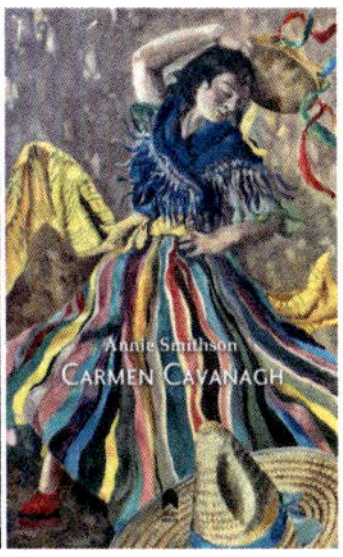
Annie Smithson
Carmen Cavanagh

A Life of No Light Toil
The Anna Maria Fielding Hall Reader

Awkward Women
Mary Rose Callaghan

Patricia O'Connor
The Mill in the North

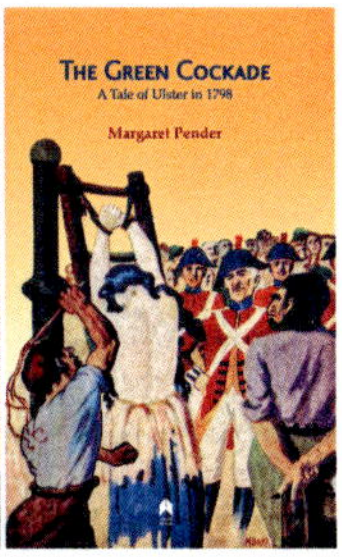
The Green Cockade
A Tale of Ulster in 1798
Margaret Pender

CoolChaint
Dolores Stewart

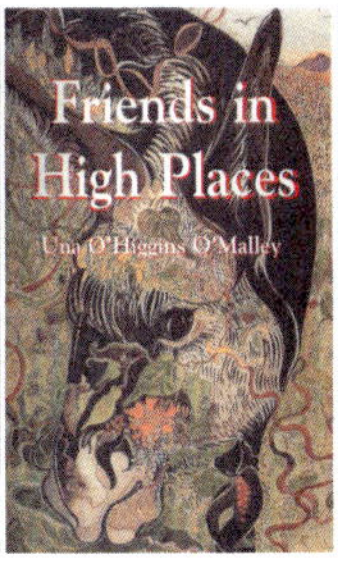
Friends in High Places
Una O'Higgins O'Malley

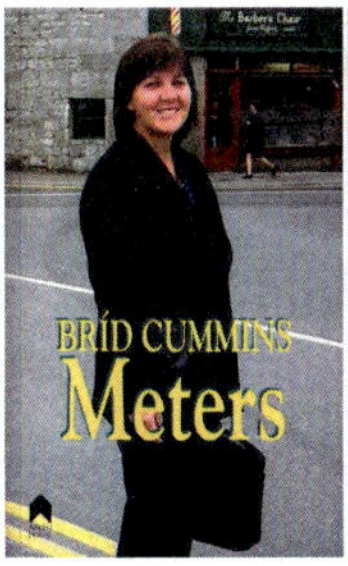
Bríd Cummins
Meters

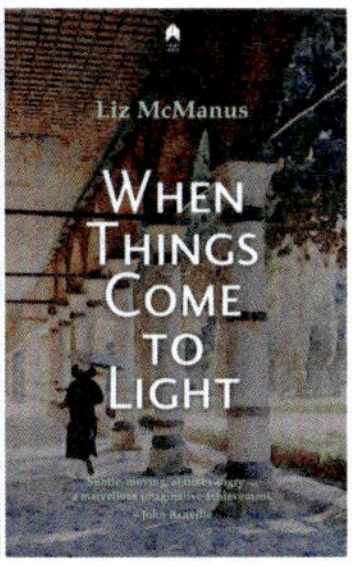
Liz McManus
When Things Come to Light

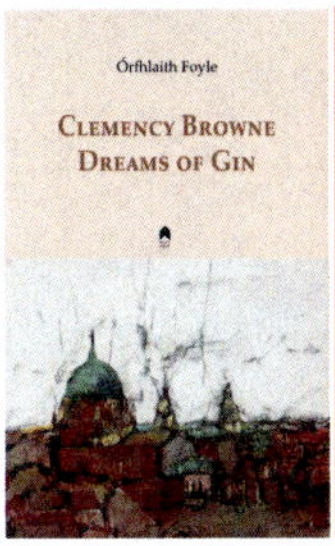
Órfhlaith Foyle
Clemency Browne Dreams of Gin

Órfhlaith Foyle
Revenge

Órfhlaith Foyle
Somewhere in Minnesota

Órfhlaith Foyle
Red Riding Hood's Dilemma

Travelling West
Rita Kelly

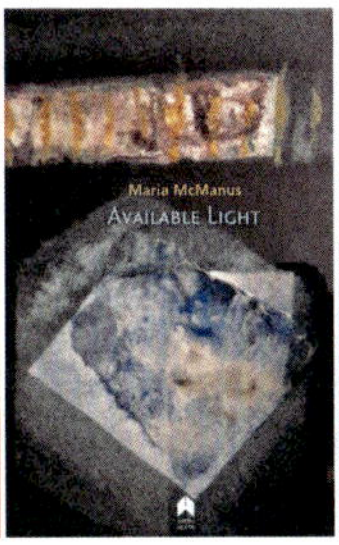
Maria McManus
Available Light

Vivienne McKechnie
A Butterfly's Wing

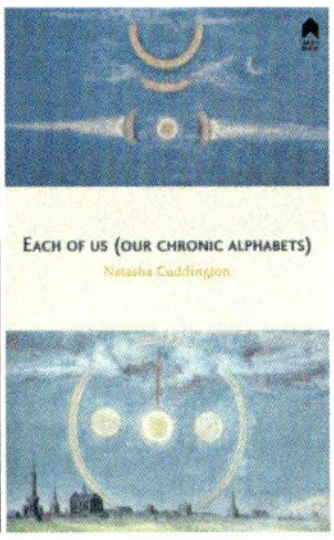
Each of us (our chronic alphabets)
Natasha Cuddington

# UNMANAGEABLE REVOLUTIONARIES

WOMEN AND IRISH NATIONALISM, 1880-1980

Margaret Ward

The Years Flew By
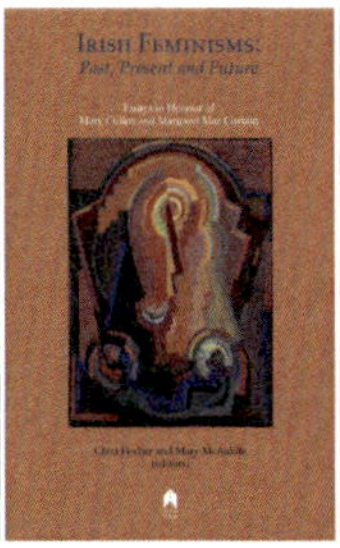
Irish Feminisms:
Past, Present and Future
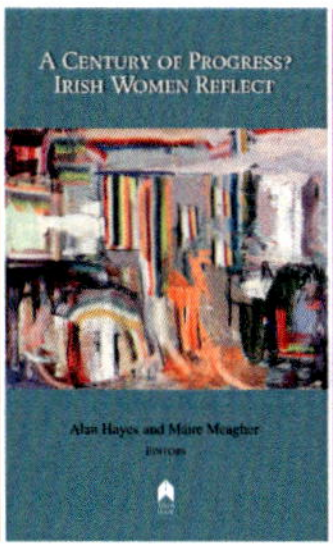
A Century of Progress?
Irish Women Reflect
Alan Hayes and Máire Meagher
Editors
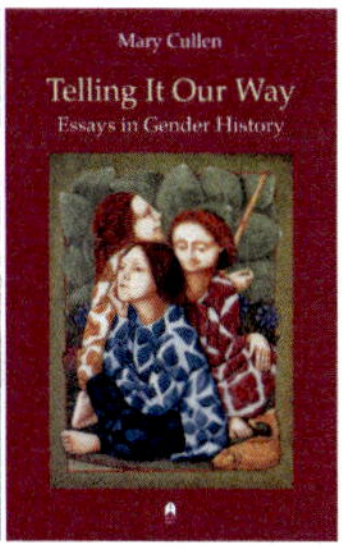
Mary Cullen
Telling It Our Way
Essays in Gender History

Joyce Padbury
Mary Hayden
Irish Historian and Feminist
1862–1942

Mary Cullen and Maria Luddy
Female Activists
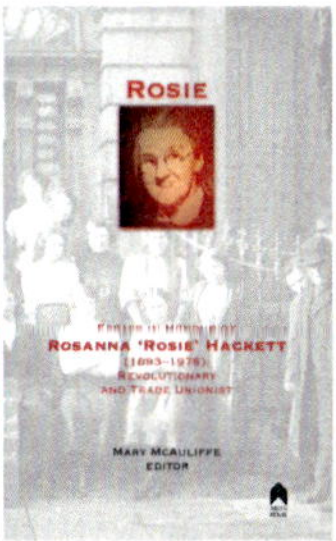
Rosie
Rosanna 'Rosie' Hackett
Mary McAuliffe
Editor

Hilda Tweedy and the Irish
Housewives Association:
Links in the Chain ...
Alan Hayes, Editor
The Children Must Be Fed

The Language of Gender,
Power and Agency in Celtic Studies

Historical Perspectives
on Parenthood and Childhood
in Ireland

Nan
Scéal a Beatha

Anne Ridge

The Women
of Galway Jail
Female criminality in nineteenth-century Ireland
Geraldine Curtin
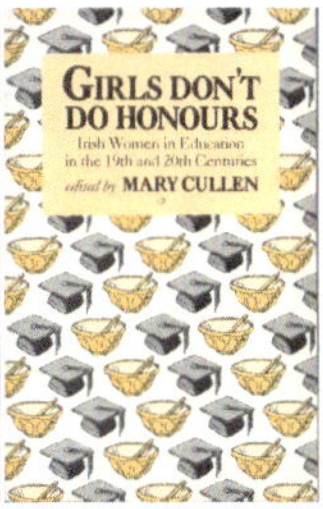
Girls Don't
Do Honours
Irish Women in Education
in the 19th and 20th Centuries
edited by Mary Cullen

Agnes O'Farrelly
Smaointe ar Árainn | Thoughts on Aran

From Pardon
and Protest
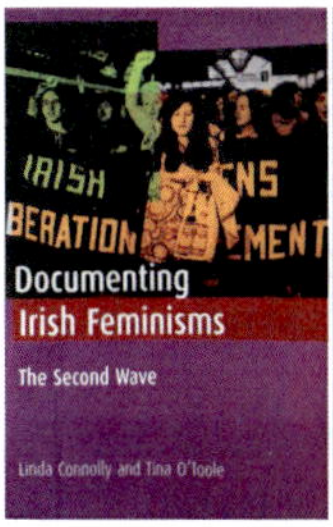
Documenting
Irish Feminisms
The Second Wave
Linda Connolly and Tina O'Toole

Dorothy
Macardle
A Life
Nadia Clare Smith
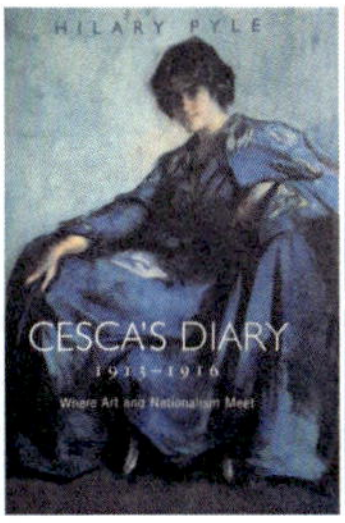
Hilary Pyle
Cesca's Diary
1913–1916
Where Art and Nationalism Meet

Hilary Pyle
Red-Headed
Rebel
Susan L. Mitchell
Poet and Mystic of the
Irish Cultural Renaissance

## Nanci Griffith
(1953–2021)
*Former resident of Dublin – never a stranger in our town*

*an extract from* SING (2009)

Still trying to find a reason,
trying to find that rhyme.
Still rolling with the rhythm,
trying to keep time.
But in the end I wouldn't change a thing.
I'd sing.

*Written by Nanci Griffith, Charley Stefl, Thomas Jutz*